God and War

God and War

AMERICAN CIVIL RELIGION SINCE 1945

RAYMOND HABERSKI JR.

RUTGERS UNIVERSITY PRESS
New Brunswick, New Jersey, and London

LIBRARY OF CONGRESS CATALOGING-IN-PUBLICATION DATA

Haberski, Raymond J., 1968–
    God and war : American civil religion since 1945 / Raymond Haberski, Jr.
        p. cm.
    Includes bibliographical references (p. 000) and index.
    ISBN 978–0–8135–5295–8 (hardcover : alk. paper) — ISBN
978–0–8135–5318–4 (e-book)
    1. Civil religion—United States.   2. United States—Religion—1945–
3. United States—History, Military—Religious aspects.   I. Title.
    BL2525.H33   2012
    201'.72730973—dc23
                                                                2011037601

        A British Cataloging-in-Publication record for this book is available
                            from the British Library.

            Visit our website: http://rutgerspress.rutgers.edu

            Manufactured in the United States of America

Dedicated to my mentors:

Charles C. Alexander, Kevin M. Shanley, Vincent P. Fox,
and my dad

CONTENTS

Acknowledgments

I THANK FIRST AND FOREMOST George Cotkin for giving me an opportunity to shift my intellectual focus and to delve into an area that is rich and fulfilling beyond what I expected. I am indebted to George for his stewardship, confidence, and, most of all, his kindness. He stands as an exemplar to those of us who work with him in the vibrant field of United States intellectual history.

Once again I have been fortunate to have comrades in ideas to call on for a frank hearing of my work, usually over good beer. Among those I am indebted to are Dave Steigerwald, Marc Selverstone, Jeff Woods, Marc O'Reilly, Steve Remy, Jeff Coker, and especially Colin Nugent for helping me make a significant investment in Café Bartof. I am forever grateful to the American and Danish Fulbright committees for bringing my family and me to Denmark for the 2008–2009 academic year; that grant gave me the opportunity to research and teach this project. In Copenhagen, I have a group of colleagues who have become dear friends; my sincere thanks to Niels Bjerre-Poulsen, Eddie Ashbee, Carl Pedersen, and Martyn Bone. Thanks also to Merete Borch and Jan Gustafsson at the Copenhagen Business School and Marie Mønsted of the Danish-American Foundation for their help and kindness. My thanks also to Gina Gustavsson and Mike Wolf, both of whom I met at the European Consortium for Political Research conference in Lisbon and who have since become my good friends.

I also thank the faculty and students at the Catholic University of Eichstätt-Ingolstad in Germany, the University of Graz in Austria, Southern Denmark University in Odenese, and the University of Copenhagen for being fine hosts and giving me opportunities to present the ideas addressed in this work.

At Marian University, where I have worked for the past eleven years, I thank my colleagues, who have helped me in numerous ways, especially Mary Ellen Lennon and the members of BOB and WAG.

I also thank the provost, Tom Enneking, and the president, Daniel Elsener, for supporting my work over the years.

My colleagues who created the Society for United States Intellectual History have been more important to my intellectual development than they can know. Through our blog, the annual conference, and now the society itself, I have had the privilege to get to know a remarkable group of scholars, among them Andrew Hartman, David Sehat, Ben Alpers, Tim Lacy, and Mike O'Connor.

My family and friends have provided encouragement and love that would be impossible to capture in a brief statement. My heartfelt thanks to my parents, my sisters and their families, and the many relatives who have given so much that is good to their children.

My wife and daughter are the greatest gifts in my life. They remind me of the happiness that exists beyond the satisfaction of completing a project such as this.

And, finally, my appreciation to the mentors who continue to play fundamental roles in my life: Charlie Alexander taught me how to be a historian; Kevin Shanley made me want to be a teacher; Vincent Fox challenged me to be a Catholic; and my dad showed me how to be a father. I thank them all.

God and War

CHAPTER 1

Lincoln's Bequest

ON VETERANS DAY 2009, just prior to his first major address on the war in Afghanistan, President Barack Obama walked through Arlington National Cemetery. James Meeks, a reporter for the *New York Daily News*, happened to be visiting Arlington that day as well. He recounted how the President and the First Lady made an unannounced stop in section sixty, a place where many American soldiers from the wars in Iraq and Afghanistan are buried. "They stopped first at the grave of Medal of Honor recipient Ross McGinnis, [the] Army private who threw himself on a grenade in Iraq three years ago to save four buddies." The Obamas then met and consoled a few other people who were in section sixty, including Meeks, who shook Obama's hand and told him of a friend who had been killed a year earlier in Iraq. The president's visit was captured in a few photographs, one of which showed a solemn Obama striding amid headstones looking resolute and contrite.[1]

Two weeks later, in a speech on the evening of December 1, 2009, Obama addressed the moral rationale for the war in Afghanistan, offering his justification for the sacrifices already made by American soldiers and providing inspiration for sacrifices yet to come. The president described the war as "a time of great trial" and reminded his audience that when it began, "we were united—bound together by the fresh memory of a horrific attack and by the determination to defend our homeland and the values we hold dear." Obama emphasized the unity that existed in the aftermath of 9/11, adding that the war in Afghanistan was about values as much as strategy. "The strength of our values ... [is] the source, the moral source, of America's authority," he declared. Obama grew increasingly passionate as he spoke about American ideals, clearly acknowledging the widespread skepticism and even cynicism engendered by the war in Iraq as well as by the ten-year-long engagement in Afghanistan. In the hope of rebuilding unity for his moment, the president called on ideas rooted in the past. "I refuse to accept the notion that we cannot summon that unity again," he declared. "I believe with every fiber of my being that we—as Americans—can still come together behind a common purpose. For our values are not simply words written into parchment—they are a creed that calls us together and that has carried us through the darkest of storms as one nation, as one people."[2]

Every president has made similar appeals to a common purpose—an American creed. Yet in a time of war the imperative to define that creed and marshal that common purpose grows exponentially. After all, Obama chose to make his address at West Point to an audience that included soldiers who might give the last full measure of devotion to their nation. And by identifying the ideals for which the nation went to war, Obama tried to justify the sacrifices that would be made by those in the war. As sociologists Carolyn Marvin and David Ingle astutely observed, "What is really true in any community is what its members can agree is worth killing for, or what they can be compelled to sacrifice their lives for. The sacred is thus easily recognized."[3]

In making his appeal, Obama echoed another politician from Illinois. In his address at the Gettysburg Cemetery, Abraham Lincoln offered a moral reckoning for the carnage of the Civil War. Looking out at the freshly dug graves of thousands of soldiers from both sides of the war, Lincoln proposed that the only suitable testament to such sacrifice was to pledge "increased devotion to that cause for which they gave the last full measure of devotion—that we here highly resolve that these dead shall not have died in vain." The war was not an end in itself, he argued; it forced the living to recognize the existential purpose for which the war was fought. For Lincoln, the tragedy of his war and perhaps any war could be redeemed if Americans rededicated themselves to the founding principles of their nation.[4]

However, Lincoln's bequest carried a terrible dilemma, that the nation might find redemption through war. For when Obama declared in his speech at West Point, "We will go forward with the confidence that right makes might," he seemed to traffic in a dangerous confidence that assumes Americans know when and how their righteousness can be deployed. In other words, American troops take more than just the flag into battle; they carry with them a set of assumptions commonly understood as American exceptionalism, or the notion that no matter what actions it takes abroad ultimately America will be redeemed by history. In a witty, hard-hitting critique of that idea, essayist David Rieff writes that "the American consensus has always been and remains that we are not an empire in any traditional sense, but rather the last best hope of humanity—which, coincidentally or not, also happens to be the most powerful nation in the world." Rieff calls this condition a "theology of American exceptionalism" and hints at, although does not explicitly identify, the faith that informs this "theology." By imagining their nation as more of an idea than a political entity, Rieff believes Americans sacralize their nation, considering it an abstraction that deserves uncritical devotion. Thus he fears that "at its most extreme, this faith—and it is faith in the sense of being a religious rather than a political construct—can lead to the claim . . . that the United States is an 'inherently' good country." Even critics of U.S. policies can buy into this argument because when Americans are faced with tragedy (as in Vietnam or Iraq or even the Civil War), it is hard to argue against the idea that "the Constitution was an inherently good document. . . . As the old joke about Communism goes, 'If the facts don't fit the theory, so much the worse for the facts.'"[5] In this way, the United States is indeed an exceptional nation, for even in failure it still succeeds.

And yet, it seems to me, there is a basic flaw in critiques like Rieff's because he and other critics of American adventurism abroad fail to delve deeply enough into the faith that sustains the nation. Of course the most dramatic expression of such faith often appears to be public support for the United States to plow across the world proclaiming the best intentions and creating the worst results. But we also know that Americans can and do reassess their support for war. To take just one example, Andrew Kohut and Bruce Stokes of the Pew Research Center for the People and the Press noted in 2006, "Contrary to widespread misconceptions, America's pride in their country is not evangelistic. . . . In reality, [Americans] are far more likely to say 'We think the American way is great; we assume you want to be like us, but, if you don't, that's not really our concern.'" And while there is little doubt that American actions have grown more consequential with the growth of the nation into a military superpower, Kohut and Stokes write, "Fully seventy percent of Americans described their fellow countrymen as greedy,

a harsher criticism than that leveled by any non-Americans in the sur-
vey[,] [and] forty-nine percent saw themselves as violent, a self-criticism
with which majorities agreed in thirteen of the sixteen other countries
surveyed." Indeed, such responses might indicate that Americans have "a
healthy self-doubt that tempers any tendencies toward imperial hubris."
Americans are, after all, heirs to both John L. O'Sullivan's 1839 term
"Manifest Destiny" as well as John Winthrop's admonition in 1630 as he
sailed for America aboard the *Arabella*: "If our heartes shall turne away so
that wee will not obey, but shall be seduced and worship . . . other Gods,
our pleasures, and proffitts, and serve them; it is propounded unto us this
day, wee shall surely perishe out of the good Land whither wee passe
over this vast Sea to possesse it."[6]

Thus, rather than dwell on the simplistic notion of American exceptionalism, we might consider Obama's speech an expression of a complicated American national faith—an American civil religion. The term *civil
religion* has had a long history, originating in the political theory of
French philosopher Jean Jacques Rousseau. But for recent American history the touchstone remains the 1967 essay by sociologist Robert Bellah.
Amid another problematic and seemingly open-ended conflict, Bellah
gained considerable notoriety in the academic world for an essay entitled
"Civil Religion in America." In it, Bellah reminded Americans that
despite the divisions they suffered during the Vietnam War they still
possessed a common heritage that they might call on in times of trial.
He argued that this "American civil religion is not the worship of the
American nation but an understanding of the American experience in
the light of ultimate and universal reality." Thus he contended that
Americans had a common creed that not only unified them but also provided a means to evaluate their nation's actions. In parlance that became
popular following World War II, the United States was a nation "under
God," meaning, as Bellah explained, that "the will of the people is not
itself the criterion of right and wrong. There is a higher criterion in
terms of which this will can be judged; it is possible that the people may
be wrong. The president's obligation extends to the higher criterion."[7]

Vietnam was the kind of moral crisis that tested the operation of civil
religion; in Bellah's argument, Vietnam was one of three times of trial.
The first time of trial was the founding of the nation; the second was the
Civil War; and the third was the period following the Second World War,

when the United States struggled in an almost constant state of war to define its role in the world. According to Bellah's version of civil religion, Obama finds himself within the third time of trial, which has been shaped by the Cold War and the limited and failed wars in Korea, Vietnam, and now Iraq and Afghanistan.

However, civil religion is a strange beast; it can often appear to mean almost anything to anyone at anytime. As a hybrid of nationalism and traditional religion, civil religion has an ideological flexibility that is intoxicating because it is so evocative, elastic, and deceptively complex. Civil religion seems to capture the intersection between faith and civic obligation in a way that allows a mixing of truth claims without manipulation—as if a president doesn't play on the religious faith of his audience and the people don't mythologize the meaning of their nation. Yet civil religion is significant precisely because its promise is so racked by peril. There is a fundamental irony of American civil religion—the nation lives with a misbegotten confidence born from a union of religion and reason.

This American confidence is symbolized in the Great Seal of the nation: the pyramid represents the new nation, the barren desert is history before 1776, and the eye of God looks down on the unfinished nation with pleasure. The Latin inscriptions read: "He has favored our undertakings" and "A new order of the ages." The other side of the seal depicts an eagle clutching arrows in one talon and an olive branch in the other, thus representing the powers of war and peace. The inscription famously declares: "Out of many, one." The seal captures the foundation of American civil religion: a diverse people join together to affirm the nation as a moral entity.[8] As historian Arthur Schlesinger Jr. pithily contended: "[The Founding Fathers] bequeathed to us standards by which to set our course and judge our performance—and, since they were exceptional men, the standards have not been rendered obsolete even by the second law of thermodynamics. The Declaration of Independence and the Constitution establish goals, imply commitments, and measure failures. . . . The conflict between creed and reality has been a powerful motive in the quest for justice."[9]

Perhaps Americans do have a political system that, while not good in some absolute sense, has the capacity for a moral accounting. The promise of civil religion helps that process by serving as a touchstone in such debates.[10] At the same time, however, civil religion is manufactured by the same people who wish to use it as a means to evaluate themselves. That arrangement is fraught with peril because civil religion is not a set of laws but a collection of myths. There is nothing verifiable about civil religion. One cannot empirically confirm whether, for example, "all men are created equal" or whether the United States is "the last best hope for mankind" or, for that matter, whether America is a source of modern evil and tragedy. And yet we know that it is precisely the mythical nature of civil religion that allows people to die for it and in their deaths the myths of civil religion become sacralized. In other words, when Obama spoke to the cadets at West Point, he did not ask them to sacrifice for him, their Commander in Chief, but for their nation—even more for the mythical understanding of that nation. It is in war, therefore, that the perils of civil religion's promise become acutely apparent.

Of course, no conflict in American history illustrated the power of civil religion—for both good and bad—better than the Civil War. Historian Mark Noll explains that in the years leading up to the Civil War, a grand alliance between the Bible and the Enlightenment encouraged Americans to believe that "they could see clearly what the world was like, what God was like, what factors drove the world, who was responsible for events, and how the moral balance sheet should be read. They were children of the Enlightenment as well as children of God." Such confidence imparted by the nation's unique intellectual consensus contained a dangerous hubris for "it also imparted a nearly fanatical force to the prosecution of war." We know the results of that fanaticism—mass violence and death on a scale never equaled on American soil. One would think that such an experience would sorely test American faith in the nation, perhaps leading to a deeper appreciation of the moral consequences of war. In short, Americans should have found God in new ways.[11]

Yet that did not happen. The Civil War did indeed spark a theological crisis, but it wasn't over competing views of God's judgment but over the nation's civil religion. As Noll contends, "The story of theology in the Civil War was a story of how a deeply entrenched intellectual synthesis divided against itself, even as its proponents were reassuring combatants on either side that each enjoyed a unique standing before

God and each exercised a unique role as the true bearer of the nation's Christian civilization." A civil religious understanding of the nation had divided against itself.[12]

No one grappled with that American struggle better than Lincoln. And he did so because he was intimately familiar with the confidence that led to dangerous delusions about reason and God. Lincoln was a devout rationalist who later in his life also acquired a significant belief in Providence. We have in Lincoln the embodiment of the two sides of civil religion: Lincoln understood that death on the scale endured during the Civil War had profound meaning, but he wasn't confident that he knew what that meaning was. Historian Harry Stout captures the first part of Lincoln's awakening well: "As the war descended into a killing horror, the grounds of justification underwent a transformation from a just defensive war fought out of sheer necessity to preserve home and nation to a moral crusade for 'freedom' that would involve nothing less than a national 'rebirth,' a spiritual 'revival.' And in that blood and transformation a national religion was born."[13]

There was no making sense of a nation with so much promise nearly committing suicide. Thus, Lincoln the rationalist had to come to terms with the transcendent experience of the Civil War. But it was also Lincoln's particular kind of faith in God that prevented him from accepting the war as some kind of blood sacrifice required by a God sitting in judgment. As Lincoln reasoned in his "Meditation on the Divine Will," "The will of God prevails," but nobody (neither side in the war, especially) could know what that will was because "God cannot be for and against the same thing at the same time." Such sentiments suggested an antidote to the hubris that caused the war. In his Second Inaugural, Lincoln took his thought a step further, pointing out not merely the obvious blasphemy of claiming God's grace in war but the irony of a nation that seemed ideologically designed to do so.[14]

Lincoln did not doubt that America was a force for good in the world, but even as he accepted that proposition he also wondered whether the nation might see the irony of a war at odds with the fundamental promise of the nation. By making this argument, Lincoln spoke from the tradition of the American jeremiad, or the practice developed by the Puritans of using a sermon to remind the members of a community that they had entered into a covenant among themselves and with

God. If community members violated this covenant—their set of moral standards—they placed not only their individual souls but the collective soul of their community in peril. The jeremiad was a call to "return home," to reorient the community and thereby redeem the community.[15] Lincoln's jeremiad had prophetic power because it recognized the existence of an American civil religion. Knowing that Americans believed themselves to be righteous—no matter what side they fought on—he posed a devastating question. At the end of the longest, most deliberative passage in his Second Inaugural, Lincoln ruminated about the will of God. "If we shall suppose that American slavery is one of those offenses which, in the providence of God, must needs come, but which, having continued through His appointed time, He now wills to remove, and that He gives to both North and South this terrible war as the woe due to those by whom the offense came, shall we discern therein," Lincoln asked, "any departure from those divine attributes which the believers in a living God always ascribe to Him?"[16]

The implications of Lincoln's question were almost as apocalyptic for the promise of America as the war itself: Had the Civil War, he asked, undermined the belief that God had any active interest in the United States? Indeed, knowing that the mixing of religion and politics was not incidental to the prosecution and interpretation of the war, Lincoln wanted to know whether the horror of the war had deflated American confidence in the grand synthesis of reason and faith. What made Lincoln the finest theologian of American civil religion was his sense of irony: he found it ironic that Americans had the capacity to be confident that while God was present in American life and His will remained a mystery, His judgment was never in doubt—America was good. Thus Lincoln saw a particular kind of American tragedy: Americans would find war, at once, both a terrible consequence of their contemporary world and a chance to redeem the nation through martial sacrifice.[17]

Lincoln's experience has acute implications for our time: generations of Americans who have fought the long Cold War and now the "war on terror" can learn from Lincoln's attempt to balance the contradictory tendencies embedded in the American proposition—the inclination to beat history chastened by the experience of succumbing to history. That legacy has hung over American efforts to define national purpose as the country has passed from the Civil War to the period following World War II. As during the Civil War, Americans in the postwar era have been at war with themselves as much as with their enemies. And, in ways similar to those of the Civil War, calls to sacrifice for the nation have complicated the capacity of civil religion to be anything close to a moral accounting of the nation's actions. Thus, Lincoln has been claimed by presidents from Harry Truman, who made the phrase "this nation under God" a fixture of presidential speeches, to Ronald Reagan and now Barack Obama, both of whom emphasized the Great Emancipator's ability to make difficult decisions that were at once nationalistic and moral. And a variety of public theologians—from Reinhold Niebuhr in the early Cold War to Martin Luther King Jr. during the Vietnam War to Richard John Neuhaus in the early days of the war on terror—found Lincoln's insights into civil religion so profound that they believed Lincoln set the standard by which all other public theologians are measured.

Lincoln's continuing relevance is this: he did not deny popular reliance on a biblical faith in God to comprehend American history because he knew that for the vast majority of Americans faith in God might be the only way they could comprehend war. Yet he offered a way to navigate between, on the one hand, using God to make norma-tive claims about the meaning of war, and, on the other, using religion to commend or condemn the nation in absolute moral terms. For Lincoln, looking to God helped bring perspective to the way war had revealed the soul of his nation while at the same time alerting him to the irony of that revelation.

Americans have long imagined that their nation is good and has a profound role to play in the world, yet, unlike any previous period, the era since 1945 has witnessed a merging of American promise and power to forge a potent civil religion. During the postwar era, American civil religion captured the faith Americans invested in the promise of their nation and the way that promise manifested itself in American power. Expressions such as "God bless America" and "one nation under God" were the popular manifestations of this civil religion. And yet politicians and preachers, theorists and theologians of this period also were benefac-tors of Lincoln's bequest: that war must change the way Americans understand their nation's moral authority—its relationship to God. During the First World War, Randolph Bourne warned that war was the "health of the state" because through war the state exercised its ultimate power to command sacrifice.[18] He probably didn't imagine that his country would enter a period of almost perpetual war. And thus, as war has become a constant presence in American society, it has also become more than the political barometer Bourne suggested. *God and War* chronicles the debate from the end of the Second World War through to the war on terrorism over a civil religion that has been forged in a union of God, war, and the nation.

CHAPTER 2

Civil Religion Incorporated

"IT IS AN AWFUL RESPONSIBILITY which has come to us," Harry Truman told his radio audience on August 10, 1945. "We thank God that it has come to us instead of our enemies; and we pray that He may guide us to use it in His ways and for His purposes." The "awful responsibility" of which Truman spoke was America's decision to drop two atomic bombs on Japan. A few days after the second bomb destroyed the city of Nagasaki, World War II was over. And a moral reckoning began. As Truman's statement suggested, America needed help understanding its new role in world affairs. Americans looked skyward and inward to find ways to makes sense of the war that had just ended and the world they had inherited. As *Time* magazine put it on August 20, 1945, "With the controlled splitting of the atom . . . all thoughts and things were split." The sense of national purpose that had existed during the war had started to come undone. A new era dawned and its title belied the ambiguity of its meaning—Americans would now be in the postwar period. War had defined relationships among the American people and between the people and the government. Yet once the war ended, so did the ideological framework that had grown up to support the prosecution of the war. Reflecting on this ambiguity, James Agee, one of *Time*'s extraordinary writers, offered a prophecy of sorts: Americans had now to consider the simple notion that "each man is eternally and above all else responsible for his own soul, and, in the terrible words of the Psalmist, that no man may deliver his brother, nor make agreement unto God for him."[1]

Such existential angst made apparent the vacuum left by the absence of war. In a way similar to the Civil War, the Second World War remade the American sense of national morality. The death, destruction, and immoral acts affected all sides in the great global struggle and could not be waved away as simply part of war. Americans from the president on down recognized that some sort of moral reckoning would follow a conflict of this size and scope, but no consensus appeared on how such a reckoning would operate. For one thing, the soldiers who fought in the war simply wanted to return home. In May 1945 there were 12.3 million men and women in the military, and 7.6 million of them were stationed overseas; ten months later there were fewer than 1.5 million in uniform. And yet the federal government had come to appreciate the phenomenal organizational benefits of wartime planning. Truman and American military leaders believed that in order to meet the threats that persisted, they needed the ability to mobilize and coordinate huge national efforts to defend the nation. Yet, unlike in the time of war itself, in the postwar era the nation had to prevent attacks and rally Americans intellectually as much as economically and militarily. In other words, the postwar era required leaders to frame rhetorically the imperative to sacrifice in order to stave off another war, for most Americans agreed that the next world war would indeed be the last.[2]

Thus a new American civil religion took shape in a way different from that in other times of trial in American history. Rather than during a war, as in the American Revolution, or after a war, as with the Civil War, civil religion in postwar America initially emerged to fight a cold war and ostensibly to prevent a real war. Of course, World War II had created a sense of unity among Americans to defeat a common enemy. Yet, as historians Paul Fussell, John Bodnar, and Wendy Wall all explain, the American war effort did not create a singular vision—perhaps the conflict was too enormous, too diffuse, too wracked by domestic turmoil to produce a civil religion that could answer with great clarity why Americans had to fight and die.[3]

The statement that came closest to accomplishing that feat was Henry Luce's brazen declaration in 1941 of "the American Century." Fighting to marshal popular support for American entry in the war, Luce declared that "it now becomes our time to be the powerhouse from which the ideals [of Western civilization] spread throughout the world and do their mysterious work of lifting the life of mankind from the level of beasts to what the Psalmist called a little lower than the angels." Bodnar observes of Luce: "This perspective saw World War II not as a human tragedy but as an opportunity for Americans to assume a position of dominance in the world and reaffirm their innate (and traditional) moral courage and bravery."[4] In time, Luce's vision prevailed, not during the war but after it, when Americans groped for purpose in an era of ambiguity.

That era began with a single incredible event: the dropping of the atomic bomb marked the end of one tragic war and, rather quickly, signaled the beginning of an almost equally perilous time. The idea that America might enjoy a period without war—and become truly *post*war—quickly diminished. America would not return to a familiar understanding of normalcy. In the shadow of the most horrific war in history and in the dusky dawn of a terrifying new era, Americans went primeval, eschewing complexity and ambiguity and pining for the simplicity of first principles.

Thus even though a diverse array of voices chattered about the war and its aftermath, the most significant were those who preached directly about the spiritual crisis into which Americans had entered. According to polls that asked, "Who does the most good for the country?" religious leaders moved from third to first place from 1942 to 1947.[5] Such data suggested the important role religion might play following World War II. But not any one denomination or even a specific faith helped Americans make sense of this juncture in their history. Rather an American civil religion did what churches could not—it incorporated the myths of the nation's past with the promise of the nation's unique position in the present to create meaning out of a time of great distress. Bodnar points out that in the end the struggle over the legacy of World War II was between those who wanted "memory without accountability and anguish" and those who "looked to undercut such myths and keep alive a legacy of misdeeds and complaints."[6]

Reckoning with the bomb made apparent that struggle. A collective opinion about the cataclysmic act of dropping the bomb illustrated how a nation with a great diversity of opinion about war and peace might, at once, condemn specific actions—whether committed by a person or the nation—but ultimately rally around the nation as an entity set apart from specific moral judgments. Over all, Americans did not second-guess Truman's decision to use the bomb and therefore gave the nation a moral pass. In August 1945, George C. Gallup asked Americans, "Do you approve or disapprove of the use of the atomic bomb?" Eighty-five percent of respondents approved. Historian Paul Boyer notes, "The belief that the atomic bomb 'saved American lives' (and, to a lesser extent, Japanese lives) quickly became an article of faith after August 6, 1945." War planners in Washington did comprehend the immorality of the bomb, but they also argued that they were in a war so barbarous that such destruction was not uniquely immoral. Thus only a minority voiced "troubled uneasiness to anguished dismay" over the atomic bombings. A few editorials registered "moral uneasiness" with the actions, wondering whether Americans had forsaken the ability to appeal to God or to a higher conscience considering the tragedy of the bombings. The *Omaha World Herald* went so far as to say that it was "almost sacrilegious" for Truman to have used "the name of a merciful God in connection with so Satanic a device."[7]

Mainline Protestant churches were generally critical of the atomic bombing but failed to make clear what they thought the nation should do to atone for its act. Catholic leaders were also critical, using just-law tradition to counter the argument that the ends justified the means. Catholic intellectual journals—*Commonweal, Catholic World, America,* and *Theological Studies*—had condemned terror bombings and the atomic bomb as morally indefensible. However, as Catholic theologian William O'Brien astutely observed, "In World War II the United States seemed to have accepted the proposition that *all* means are permissible in total conflict with a truly evil enemy. This may turn out to be the most tragic of the many bitter legacies left us by the Axis powers—an adversary so patently evil that the habit of unlimited response was inordinately encouraged."[8]

Indeed, most American religious leaders demurred at a crucial moment when they could have served as moral checks on the actions of the nation. But because, by and large, American churches had not opposed U.S. prosecution of World War II and had, in fact, provided a moral rationale for defeating regimes that most people agreed did not deserve much mercy, it would have been quite a twist to suddenly condemn the nation post hoc. Arthur Compton, a Protestant layman and religious leader, summed up this position in an essay entitled "The Moral Meaning of the Atomic Bomb." Compton argued that the greatest moral obligation that the United States had inherited from World War II was "the responsibility to protect the world from [another] suicidal war," even if that meant going to war. "Most Americans," he asserted, "freely chose war with all its agony and evil rather than have their consciences bear the burden of refusing to share in protecting the world against great disaster." Compton's position echoed a kind of confidence reminiscent of religious belief just prior to the Civil War in the way he suggested religious Americans could accede to the nation's use of force to reach moral ends. The moral crisis of the early Cold War apparently offered two options: the protection of liberty or the abdication of responsibility. Compton had identified how postwar America would use religion to certify the nation's moral nature, much like the two sides of the slavery issue had in antebellum America. Except this time there was little dissent over what constituted the proper moral position. In other words, the nation had moral authority and those who dissented from it were in moral jeopardy. For the few critics of the American war effort, there was great peril in such consensus.[9]

A. J. Muste was one of them. Like Compton, Muste was a Protestant layman with considerable influence. Yet, unlike Compton, Muste was a pacifist. He served as executive director of the Fellowship of Reconciliation, a pacifist organization that came to prominence during World War II. Muste believed that in order for America to claim moral authority in the postwar world it had to account for the atomic bombings. In his influential 1947 book *Not by Might*, Muste offered an alternative to moral equivocation regarding war's brutality. "Thus it has fallen upon this 'Christian' nation, incessantly declaiming against the perpetrators of atrocities, and still doing so, to perpetuate the ultimate atomic atrocity—needlessly—and so to remove all restraint upon atrocity. That is the logic of the atrocious means," Muste declared. "With fatal precision the means in war become more destructive, both of physical life and of moral standards and spiritual values." "Has it come to this?" he asked. "The atomic bomb is the symbol of power to destroy and kill raised to demonic proportions. What shall be set against it? What shall overcome it? A still greater power to destroy and kill? Obviously, there is nought but still more awful destruction in that. In this extremity, is it not at last clear that our sole alternative is the love that absolutely refuses to destroy, will not be tempted to violence and is able and willing to die in order that the diabolical chain of evil linked to evil may be broken?"[10]

Muste made clear that pacifism offered the only hope for Christians in Cold War America, just as Dorothy Day had preached pacifism during the Second World War. Both demanded that the church bear witness to the last war in order to prevent what they viewed as a dangerous morality of war to prevail in the period that followed. Day wrote in the *Catholic Worker* a month after Pearl Harbor:

> We are still pacifists. Our manifesto is the Sermon on the Mount, which means that we will try to be peacemakers. Speaking for many of our conscientious objectors, we will not participate in armed warfare or in making munitions, or by buying government bonds to prosecute the war, or in urging others to these efforts.
>
> But neither will we be carping in our criticism. We love our country and we love our President. We have been the only country in the world where men of all nations have taken refuge from oppression. We recognize that while in the order of intention we have tried to stand for peace, for love of our brother, in the order of execution we have failed as Americans in living up to our principles.[11]

Most Christian churches and theologians in the United States opted to express their "love of country" by supporting the war and rejecting pacifism, not because they had given up on peace but in order to take part in the exercise of American power in a world fraught with danger. It was a position that both Day and Muste believed placed the soul of the nation in great peril.

The religious leader who best grappled with the implications of that irony was Reinhold Niebuhr, the Protestant theologian, scholar, and public intellectual. Niebuhr's significance lay in his willingness to acknowledge the promise of American power and the perils embedded in taking that promise too sincerely. During World War II, Niebuhr had grown to prominence in part for publicly breaking with pacifism and offering a rigorous moral defense of America's war against fascist Germany and Japan. "A simple Christian moralism is senseless and confusing," he exclaimed. "It is senseless when, as in the World War, it seeks to uncritically identify the cause of Christ with the cause of democracy without a religious reservation. It is just as senseless when it seeks to purge itself of this error by an uncritical refusal to make any distinctions between relative values in history." Niebuhr challenged both pacifism and patriotism by attacking the tendency they both shared to see their nation as simply a moral agent for good. In this terrible war there was no moral position. Trying to find one only made more apparent the fact that, as Niebuhr argued, "the whole of human history is involved in guilt." But such guilt should not paralyze Christians into inaction, for God's grace prevailed above the moral temperament of his children. "The Christian is freed by that grace to act in history, to give his devotion to the highest values he knows, to defend those citadels of civilization of which necessity and historic destiny have made him the defender; and he is persuaded by that grace to remember the ambiguity of even his best actions." And in a statement that echoed the kind of wrestling Lincoln had engaged in during the Civil War, Niebuhr concluded: "If the providence of God does not enter the affairs of men to bring good out of evil, the evil in our good may easily destroy our most ambitious efforts and frustrate our highest hopes."[12]

However, the atomic bombing of Japan revealed the difficult balancing act Niebuhr attempted in his political theology. In an exchange with James Conant, Niebuhr elucidated his paradoxical counsel for the atomic age. On March 6, 1946, Conant, Harvard's president, wrote a pointed letter to Niebuhr. Conant had read a front-page article in that morning's *New York Times* about a declaration made by the Federal Council of Churches (FCC) that called the use of the atomic bomb on Japan "morally indefensible." Among the religious figures who had signed the statement was Niebuhr.

For Conant, Niebuhr's theological support for America's war effort had contributed ethical and moral legitimacy for the force America and its allies had used on enemy cities, including the atomic bomb. But now it appeared that Niebuhr had second thoughts regarding the use of immoral means to achieve what Conant believed were moral ends. The tone of Conant's letter suggested that without the type of moral support Niebuhr provided, America's actions might be considered immoral. "If the American people are to be deeply penitent for the use of the atomic bomb, why should they not be equally penitent for the destruction of Tokyo," Conant asked. "If we are to be penitent for this destruction of Japanese cities by incendiaries and high explosives, we should have to carry over this point of view to the whole method of warfare used against the axis powers." Taking his reasoning a step farther, Conant wondered whether the statement Niebuhr had signed also implied a renunciation of America's fearsome postwar military arsenal. "Are we to rule out strategic and area bombings . . . and are we to rule out the use of the atomic bomb, even in retaliation?"[13]

Niebuhr's response to Conant illustrated the vexing role a theologian played in this new era. Niebuhr made clear that he believed the use of the atomic bomb in certain circumstances was morally justifiable: "The pacifist always declares that we cannot do good if it involves the doing of evil, which is an impossibility." However, Niebuhr then turned to one of his characteristic arguments regarding the paradox of American power. "On the other hand," he reasoned, "it seems to me there is too general a disposition to disavow guilt because on the whole we have done good—in this case defeated tyranny. I was ready to sign the report on the expression of guilt—particularly because I thought it important from the Christian standpoint to admit the moral ambiguity of all righteous people in history, who are, despite the good they do, involved in antecedent and in marginal guilt."

Niebuhr did not object to the bomb as a viable weapon, only to its use without considering the implications of such an act. Niebuhr told Conant, "To judge from several letters I have received, it seems to me that the section of our report dealing with the irresponsible use of the bomb, is subject to misunderstanding, at least the misunderstanding of those of us who are not pacifists. We objected to the use of the bomb without warning, but could not have said that it should in no case have been used."[14] In that case, then, what was Niebuhr's point? In short, what was the point of admitting guilt? For Niebuhr the point was to anchor oneself in time—a terrible event had taken place, someone was responsible for it, and it could not be rationalized or justified before being recognized as a sin.

The sense of sin that Niebuhr carried into politics formed the core of a war-hardened theology that came to be called Christian realism. What Niebuhr offered was more than simple moral affirmation of America's special mission in the world; it was rather a morally rigorous, complex, and tragic understanding of the difficult but ultimately defensible position of a nation that was forced to commit acts of extraordinary violence in order to protect its citizens and to defeat the monstrous systems that led to wars of catastrophic destruction. He argued, as he had in his 1934 book *Moral Man and Immoral Society*, that man might have the luxury to be moral; society or the state did not. The anxiety that characterized the early postwar period provided Niebuhr with an opportunity to act as a theologian to the nation. One of his best biographers explained, "Niebuhr is the father of us all in the . . . sense that his confrontation with the events of his time was paradigmatic, a critical model for our generation as a whole. In helping to shape his own world, he helped shape our worldview—above all our inner conviction that all social endeavor is circumscribed by strict limits in a sinful, fragile, imperfect world."[15]

Niebuhr and his Christian realism became a touchstone for Cold War faith—a distinction ratified by *Time* magazine in 1948, when it put him on the cover of its twenty-fifth anniversary issue. Under a dark and ominous illustration of Niebuhr ran the subtitle: "Man's story is not a success story." In an essay the former communist turned devout American Whittaker Chambers argued that Niebuhr's jaded theology was apt for a time defined by the atrocities of the recent past and the foreboding of the future. As a counselor to his age, Niebuhr preached that neither the United States nor any other nation was blessed and that the Second World War coupled with the necessities of waging a cold war had forced Americans to recognize that they existed perilously between the poles of redemption and sin. Chambers declared, "Against the easy conscience Dr. Niebuhr asserted: 'man is by the nature of his creation sinful' and at the height of man's perfection there is always the possibility of evil. Against easy optimism, he asserted that life is inevitably tragic."[16]

While Chambers might have appreciated Niebuhr's complicated relationship to America, the former communist also played a specific kind of game with Niebuhr's theology. Niebuhr's use of contradictions and paradoxes provided a way to frame the postwar period in binary terms: good and evil, democracy and communism, the United States and the Soviet Union. However, Niebuhr contended that America too contained its own set of binaries—it could also be both good and evil. Yet that insight was largely lost when Niebuhr's moral language was abstracted from his theology. *Time* regarded Niebuhr as a figure who was suitably dark and brooding for his time, a voice for a kind of religion that was relevant but not too complicated or judgmental.

Niebuhr preached to an America that accepted his faith but not necessarily his theology. That was not surprising considering that in the early postwar Americans seemed always to be balanced precariously between falling into despair because of recent history and present challenges and rising to a new, almost unprecedented moment of moral clarity. "These visions gave urgency to the tasks at hand," sociologist Robert Wuthnow observed. "They comprised a cultural model that was also to play a continuing role in inspiring religious action in the years to come." It was a time filled with an imperative to act, and religious people felt this imperative acutely when they considered themselves part of a heroic, millennial struggle between good and evil. "Some would argue for great moral crusades, confronting evil head-on; others, for quiet, sustained, individual contributions; still others, for various escapes, withdrawals, or idealistic alternatives."[17] The Kingdom of God was a reality to the faithful, but understanding it had not yet been reached. The early Cold War offered a unique moment for religious people: it was a moment that could be understood almost only through religion.

In his book on religion and American foreign policy, William Inboden contends religion helped clarify what was at stake in the Cold War and how the United States should act based on those stakes. In the abstract, the use of religion and moral arguments was supposed to check as well as justify the American exercise of power. Thus, according to Inboden, "Godspeak" provided more than merely rhetorical cover for those policies. "Differences over political structures and economic systems and even national interests, though important in their own right, paled in comparison with the prospect of a world ruled by evil, a world devoid of spiritual values, a world without God," Inboden contends. "If ever there was a cause to fight, this was it."[18]

The imperatives of the Cold War pressed religion into the service of the nation. Amid a semblance of hand-wringing, religious organizations spoke confidently about the role the United States had to play in a struggle with theological overtones. The Cold War was about souls, and the secular state not only had to comprehend such moral gravity but had to act on it. This is not to say that the historic tensions among faiths had faded—there were still conflicts among Catholics and Protestants and Jews and within Protestantism itself. However, where denominational ecumenicalism failed, the emergence of a postwar civil religion afforded common ground. Where all sides sounded alike was in the general assessment that the Cold War was a moral crisis and the United States had a responsibility to engage it.[19]

The Cold War revealed something about the soul of the nation, and religious leaders fell in line. For example, the FCC in its 1950 report entitled *The Christian Conscience and Weapons of Mass Destruction* dismissed any residual pacifism in its position, arguing that "most of us find ourselves called to follow a course which is less simple and which appears to us more responsible because more directly relevant to the hard realities of our situation. And we believe it is the way in which most Christians must go." Compared with its previous position on the use of the atomic bomb, this position might have sounded like moral equivocation. The FCC stated, "We have no clever new political strategy to offer. But in sight of God we are persuaded that our desperate times call for a mighty and costly drive for the political and moral revival and uniting of the free world and beyond that for reconciliation." Churches turned to the moral power of self-sacrifice rather than judgment as the Cold War deepened. By doing so, they signaled a willingness to suspend judging the nation in order to shape the nation. A few notable and influential religious leaders did this by helping to forge a new national faith.[20]

Among the most visible religious leaders of this faith were Protestant evangelical Billy Graham and Catholics Francis Cardinal Spellman, Bishop Fulton Sheen, and theologian John Courtney Murray. Of this group, Graham was the youngest when World War II ended; he would become the most significant religious leader in postwar America.

Graham began his rise to stardom as a revivalist, but consolidated his popularity by working across denominational lines. He understood the relevance of the Cold War to his religion early in his career: it was a moral crisis that demanded a return to religious fundamentals before it was too late to save the nation he loved. Mark Silk writes of Graham, "Here was a man of faith, a tall blond evangelical Galahad whose earnest speech and clear-eyed gaze banished all thoughts of hypocrisy." He grew to become the most influential American preacher in the world—the combination of his appearance, rhetorical style, and, most of all, his faith made him something Americans hadn't seen for a while, a minister to the nation. While other theologians were practicing theology, Graham systematically and efficiently established a religious-based global network that ran through his ministry. Graham provided counsel—political as well as spiritual—to a world beset by crises.[21]

A paradigmatic example was Graham's Los Angeles revival in 1949. A couple of days after Americans found out that the Russians had entered the atomic age by detonating their first atomic weapon, Graham channeled popular anxiety over this news to implore his listeners to turn to God. "Unless the Western world has an old-fashioned revival, we cannot last!" he declared. Initially though, Graham's message did not attract many more than a few thousand people. That changed when he caught the attention of a new benefactor. Publishing tycoon and rabid anticommunist William Randolph Hearst commanded his newspapers to give Graham front-page coverage. The preacher's willingness to cast the Cold War in stark Manichean terms appealed to Hearst's personal worldview, and, as Hearst well knew, it could also clearly be connected with an American *Zeitgeist*. By the end of the preacher's revival he had spoken to upward of 350,000 people. In a sense this confluence of message and money made Graham the opposite of Niebuhr in his ability to channel his popularity through his ministry.[22]

From his first great success in the 1949 Los Angeles revival, Graham shrewdly made friends with another media giant, Henry Luce, and with politicians. By the summer of 1950, Graham and a few of his associates visited Harry Truman, though this encounter ended in a blunder when the evangelist played up the visit to the press, which published a photograph of him and his entourage kneeling in prayer on the White House lawn. Truman was furious that Graham had seemingly used his visit to promote himself. Truman did not need Graham to pray for him—which was how it looked in the press photo. After all, like other presidents, Truman's obligation extended to the spiritual well-being of the nation as well as the political and martial state of the union.[23]

Two years later, though, Graham had accumulated enough friends in high places to hold a revival in Washington, D.C., that culminated with a religious service on the steps of the U.S. Capitol. Besides scoring a first-of-its-kind religious ceremony, Graham also preached daily at the Pentagon. In early 1952, Graham squarely entered presidential politics when in Paris he met with Dwight Eisenhower for the first time. At this meeting, he encouraged the American war hero to run for president, advised him to become a Presbyterian, and subsequently told the millions of his followers on his weekly radio show, *Hour of Decision,* that he was deeply impressed by the general. This encounter began a life-long relationship between the occupants of the Oval Office and Graham.[24]

Graham became a trusted spiritual counselor to successive ministers-in-chief because of his vision of the Cold War as a moral crisis rather than a moral paradox. Throughout Graham's preaching, whether in person or on his radio show, he denounced communism as a "battle to the death . . . between Christ and the Anti-Christ" in order to fortify his listeners and their nation. Through his Manichean jeremiads, Graham fostered a muscular Christian patriotism that made clear that America would be judged almost solely on the strength of its devotion to an anticommunist crusade. Historian Angela Lahr points out that it was not just that Graham seemed well-suited to the atomic age but that American culture was eager to accept Graham's message. "This zero-sum struggle," she writes, "fit firmly into a premillennial worldview where the fight between good and evil intensified until the end, when good, not compromising, would prevail. The implications of the merger of the Cold War and premillennial worldviews meant that evangelicals could easily join the American anticommunist consensus."[25]

Graham was far from the only preacher with an apocalyptic message however. On the far right Fred Schwarz, creator of the School of Anti-Communism, Billy James Hargis of the Christian Crusade, and Carl MacIntire of the American Council of Christian Churches consciously countered the work of more moderate Christian evangelicals. Thus, in an anxious time, when the National Council of Churches (NCC) responded with ambivalence and Niebuhr with ambiguity, the Manichean Christian churches offered clarity: the world had been reduced to a struggle between the evil Soviet Union versus righteous America. In McIntire's anticommunist program, *The 20th Century Reformation Hour,* he led listeners to "exalt Jesus Christ as Savior and Lord, honor the scriptures as the inerrant Word of God, stand for the historic American heritage of freedom, promote personal righteousness and patriotism, warn of threats to our faith and freedom, and inspire enthusiastic service to our Lord and land."[26]

That fundamentalist Christians became ardent patriots was remarkable since only a generation earlier such churches had been marginalized from American politics and thought by taking decidedly antimodern views of evolution and contemporary mores. But the Cold War seemed especially well-suited to premodern views of the world. Niebuhr's idea of complexity and ambiguity might have captured a central dilemma of modernity, but his theology made apparent fault lines and fractures at a moment when unity and universalism seemed required. Perhaps no religious development in postwar America illustrated that better than the inclusion of the Catholic Church into a Cold War civil religion.

The cover story of the December 14, 1953, issue of *Time* magazine began with a brief and notorious exchange: "Joseph Stalin (at Teheran): How many divisions has the Pope? Pius XII (later, to Winston Churchill): Tell my son Joseph he will meet my divisions in heaven." The magazine described the Roman Catholic Church as the oldest witness of Western civilization. Pious XII was described as a man of time and, most significantly, as "a man of reality, for he is one of the world's leading spiritual fighters against Communism." Thus within the first two paragraphs of a story in America's leading political journal, a magazine read by far more Protestants than Catholics, the head of the Catholic Church was associated with the two great causes of the Cold War—the promotion of Western civilization and the fight against communism. This was no small feat. The magazine marveled:

> The Pope is chief executive of a unique organization. No secular government, no other church is comparable to it. It includes some 1,500 dioceses, 2,500 bishops, 500,000 priests, nuns and brothers in religious orders, with some 100,000 of them serving in the Church's missionary areas throughout the world. Into the brocaded offices of the Vatican Secretariat of State, cables carry news from its nunciatures around the world. To this organization, nothing can be unimportant, be it a new philosophical school in France or new playgrounds in an American diocese. It must deal with God and Caesar, with salvation and with society, with Freud and Marx, with hydraulic elevators and the levitation of saints.[27]

At this moment, though, the Catholic Church was seen as both a great bulwark against communism and, in the United States, perhaps the greatest single impediment to modern democracy. However, the *Time* article signaled that a transition of the church's image was under way.[28]

This transition was in large part a result of three different but visible leaders of the Catholic Church: Francis Cardinal Spellman, head of the New York Archdiocese; Bishop Fulton Sheen, whose popularity spanned radio and television as well as work among the laity; and a quiet, yet fiercely nationalistic, intellectual Jesuit priest named John Courtney Murray. Spellman took the crusade of anticommunism literally to the battlefield as the chaplain of the American military services from World War II to his death in 1967. Sheen too joined the anticommunist crusade but did so through a vigorous and at times remarkably eloquent defense of Western civilization. These two lighting rods of anticommunism were joined by Murray, who made a forceful argument for including Catholics in the period's "ecumenical rapprochement with the nation."[29]

The fact that the imperatives many Americans and their leaders had come to accept about the Cold War aligned with a set of Catholic assumptions made it easier to accept Catholicism as something other than a threat to the nation's dominant Protestant churches. Catholics accepted the idea of a moral order in which certain ideas about good and bad, rights and wrongs were immutable or inalienable. They understood the importance of tradition and saw the necessity of ceremony for unifying a disparate people through sacrifice of individual needs for service to a greater good. During the Cold War, such positions remade the image of Catholics into "champions of the West and the United States as Christendom's last great guardian." The significance of that transition was not merely that Catholics became accepted as allies in the fight against communism or the defense of Western civilization but, as Murray's work suggested, that the United States as a nation offered Catholics the best possible conditions to carry out their mission. If Catholics were to engage in this fight against communism they would need to do so through the nation itself. The church revealed the dynamic potential of the idea of national sacrifice.[30]

Cardinal Spellman was especially good at being both virulently patriotic and religiously pious in his anticommunism. For example, at an American Legion conference in August 1954, Spellman warned of another "Pearl Harbor" and declared, "War to the hilt between Communism and capitalism is inevitable." In his final benediction, Spellman asked the Legionnaires to pray: "Be with us, Blessed Lord, lest we forget and surrender to those who have attacked us without cause, those who repaid us with evil for good and hatred for love." Known as the American Pope, Spellman had a degree of influence unmatched by any other figure in the Catholic Church except the head of the Roman Church itself. In a clash between the Vatican and Spellman's ideological anticommunism, his biographer John Cooney writes, "Spellman, the American, in time would place the foreign policy goals of his government above those of the Vatican." He actively supported authoritarian dictators in Latin America, the homegrown demagogue Joseph McCarthy, and, most perilously, Ngo Dinh Diem of South Vietnam.[31] Yet Spellman was a product of the Cold War—a patriot both because of and despite his authoritarian proclivities. In an earlier era, his denunciation of liberalism and what he considered weak-willed Protestant confrontations with sin would have earned him and the Catholic Church categorical denigration by many Americans. But the Cold War made him a national religious leader, a chaplain in fatigues.

Bishop Sheen was no less strident in his anticommunism but was more appealing to broader audiences. Sheen was a well-educated, well-spoken Catholic priest who served a unique ministry: in the 1950s, he reportedly reached as many as thirty million Americans through his weekly prime-time television program *Life Is Worth Living*. One Catholic journal claimed that Sheen was "the most influential voice in Christendom next to that of Pius XII." He too believed that the Cold War was a spiritual war of cataclysmic proportions, but he also argued that the Soviet Union was not an alien human entity. It was "the final stage of degeneration of Western society." It was "Satan's answer to religion."[32]

Sheen defended the United States as the best earthly agent to oppose and defeat the communist menace. His rhetorical eloquence made his call for sacrifice sound even more imperative than Spellman's. In a sermon entitled "God and Country," Sheen declared, "We want to keep the United States a leader in the world and we believe that all God-believing people of the United States should unite to keep the country under Providence as the secondary cause for preservation of the liberties of the world." In Sheen's mind, America did God's work on earth, and because there was no more profound cause than this, all Americans, especially Catholics, had to contribute. In his most famous book, *Communism and the Conscience of the West* (1948), Sheen provided a discourse on communism as the enemy of the Western world. He asserted,

"*Communism is not to be feared just because it is anti-God, but because we are Godless*, not because it is strong, but because we are weak, for if we were under God, then who could conquer us?"[33]

Not many Americans disagreed with Sheen's strong religious message. Religion mattered in the early Cold War because through faith in God the United States could both confirm its fundamental rightness and comprehend the sacrifices it needed to make to be righteous. However, Sheen was like most other religious leaders of his day in that his apparent prophetic public theology—his calling on Americans to be more godly—was circular. If Americans moved closer to God, they more closely affirmed the good origins of the nation itself, for the nation's cherished rights came first and foremost from God. Sheen explained, "We believe that religion and morality are indispensable supports of democracy and that religion and patriotism go together." If Sheen and Spellman maneuvered American Catholics into the martial culture of the Cold War, Murray helped justify that culture through Catholic thought. For that reason, Murray's thought provided vital support to the Manicheanism of his fellow Americans.[34]

Murray operated in intellectual and religious circles inhabited by Niebuhr, not Graham. His greatest effort and achievement was to develop "a Catholic defense of religious liberty." This issue more than any other would placate Catholicism's most intelligent critics. His work on this issue came forth in a series of essays in the late 1940s and early 1950s; these essays were subsequently published in the book *We Hold These Truths* (1960). Murray hammered the point that the United States was the protector of the Judeo-Christian tradition far more than any European country. Through the American Revolution, the American founders made it possible for Catholicism to flourish in the modern world.[35]

Murray's contention was simple: Americans had a public philosophy that could help guide them through moral crises—such as the Cold War—because it united them not merely as citizens under a government but as persons under God. Whereas clergy such as Graham, Spellman, and Sheen used religion to unite Americans against the Soviet Union, Murray offered a more complex form of civil religion. He reasoned that the trend toward religious pluralism in the 1950s suggested both the imperative to unite (in this case, against communism) and a way to comprehend the moral purpose for such unity. This purpose was, he told *Time* magazine, a "kind of spiritual charter by which all Americans can live together. It is 'the constitutional consensus whereby the people acquires its identity as a people and the society is endowed with its vital form . . . its sense of purpose as a collectivity organized for action in history.' "[36]

Like Niebuhr and Graham, Murray also graced the cover of *Time* magazine, as a sign that he too represented a way for religion to go beyond the specific church in which he worshiped. In a long cover story entitled "City of God and Man," Murray was compared to Saint Augustine and his project to Augustine's reflections on the role the church played as the Roman Empire collapsed. However, rather than barbarians with axes, Murray argued that the contemporary danger came from the children of the Enlightenment, progeny of the scientific revolution, and offspring of the modern industrial state who are "engaged in the construction of a philosophy to put an end to all philosophy . . . to corrupt the inherited intuitive wisdom by which the people have always lived, and to do this not by spreading new beliefs but by creating a climate of doubt and bewilderment in which clarity about the larger aims of life is dimmed and the self-confidence of the people is destroyed."[37]

Even though Murray was often portrayed as a cool intellectual and the Catholic whom Protestant intellectuals could safely admire, his critique of American liberalism was as pointed as any sermon from other prominent religious firebrands. However, Murray's project aligned with the role for religion peddled by Cold War politicians. "Can we or can we not," he reasoned, "achieve a successful conduct of our national affairs, foreign and domestic, in the absence of a consensus that will set our purposes, furnish a standard of judgment on policies, and establish the proper conditions for political dialogue?" He told *Time* that unifying to fight communism wasn't enough—America needed "a new moral act of purpose [beyond the] small-souled purpose of mere survival." Therefore, as Robert McElroy wrote of Murray, "it was no exaggeration for *Time* magazine to designate Murray and Reinhold Niebuhr as the primary architects of a renewed role for religion in American public life at mid-century, a role that recognized the pluralism and freedom of the United States as a source of moral strength and direction." Indeed, unlike Niebuhr, who could argue from a position at the center of the nation's most dominant faith tradition, Murray made Catholics at least competitive in the construction of a national faith when he argued that it must be based on what he called "the public philosophy—natural law."[38]

Natural law was not exclusively Catholic, although Thomas Aquinas historically gets credit for making it the foundation of Western civilization. More important, Murray contended that it was not incidental to American history. Murray argued that the United States owed its ideological existence to this philosophy because, as the Founding Fathers clearly believed, the natural rights of man are located in the one place above yet also accessible to all, God. McElroy notes that, for Murray, "the American experiment in democracy rest[ed] primarily upon a moral consensus rooted in the transcendent rights of the human person." This consensus was not provided by divine revelation but was comprehended and constructed out of "substantive and civil dialogue within American society concerning the key issues of the day." According to Murray, the American religious heritage inspired the notion of democracy rightly understood—meaning that "there are truths that we hold in common, and a natural law that makes known to all of us the structure of the moral universe in such ways that all of us are bound by it in a common obedience."[39]

In submitting to this higher law, Murray suggested Americans would find the kind of prophetic faith that would allow them to act in a dangerous world—and thus defend themselves from destruction—while also rein in the worst impulses of unbounded human ambition. In regard to war, Murray explained that natural law dictated limits to military action but did not tend toward either pacifism or moral relativism. The natural law tradition illustrated, according to Murray, that "policy is the meeting place between the world of power and the world of morality." In perhaps its most calibrated form, American civil religion would function as a manifestation of Murray's public philosophy by forcing state action to be consonant with the best traditions of the United States without employing American history as if it were merely de jure rationalization for such action.[40]

Murray was one of a few public intellectuals during the period advocating a revival of natural law. Mortimer Adler, Walter Lippmann, and Leo Strauss all advanced the necessity of a public philosophy that would

fortify free societies in their struggle against totalitarianism and the shal-
lowness of modern consumerism. As Murray had suggested, one might
make people aware of the dangers lurking outside their borders but
one was hard-pressed to make them understand the existential threat
that communism and modernity posed to a nation that had lost its soul.
Thus internal decay might be arrested if a godly people unified against
totalitarian threats for expressly moral reasons.[41]

Clearly religious leaders had become important in framing the Cold
War, but merging that faith to a prosecution of war itself fell to political
leaders. America's first Cold War presidents, Truman and Eisenhower,
found it necessary to make official a theology that could exist beyond the
nation's churches. Inboden explains that such political leadership became
necessary because ultimately the nation's religious leaders "differed on
just how pernicious a threat [communism] posed, and how and where
and to what extent America should oppose it."[42] The first president to
take up "the cross" of the Cold War was Truman.

Truman had ordered the atomic bombing of Japan and led the
United States in the early, anxious days of the Cold War. To help him
in his endeavors, he developed a theology of American exceptionalism
based on two basic assumptions: first, the United States was nothing if
not a creation of the Judeo-Christian tradition; and, second, this tradition was absolutely vital to the successful comprehension of the postwar
world. Undoubtedly this theology framed how he prosecuted the Cold
War against Soviet communism, but his thinking went beyond strategic
to existential considerations.

During World War II, an assumption emerged that one of the pillars
of American moral authority lay in its historic attachment to the Judeo-
Christian tradition. The idea that the nation could draw on its three
largest faiths—Protestantism, Catholicism, and Judaism—not only made
the nation sound Godly but also covered all the ethnic groups that made
up the diverse population then at war. Using religion in the war also
provided another point of unity for soldiers and a point of contrast with
the enemy for those at home. After the war, calling upon the Judeo-
Christian tradition adapted to the new struggle against communism by
constantly and pointedly linking the enemy's ideology to atheism.[43]

In the State of the Union address Truman delivered in January 1948,
the president reasoned that while the United States was a great nation,

possessing great economic and military power, the most significant source of its strength was "spiritual." "For we are a people of faith," Truman declared, and that provided the imperative for Americans to act in a world beset by "great questions, great anxieties, and great aspirations." Answering these questions would of course require an enormous commitment of material wealth. But such sacrifice made no sense, Truman explained, unless Americans understood that "it is our faith in human dignity that underlies these purposes. It is this faith that keeps us a strong and vital people." Thus it was this faith rather than mere strategic necessity that would obligate the United States to face down whatever problems arose around the world, including the growing threat posed by Soviet communism, because ultimately the question was not who would dominate the world in a material sense but which system of ideals would prevail. "Today the whole world looks to us for leadership. This is the hour to rededicate ourselves to the faith in mankind that makes us strong. This is the hour to rededicate ourselves to the faith in God that gives us confidence as we face the challenge of the years ahead."[44]

Truman's idealism sounded similar to the rhetoric of Woodrow Wilson and Franklin Roosevelt, and like theirs his vision underscored the American ideological commitment to remake world politics. Truman believed that the United States did not create an ideology for itself but, rather, successfully built a nation on ideas available to and suitable for all people everywhere. His faith in the universal application of what were American ideals transformed his vision from strategic to what he imagined was prophetic. The world was engaged in a historic struggle between two competing systems of thought—one was moral and democratic, the other was immoral and antidemocratic. The United States could do nothing less that advance those ideals that were universal and for which the nation had sacrificed in World War II. Unlike Wilson and Roosevelt before him, though, Truman inaugurated an era in which American power matched the ambition of American ideals. He could turn vision into a reality by establishing America's moral commitment to world affairs and doing so in decidedly religious terms.

In his only inaugural address, Truman recited the American creed as he understood it, with phrasing that sounded much like the Nicene Creed: "The American people stand firm in the faith which has inspired this Nation from the beginning. We believe that all men have a right to equal justice under law and equal opportunity to share in the common good. We believe that all men have a right to freedom of thought and expression. We believe that all men are created equal because they are created in the image of God." This profession of faith made clear why Truman thought a clash with communism was inevitable. But the tone and intellectual construction of Truman's statement echoed another fundamental belief of the day: that the United States was a product of both the Judeo-Christian tradition and the Enlightenment. As Truman argued, the faith Americans had in their nation came from their acceptance that "all men are created in the image of God." One need not be a Baptist, as Truman ostensibly was, to grasp this principle. But this was a religious understanding of the nation, not a theocratic or denominational one. In short, it mattered that at the outset of the Cold War President Truman constantly couched America's moral obligations to the world in religious terms. He advanced and clarified a faith in an American civil religion by establishing that American actions abroad emerged from and would be evaluated by the nation's commitment to certain fundamental ideals. War had established America's preponderance of power, but civil religion would guide the nation's projection of it.[45]

The most consequential policy based on that faith appeared in a master strategy laid out in a national security document, NSC-68. In 1950, Truman's national security team, led by Paul Nitze, drafted a top-secret memo that advocated the largest peacetime expansion of military might in U.S. history in order "to make ourselves strong both in the way in which [we] affirm our values in the conduct of our national life, and in the development of our military and economic strength." NSC-68 dramatically expressed the imperatives under which an American civil religion operated in the Cold War. The document has rightly been credited (or blamed) for militarizing the American state, but NSC-68's authors argued forcefully that a military buildup made sense only in connection with the projection of American ideals. The Cold War was about competing faiths defended by massive arsenals. "Every consideration of devotion to our fundamental values and to our national security," Nitze and his team declared, "demands that we achieve our objectives by the strategy of the cold war, building up our military strength in order that it may not have to be used." Was such rhetoric disingenuous?

Consider: the document was not made public but was intended for and was acted upon by the president and his national security advisors. Moreover, NSC-68 was, as intellectual historian Bruce Kuklick suggests, a modern-day jeremiad written by intellectual elites to press American political leaders into action as warriors in a world in which the United States defended what was right against forces that had done and would do great wrongs.[46]

Such nobility, though, came at a price in material and lives. In June 1950, communist North Korea invaded the American-supported authoritarian state of South Korea. The United States appealed to the young United Nations to take a stand against communist aggression in Asia based not on American national interests but in the interest of universal ideals. This "peace action," as it was known, lasted three years and one month; included troops from both Koreas, the United States, China, the Soviet Union, and seventeen other nations; cost billions of dollars to fight; and took hundreds of thousands of lives.

A news report from March 1951 that recounted the first transport of dead American soldiers from Korea quoted General Doyle O. Hickey, who claimed that these men represented "all the peoples of the earth who prefer death to bondage." As if to emphasize the universality of this sacrifice, the report also mentioned that these men "were of all ranks, from private to general, of various creeds and races. They died on many scattered battlefields."[47]

Historian James Stokesbury has called the Korean War a "half-war," for unlike the two world wars that preceded it this one failed to provide anything approaching conclusive, even cathartic, lessons. Soldiers died, but the nation as a whole did not need to participate in the sacrifice. In speeches throughout 1951, Truman attempted to make the nation aware of a larger meaning of the war.[48]

The president used the dedication of a chapel in Philadelphia honoring four chaplains—two Protestant, one Jewish, and one Catholic—who famously and heroically prayed together while their military ship sank during World War II to remind the nation that through religion Americans could comprehend the transcendent meaning of their nation. "Their belief, their faith, in His word enabled them to conquer death," he said. "This is an old faith in our country. It is shared by all our churches and all our denominations." It was not incidental, therefore, that these men practiced their faith as chaplains in the U.S. military, for their sacrifice in service to United States was religious. Truman declared, "We must never forget that this country was founded by men who came to these shores to worship God as they pleased. . . . They did not come here to do as they pleased—but to worship God as they pleased, and that is a most important distinction. The unity of our country comes from this fact. The unity of our country is a unity under God." Thus the deaths of soldiers in Korea, Truman argued, were "in the spirit of the four chaplains." Men were dying "in defense of the great religious faiths which make this chapel a place of worship," he said. "I have faith that the great principles for which our men are fighting will prevail."[49]

However, the war in Korea did not consolidate a civil religion for the post–World War II generation. Americans did not want to sacrifice actual lives in order to substantiate the ideals of the nation. They wanted to struggle over abstract notions of right and wrong against a foe that was both real enough to scare them but not enough of a threat to engage with militarily. In polls taken throughout the war, Americans demonstrated their ambivalence toward waging war against communism. Immediately after Truman sent troops to South Korea in June 1950, 78 percent of those polled said they approved of the president's decision to send military aid and only 15 percent disapproved. By June 1951, 43 percent of those polled thought that going to war in Korea was a mistake, and 40 percent said it was not. Numbers fluctuated throughout the rest of the war until it ended; in January 1953, 50 percent of Americans said that it had not been a mistake to go to war in Korea, while 36 percent said it had been. Weighing on the minds of those polled was a widely shared fear that the war in Korea would lead to World War III. In July 1950, 53 percent of those polled thought this; a little more than a year later 49 percent continued to believe that the United States was actually in the early stages of World War III.[50]

The Korean War would ultimately amass millions of casualties, including the deaths of close to thirty-five thousand Americans. And yet it was never declared a war by the United States. Truman did not go to Congress to ask for a declaration of war, rather he went to the United Nations and through it coordinated a coalition of forces to fight what amounted to an ideological battle in a place far from American shores. In his farewell address, Truman justified this mission in familiar terms: "Our men are fighting as valiantly as Americans have ever fought," he explained to his radio audience, "because they know they are fighting in the same cause of freedom in which Americans have stood ever since the beginning of the Republic." It was a "test" that Truman assured Americans they had to meet. In turn, most Americans understood that the struggle in Korea was not an end in itself. It was part of a larger, more ambiguous, but still very dangerous, war against communism. Truman made clear that it was a struggle that required sacrifice and determination. It required American unity but, he hoped, not many American lives. The point seemed to be, as Stokesbury has suggested, to fight a half-war that was framed in Manichean terms.

For example, Truman told his audience, "Once in a while I get a letter from some impatient person asking, why don't we get it over with? Why don't we issue an ultimatum, make all-out war, drop the atomic bomb?" Truman added that for most Americans "the answer is quite simple":

> We are not made that way. We are a moral people. Peace is our goal, with justice and freedom. We cannot, of our own free will, violate the very principles that we are striving to defend. The whole purpose of what we are doing is to prevent world war III. Starting a war is no way to make peace. But if anyone still thinks that just this once, bad means can bring good ends, then let me remind you of this: We are living in the 8th year of the atomic age. We are not the only nation that is learning to unleash the power of the atom. A third world war might dig the grave not only of our Communist opponents but also of our own society, our world as well as theirs.
>
> Starting an atomic war is totally unthinkable for rational men.

The point was not to blow the other side off the map, even though the United States had decided by this point to accelerate its production of nuclear weapons. Rather, Truman asserted, the communist world contained a fatal flaw—"theirs is a godless system, a system of slavery." Defeating a foe like that would not happen in a great conflagration but through a contest of ideas. And Truman believed that "in the long run the strength of our free society, and our ideals, will prevail over a system that has respect for neither God nor man." Yet Truman left office with both the Cold War and the Korean War unfinished. The world torn apart by the bomb remained fractured.[51]

Eisenhower echoed Truman's belief that ideas were as important to the Cold War as bombs. From his military experience, Eisenhower appreciated the contrast between death in war and the moral justification assigned to such sacrifice by a grateful nation. As president, he needed to emphasize the moral rationale for the struggle against communism in order to stave off war that would bring slaughter on a scale unseen even in Ike's war-hardened experience. Yet Eisenhower also understood the need for Americans to feel some imperative to unify: if not to kill and die for the nation then to prevent the need to do so. While it is undoubtedly the case that under Eisenhower American defense budgets swelled, the old general also went far in incorporating an American civil religion into the nation's plans for defense.

Eisenhower expressed the significance of this national faith most famously in remarks he made shortly after his first election as president in the winter of 1952. In a brief speech before the Freedom Foundation, Eisenhower recalled an encounter with his World War II counterpart, Soviet general Georgy Zhukov, that underscored the inability of Americans and Soviets to understand one another. Ike asserted that because Zhukov belonged to a political system that rejected religion, he would never be able to comprehend American aims in the world. "Our form of government has no sense unless it is founded in a deeply felt religious faith, and I don't care what it is," Eisenhower explained. "With us of course it is the Judeo-Christian concept but it must be a religion that all men are created equal."[52] That statement captured well Eisenhower's sincere belief that a national faith required an understanding that because of the existence of God the United States was under an obligation to do good. And so, as president, Eisenhower believed it part of his duty to emphasize the role religion played in the history and operation of the nation.

Eisenhower's public image was unlike that of any other person at the time: as commander of the Allied forces in World War II, Ike was present at the creation of America's global rise to power and responsibility, and as president he got out of Korea and stayed out of an emerging struggle in Vietnam. In his first inaugural address, Ike made the important decision to ask Americans to pray. He remains the only president to begin an inaugural address with a prayer, and during the speech that followed he used the word "faith" thirteen times. Eisenhower asserted, "This faith is the abiding creed of our fathers. It is our faith in the deathless dignity of man, governed by eternal moral and natural laws. This faith defines our full view of life. It establishes, beyond debate, those gifts of the Creator that are man's inalienable rights, and that make all men equal in His sight." In a speech that minced few words, he also addressed the need to sacrifice: "We must be ready to dare all for our country. For history does not long entrust the care of freedom to the weak or the timid. We must acquire proficiency in defense and display stamina in purpose. We must be willing, individually and as a Nation, to accept whatever sacrifices may be required of us. A people that values its privileges above its principles soon loses both."[53]

A signature illustration of Ike's views on this specific kind of national sacrifice appeared in a radio address the president made as part of the American Legion's "Back to God" program. In his brief remarks, Eisenhower explained the need to strengthen American resolve in the struggle against communism. In battle, the former World War II commander intoned, "there are no atheists in foxholes[;] . . . in a time of test and trial, we instinctively turn to God for new courage and peace of mind." In short, the Cold War made the entire country into one large foxhole, and Americans had to act because they were under God's judgment. However, it wasn't clear to Eisenhower whether Americans understood that.[54]

Earlier that same day, Eisenhower had attended a Sunday morning service at the New York Avenue Presbyterian Church with his wife. He listened to the Reverend George M. Docherty deliver a sermon commemorating Abraham Lincoln's birthday. The topic of his sermon was the significance of the phrase "under God." Docherty argued that Lincoln had triumphed over slavery, the great scourge of his day, by calling on the moral authority of the nation. By reaffirming that the United States was created "under God," Lincoln's address at Gettysburg had reminded Americans that they had the spiritual resources to win a war that was ultimately more about their souls than their soldiers. Reflecting on the cold war, Docherty intoned, "We face, today, a theological war. It is not basically a conflict between two political philosophies. . . . Nor is it a conflict fundamentally between two economic systems. . . . It is a fight for the freedom of the human personality. It is not simply, 'Man's inhumanity to man.' It is Armageddon, a battle of the gods." In Docherty's view, God was consequential to American history and destiny; faith in God was fundamental to the ideals on which the nation was based and, equally important, vital to renewing those ideals through public rituals like the pledge of allegiance. The minister declared, "To omit the words 'under God' in the Pledge of Allegiance is to omit the definitive character of the 'American Way of Life.' "[55]

Eisenhower told Docherty that he agreed with the sermon "entirely." Docherty's words were reprinted widely in newspapers, and he received hundreds of letters of support. The moment was ripe for a campaign begun in the early 1950s to insert "under God" in the pledge of allegiance. A few months later, on Flag Day, June 14, 1954, Eisenhower signed a bill that made "under God" an official part of the pledge. In his prepared remarks, the president declared, "We are affirming the transcendence of religious faith in America's heritage and future; in this way we shall constantly strengthen those spiritual weapons which forever will be our country's most powerful resource, in peace or in war."[56]

The phrase "under God" has a long history, with its point of origin in Lincoln's Gettysburg Address, when he declared "that this nation, under God, shall have a new birth of freedom and the government of the people, by the people, for the people, shall not perish from the earth." However, not until the Cold War did the phrase begin to get regular use. Calling upon Lincoln fit the Cold War; after all, the sixteenth president used the phrase "under God" in his Gettysburg Address to reframe a conflict that deeply divided Americans into a cause that could ultimately unite them. Likewise, Eisenhower hoped to unite Americans in a war that had to be fought—it could not be avoided—but that also had to be more ideological than martial. Lincoln had appealed to God in order to make sense of mass death, to eulogize mass sacrifice. Eisenhower used God to make sense of widespread fear of the next war, which would, if it came, bring apocalyptic destruction. In Lincoln's time, Americans felt war—it destroyed their families, their farms, and, for some, their faith. In Eisenhower's Cold War, Americans imagined war—it created both mass anxiety and mass apathy. Thus, for both presidents, faith in the nation became an imperative: Lincoln used God to bring meaning to a war that had torn apart the nation; Eisenhower used God to unite Americans in an effort to prevent a war that would annihilate the nation.

A significant difference separates these two examples however. For Lincoln, sacrifice in the Civil War was so widely shared that he could use it to unify the nation: the war incarnated civil religion.[57] Eisenhower wanted to use the civil religion to avoid the ritual of mass sacrifice. To do this, Eisenhower used the conditions of the Cold War to incorporate civil religion. In other words, through the kind of rhetoric illustrated above Eisenhower made official what had been merely apparent, that in a time of war—even a cold war—Americans could not be atheists; they had a national faith.

Eisenhower had a Congress that largely agreed with him, as it illustrated during the mid-1950s by passing acts that did much to affirm the president's view of American civil religion. In the spring of 1954, the Eighty-third Congress voted to add the words "under God" to the pledge of allegiance; in 1955, Congress passed a law that required the statement "In God We Trust" placed on all U.S. coins and currency; and in 1956 Congress made the official motto of the nation "In God we trust," which replaced "E pluribus unum." Almost as important was a declaration made by a sitting United States Supreme Court justice, William O. Douglas. Douglas wrote in the majority opinion in *Zorach v. Clauson*, "We are a religious people whose institutions presuppose a Supreme Being." And he contributed an essay to Edward R. Murrow's popular and widely syndicated radio show, *This I Believe*. Douglas said, "These days I see America drifting from the Christian faith . . . acting abroad as an arrogant, selfish, greedy nation interested only in guns and in dollars . . . not in people and their hopes and aspirations. We need a faith that dedicates us to something bigger and more important than ourselves or our possessions."[58]

In a speech to the General Board of the NCC, Eisenhower made a similar appeal. In a series of remarks that were extraordinary in their candor and revealing in their epistemological construction, he acknowledged a certain uneasiness addressing a body of religious leaders because he took religion so seriously and felt self-conscious in front of people who had dedicated their lives to it. He explained in his somewhat folksy way: "Now I feel a very definite reason for being here. I happen to be the Chief Executive of a nation of which the Government is merely a translation in the political field of a deeply-felt religious faith. . . . So the fact that our Government rests and is founded on a deeply-felt religious faith gives to my appearance, even before such a body, a certain validity—say, a certain fitness." As the president of a country founded on religious faith but not unified by a single church, Eisenhower found an organization such as the NCC significant, for it could perform a task fundamental to managing the Cold War. The NCC could create interchurch cooperation by focusing on religion as the wellspring of the American character.

> As I understand it, this body is met to devise ways and means to cooperate in the great religious life of America, so that differences in dogma, or ritual—as a matter of fact, I am not sure just exactly how you describe it—will be minimized and cooperation will center around those things that are at the bottom of the life of this country: that is, the readiness to cooperate, the recognition that man is a person and an entity of dignity in front of his God, regardless of his religion or his race, or any other such things of inconsequential character. You are cooperating in order that this great recognition that man is after all basically a spiritual being and not merely an animal, or physical thing, you are cooperating to bring that under-standing home with more force to each of us. In doing so, I thoroughly believe that not only will it operate better and more effectively to the advancement of religion in the United States, it will advance all of us in the practice of democracy as it should be practiced in this country.[59]

Eisenhower's statement illustrated the promise and peril of civil religion. In his almost innocent contention that cooperation among churches got to the "bottom of the life of this country" because it moved beyond "inconsequential" things such as religion and race, he betrayed a confidence—naive perhaps—that there was a purpose to the nation that transcended the elements of identity and ideology that divided it. Ike propounded a civil religion that he hoped would enable the public as a whole to triumph over the selfishness of individuals.

Yet was this national faith, this civil religion, a bunch of bunk? At the time, journalist William Lee Miller thought so. He wrote scathing critiques of revivals such as the "back to God" campaign for promoting religion as a means to national rather than religious ends. "As a man can be converted, in a moment, so the world can be changed, by a crusade," Miller observed about the popular piety of these campaigns. "The 'illusion' of American omnipotence, that America can do whatever she wants to, is part of the same ethos which a conversionist and revivalist heritage helped to produce. In short, the American religious tradition is geared to arouse enthusiasm and passion, not to produce wisdom and patience; it is more at home with single, simple, moral choices, than with complex, continuing political problems."

Miller was not antireligious so much as anti–popular piety. He believed that religion under Eisenhower had become little more than a caricature of revivalism: the American people had gone back to God but didn't know what do with Him. Miller lamented that there was "no figure . . . who is at once a popular and a theological leader." In his view, Ike's work as the nation's pastor didn't qualify. The nation needed a theologian to complicate that faith in the nation. The promise of America became an end in itself when placed alongside the perceived cruelty of communism. In a war of faiths, American civil religion was remaking the nation into a god that could not be allowed to fail.[60]

That situation seemed especially ironic in light of a stunning book that appeared in 1950. *The God That Failed: A Confession* sounded a clarion call. Here were six writers who either had been part of the Communist Party or had been friendly to (and therefore fellow travelers of) communism confessing their "sin" of following a false god. The editors of this collection were Richard Crossman, a British member of Parliament and leader of the British left, and Arthur Koestler, a Hungarian émigré and author of a well-received novel that depicted the horrors of Stalinist Russia, *Darkness at Noon* (1940). While each essay was personal and distinct from the rest, the thread that joined them together was a simple appeal to compatriots on the left to renounce communism and acknowledge the moral superiority of Western democracy. Crossman announced, "No one who has not wrestled with Communism as a philosophy, and Communists as political opponents, can really understand the values of Western democracy. The Devil once lived in Heaven, and those who have not met him are unlikely to recognize an angel when they see one."[61]

The book's title was brilliant—it captured the crux of the Cold War as a struggle. It also sold well; 160,000 copies in English in the first four years of publication. The book's sales were undoubtedly boosted by the fact that the Cold War was not so cold between the god of communism and the God of Christian democracies in the West. Thus the collection of essays was "hatched" as way to contribute to the intellectual and cultural struggle against communism. As Koestler explained in his memoirs, " 'The God That Failed' became a kind of household word and seemed to have been quite effective in 'swelling the flood of anti-Communist propaganda,' to judge by the number of reprints and foreign translations."[62] Koestler acknowledged that the book's title was intentionally provocative; it suggested that in the wake of communism's failure there was a god that didn't fail or couldn't fail or perhaps couldn't be allowed to fail. That god, the alternative to Soviet communism, was not the God of the Hebrew Bible or Christian New Testament but of Western democracy. Thus the title of this book at least captured a duel between competing secular gods, an allusion that most reviewers at the time missed, except for two, Niebuhr and the Jewish sociologist Will Herberg.

Niebuhr was by far the better known of the two. And like the essayists in *The God That Failed*, Niebuhr could also relate to the journey away from the left. He had been a socialist in the late 1920s and early 1930s, though never a member of the Communist Party. In his review, Niebuhr observed, "The moving power of their several chronicles derives not merely from the unity of the theme embodied in significant variations but also from the reader's sense that they are recording a tragedy in which all of us have been involved. That tragedy is that the moral protest against the injustices of our civilization should have been organized in a movement which replaced the whips of injustice with the scorpions of tyranny." Here was a principle Niebuhr made the crux of his contribution to world politics—the best and brightest of any generation are at the mercy of history. "The whole drama of human history," Niebuhr preached, "is under the scrutiny of a divine judge who laughs at human pretensions without being hostile to human aspirations."[63] And by 1950 Niebuhr had become recognized as an outspoken critic of the naive optimism that pervaded the religiosity of his fellow churchmen. History, he repeatedly stated, had humbled him: "Was not the pilgrimage of the several authors of the symposium to the Utopia of Moscow a symptom of the false yearning in our whole culture for absolute goals in history, whereas we must be content with fragmentary and tentative achievements of the good in all our historical striving? Does not the charity that Koestler calls the 'gravitational force which keeps history in its orbit' derive from a humility that recognizes the incomplete and fragmentary character of every scheme of justice so that the highest form of perfection in history is incompatible with any claim that we have the final form of perfection in our keeping?"[64]

Niebuhr believed that the central sin identified by the essayists in *The God That Failed* was the original sin of the nation-state—the expectation that progress would become apparent and unstoppable once the natural rights of man and citizen had harnessed the power of popular politics. Niebuhr worried that as Western democracies celebrated the righteousness of inalienable rights in the fight against Soviet tyranny, their cause would mock equally inalienable obligations such as charity and humility. Indeed, Enlightenment thought inspired both Soviet communism and American democracy. Religion might check the excesses of modern man, but such a religion could not be a civil religion that certified the most successful nation-state in history. It had to be an ancient religion that put modern man and his modern society in the proper perspective.

Like Niebuhr, Herberg recognized that *The God That Failed* was not simply about the failure of communism but about the danger of all false gods. Thus when he asked, "And after the collapse of the Communist faith, what then?" his answer wasn't merely anticommunism. "What is to take the place of the 'god that failed'? Without some ultimate allegiance to give meaning of life, men cannot go on. . . . The ex-Communist, the passionate idolater who has lost his god, is thus confronted with the ultimate problem of human existence. If he does not turn to the living God, the God who by his holiness shatters all earthly pretensions and claims to absolutization, he will in the end inevitably find another idol to worship, and the fruits of idolatry of whatever kind are despair, disillusionment and demonic self-destruction." To prevent such a fate, Herberg argued that the ex-communists and one presumes those who never fell for the communist god but could still fall for another false god had to find humility. "Only a philosophy that understands its own inherent limitations and seeks grounding in the Prophetic faith of Judaism and Christianity can serve man amidst the perils and frustrations of existence."[65]

In the mid to late 1930s Herberg found Niebuhr's understanding of original sin the explanation he needed to understand how socialism had gone so terribly wrong. Thus, by the late 1930s and early 1940s, Herberg had taken a decidedly religious turn, and he became in the decades that followed the "Jewish Niebuhr." Herberg praised the contributors of *The God That Failed* for illustrating that "Communism is in fact a religion, a demonic idolatrous religion, but a religion nevertheless." But in the end he found the book disappointing because it lacked existential pondering: "It tells us nothing, or next to nothing, about the secret mechanism by which subconscious processes which have been going on for years are suddenly precipitated into consciousness under the impact of some great event. . . . It is more than a political, more even than a psychological problem; it is a problem deeply existential, ultimately perhaps theological."[66]

In their reviews of *The God That Failed*, Niebuhr and Herberg acted as prophets against optimism—they stood in judgment of the developing civil religion. They feared that the struggle against a foe as terrible as communism would create a one-dimensional moral world, in which those opposed to communism got to determine good and evil. Niebuhr and Herberg clearly believed communism had catastrophic consequences for people and humanity in general, yet they also understood and sought to emphasize that this disaster had not been caused by some force alien to human nature. Communism had been attractive because it satisfied a human longing for faith in something transcendent. The danger in the early Cold War, then, was that the struggle against communism would itself become a totalistic faith.

In 1955, Herberg's book *Protestant, Catholic, Jew* made him into the most prominent critic of the civil religion in the early postwar period. To be fair, Herberg did not call his target "civil religion." He called it "the American Way of Life." He capitalized each word to emphasize that this idea, as he explained, was "a spiritual structure, a structure of ideas and ideals, of aspirations and values, of beliefs and standards; it synthesizes all that commends itself to the American as the right, the good, and the true in actual life." He described this common religion as one that formed organically (or politically) and was informed by the official religions of the nation. "Insofar as any reference is made to the God in whom all Americans 'believe' and of whom the 'official' religions speak, it is primarily as sanction and underpinning for the supreme values of the faith embodied in the American Way of Life. Secularization of religion could hardly go further." Accordingly, within the American Way of Life, "religion is a 'good thing,' a supremely 'good thing,' for the individual and the community. And 'religion' here means not so much any particular religion, but religion as such, religion-in-general." Herberg argued that this common faith made no pretense to trump official religions; it didn't need to. It operated at a lower level—deeper, more pervasive and influential. The common faith goes beyond a belief in democracy and the nation and works most effectively as personal faith; it unites disparate people in a way that is unconscious and therefore personal to each individual. "This inner, personal religion is based on the American's *faith in faith*."[67]

In the middle of a religious revival, Herberg's critique was utterly and boldly anachronistic; after all, he thought that what passed for religiosity was just vacuous. Americans had accepted, even embraced, idol worship—and the idol they worshipped was themselves. Herberg had taken a step beyond his evaluation of Koestler and his comrades— once one had given up on a false god the danger became settling for a faith that was safe and affirming in ways that the other faith had been bold and exciting. Thus, Americans were cultivating a religion "which validates culture and society, without in any sense bringing them under judgment. . . . Religion becomes, in effect, the cult of culture and society, in which the 'right' social order and the received cultural values are divinized by being identified with the divine purpose." Herberg was quite unrelenting. He didn't merely hit easy targets like the facile pronouncements of the American Legion or the politically motivated truisms of congressional acts that placed God all over the currency and into the pledge. He saw this religious revival as a national pathology: he nearly scoffed at the popular notion of a nation built on a religious tradition, on rights granted by God. "Aside from occasional pronouncements by a few theologians or theologically-minded clergymen," Herberg observed, "religion in America seems to possess little capacity for rising above the relativities and ambiguities of the national consciousness and bring[ing] to bear the judgment of God upon the nation and its ways. The identification of religion with the national purpose is almost inevitable in a situation in which religion is so frequently felt to be a way of American 'belonging.' In it crudest form, this identification of religion with national purpose generates a kind of national messianism which sees it as the vocation of America to bring the American Way of Life, compounded almost equally of democracy and free enterprise, to every corner of the globe; in more mitigated versions, it sees God as the champion of America, endorsing American might." This led to one conclusion: "The God of judgment has died."[68]

Herberg had not set out to write a book that took on an American civil religion. It became so only as he addressed the consequences of religious pluralism. For most of U.S. history, Americans of the three big faiths struggled over national identity—the dominant Protestant population denied that Catholics and Jews could be full Americans. But in the postwar period, the cause of the Cold War required more unity than had been traditionally allowed, and thus it became possible for Catholics and Jews to enter the national "club." Yet, as Kevin Schultz notes, "upon its release, *Protestant, Catholic, Jew* was an immediate success, although then, as today, most people ignored Herberg's second, more indicting thesis." Herberg had identified a problem that threatened religion in America, and this force—civil religion—created its own moral crisis. Americans had grown unwilling to be (not merely to act) religious.[69]

Herberg was, of course, not alone in denouncing the religious revival of the 1950s. He was joined by religious historian Martin Marty, who described American religiosity as "religion-in-general" and as being so devoid of specific meaning that religion no longer carried prophetic significance. And Peter Berger in his book *The Noise of Solemn Assemblies* blasted the growing irrelevance of churches—denominational, institutional religion—at the moment that religion had grown so popular that it had effectively become established in the United States. Berger followed Herberg in decrying this weak-willed religion as nothing more than a faith in the American Way of Life, except he called it cultural religion. "The implications of this attitude were clear," he argued. "Religious institutions no longer generated their own values; rather, they ratified and sanctified the values prevalent in the general community."[70]

But such critiques contained an irony: the seriousness attached to religion did not come from theologians or even churches but from the popularity of faith. Postwar American religiosity gave rise to debates over the morality of this religious nation and the role religion should play in counseling a nation that was made great in large part because of its religious history. Thus, many secular critics of the 1950s "decried social developments on moral grounds, used religious language to call America to account for its sins, and reserved some of their harshest criticisms for the churches and synagogues for failing to take a stand against the prevailing secular culture."[71]

Indeed, the question boiled down to morality—how should Americans employ moral arguments? For Americans, biblical religion was supposed to be the guide. Yet for all the mighty and weighty declarations about the Judeo-Christian tradition during the early Cold War, the religious revival was like an advertisement for God rather than the real thing. The great Jewish theologian of the period Abraham Joshua Heschel harangued: "Little does religion ask of contemporary man. It is ready to offer comfort; it has no courage to challenge. It is ready to offer edification; it has no courage to break the idols, to shatter the callousness. The trouble is that religion has become 'religion'—institution, dogma, securities." Even though Heschel was a figure central to the development of religious pluralism and someone who didn't shy away from exercising public theology, his response to America's God problem was, like Herberg's, more God. "Our effort must involve a total reorientation about the nature of man and the world. And our hope lies in the certainty that all men are capable of sensing the wonder and mystery of existence, that all men have a capacity for reverence. . . . We must grow in awe in order to reach faith."[72]

For devout secularists such as American philosophers John Dewey and Sidney Hook, the trouble was too much awe and not enough reason. Dewey proclaimed that his generation had lost its "intellectual nerve" by turning (or returning) to religion as the source and savior of Western civilization. Dewey contributed to a symposium organized by the *Partisan Review* in January 1950 on "Religion and the Intellectuals" and harbored no illusions that some alternative faith in science would solve the world's problems. He observed that the use of religion seemed to eliminate the need for debate over what was worth defending and dying for in the modern world. American intellectuals opposed using religion in the American struggle against communism because it often seemed that faith flattened out the complexity of the problems Americans actually faced in the Cold War.[73] However, many more Americans retreated to a kind of religion that would sustain them in a time of anxiety, that would make simple what was complex and distressing. But for a theologian like Niebuhr the development of a national faith created dangerous portents that undermined its presumed benefits.

He once remarked to his friend and first biographer June Bingham that "bad religion can be worse than no religion . . . [because] even good religion can become a source of hidden pride, of what we might call original sin." Secularists were usually uncomfortable with the concept of original sin except when Niebuhr spoke about it. But then Niebuhr wasn't interested in theology in order to condemn unbelievers; he was much more interested in attacking true believers, whether their faith was liberalism, communism, or Protestantism. Niebuhr was part of the neo-orthodoxy movement, meaning that he "insisted on the limited and historically conditioned character of all earthly institutions," Silk explains. "The great sin, endemic to humanity, lay in treating the contingent as absolute; this was idolatry. The great virtue, embodied in the prophetic tradition, was constantly to question society's false absolutes in the name of the only true absolute, the God who transcended history." Herberg counted himself a part of this school of theology as well. It was the place best suited for critiquing civil religion.[74]

Niebuhr was America's most astute theologian because, as Marty concluded, he was "a prophet to America-in-*praxis*." With Niebuhr two strands of American intellectual thought came together: religious intellectuals' tradition of interpreting the "nation's religious experience, practice, and behavior in the light of some sort of transcendent reference" and the ability to use "specifically theological materials in order to make sense of the American experience."[75] Obviously, Niebuhr was not the only intellectual to combine these two strands in the early Cold War. And he was certainly not the most popular or perhaps even most influential theologian of the period. He was not on television; he did not speak to packed stadiums in mass revivals; and he was never a guest of the president of the United States. He did not have the power of a two thousand-year-old church behind him issuing encyclicals based on a singular reading of natural law; nor did he believe that he knew the way Jesus's love would manifest itself in relation to nuclear weapons and war.

Rather he looked ironically at the collective use of religion in America to interpret the historical position of the United States.

The book in which Niebuhr dealt most directly with America's Cold War imperatives was *The Irony of American History*, published in 1952. He argued succinctly that a people who had only sporadically shown any kind of humility in the face of power now had to recognize that there was nothing necessarily righteous about their emergence as a superpower. The question was: Could Americans effectively grapple with the fact that their new role existed within a moral paradox? Niebuhr hoped so. "We take, and must continue to take, morally hazardous actions to preserve our civilization. We must exercise our power. But," Niebuhr counseled, "we ought neither to believe that a nation is capable of perfect disinterestedness in its exercise, nor become complacent about particular degrees of interest and passion which corrupt the justice by which the exercise of that power is legitimized. Communism is a vivid object lesson in the monstrous consequences of moral complacency about the relation of dubious means to supposedly good ends."[76]

Reflecting on the culture swirling around him, Niebuhr had originally wanted to title *Irony* "This Nation under God" because he wanted to emphasize that religion was at the root of both the nation's promise and its peril. In this way, Niebuhr did not push for a more limited role for religion in American life but rather for a more prophetic one.[77]

Unlike Miller and other critics of American civil religion, Niebuhr understood that in a time of war (yes, even a cold war) faith in the nation was a product of such historical circumstances, not simply a political or rhetorical gimmick. He offered, though, a particular reading of that history. For Niebuhr, all nations committed the sin of self-righteousness in some way, so it became imperative for nations to find a way to discern, he said, "the element of vanity in all human ambitions and achievements." Such perspective would be a check on the "perils of moral and spiritual self-complacency" that "even the wisest of nations" could not escape. Niebuhr provided a necessary alternative to the theology that developed in the United States to contend with the Cold War. While Niebuhr did not always agree with the positions taken by religious organizations and various denominations—especially when they offered platitudes that seemed disconnected from the unpleasant realities of the Cold War—he did not think churches had somehow failed because they hadn't developed a theology useful to American foreign policy.[78]

Niebuhr believed that the quickest way to irrelevancy for a theologian was to wave away the combination of religiosity and patriotism that created campaigns such as the one to insert "under God" in the pledge. The impulse that pushed such statements came from a popular—and anxious—reading of American history. For Niebuhr, that reading was politically potent but also ironic. He explained: "There are so many ironic elements in current history, particularly our own national history, because a nation which has risen so quickly from weakness to power and from innocency to responsibility and which meets a foe who has transmuted our harmless illusions into noxious ones is bound to be involved in rather ironic incongruities." Niebuhr acknowledged that seeing American history as ironic and doing something with that irony were not the same. "The knowledge of irony is usually reserved for observers rather than participants," he wrote. But, he noted at the end of his book, "we might well consider the spiritual attainments of our greatest President during out Civil War" as an example of one whose "responsibilities precluded the luxury of the simple detachment of an irresponsible observer."[79]

It is significant Niebuhr chose Lincoln as a model for his era, for just as Docherty and, by extension, Eisenhower had paid tribute to the sixteenth president's legacy, Niebuhr saw something transcendent in Lincoln's theology. However, Niebuhr also sensed that Lincoln had provided the best theological account of the Civil War because the era's churches had failed to do so. In short, Lincoln spoke to Niebuhr's moment because the civil religion of an earlier period had been reborn in his. "Lincoln's awareness of the element of pretense in the idealism of both sides," Niebuhr observed, "was rooted in this confidence in an over-arching providence whose purposes partly contradicted and were yet not irrelevant to the moral issues of the conflict." In this way, Lincoln could condemn slavery as a moral abomination without sentencing those involved in the war to an ultimate fate. Niebuhr suggested that Lincoln's "combination of moral resoluteness about the immediate issues with a religious awareness of another dimension of meaning and judgment must be regarded as almost a perfect model of the difficult but not impossible task of remaining loyal and responsible toward the moral treasures of a free civilization on the one hand while yet having some religious vantage point over the struggle."[80]

Niebuhr believed that communist tyranny was "as wrong as the slavery which Lincoln opposed." And he warned against attempts to soften the profound differences between the two systems. While neither was perfect, one clearly created evil, while the other made tactical errors based on misguided assumptions. However, Niebuhr contended that Lincoln's irony also ruled out "our effort to establish the righteousness of our cause by a monotonous reiteration of the virtues of freedom compared with the evils of tyranny. This comparison might be true enough on one level," Niebuhr noted, "but it offers us no insight into the corruptions of freedom on our side and it gives us no understanding of the strange attractive power of communism in a chaotic and impoverished world."[81]

Niebuhr offered irony at a moment when American life seemed to drift away from any self-reflection. In a review for the *New York Times*, Peter Viereck predicted that such insight would indeed make Niebuhr his era's most influential social thinker. However, Viereck added, he would earn this distinction "not because of his deserts but despite them, and because of the accidental confluence of three fads." Those fads, "progressivism, artiness, and pseudo-religion" would turn Niebuhr's prophetic position into an intellectual fashion.[82] In other words, one consequence of Niebuhr's ironic stance was that many readers would end up missing the irony altogether and instead simply pretend to understand the pitfalls of man and nation. An irony of *Irony* was that it might produce a kind of stealth hubris; one could take on the Niebuhrian pose of being troubled by the implications of power—only without remorse or charity.

Another reviewer hinted that *Irony* would provoke resistance from both secular and religious readers who wanted to hear something about the momentous role of their nation but not about how ironic that moment was. Robert Fitch, a professor of Christian ethics at the Pacific School of Religion, noted that Niebuhr's subject and his fluid prose made the book timely and accessible and most likely popular. However, Fitch predicted Niebuhr's prophetic critique would be far less palatable.

The book was a religious text and as such had put off Anthony West of the *New Yorker,* who disliked Niebuhr's use of original sin. Fitch quipped that "surely this is what must happen when the irony of the 'civilized' man is confronted by the irony of the Christian man." But even Christians would have a hard time with Niebuhr's irony because he employed it to undermine any divine support for the American mission. In this context, *Irony* would fail because its readers would resist the use of irony; all they really wanted was patriotic sincerity.[83]

Just a few years later, in a profile entitled "The Irony of Reinhold Niebuhr," William Lee Miller captured the paradox of Niebuhr's prophecy: while it rang with truth about the American condition, it failed to change that condition in any substantive way. Like Viereck, Miller believed that *Irony* would simply be misunderstood. "Niebuhr may find himself the victim of his own greatness," Miller concluded, "admired but misunderstood, praised but not followed." As evidence, Miller pointed to Niebuhr's appearance on the cover of *Time* and in profiles for *Life.* "Certainly," Miller offered, "the admiration of the Luce enterprises has its ironical aspects. *Time* and *Life* themselves provide excellent examples of much that Mr. Niebuhr criticizes."[84]

Miller's assessment of Niebuhr served as an apt warning for the United States as it moved into the 1960s. But so was the farewell address of the man whom both Niebuhr and Miller dismissed for his patriotic piety. Dwight Eisenhower left the presidency in a condition that it has largely remained in ever since. Ike presided over the development of forces vital to American identity in the postwar era: the conflation of God and country, and the growth in the influence and use of military might to defend the nation. Already by the end of the 1950s, the United States was both the most "God-fearing" country and the mightiest of the nations. In his last address, Eisenhower underscored the connection between these two notions: a strong military kept Americans free to worship their God. The stakes were that simple. But the consequences of this struggle were complex, Eisenhower explained, and he cautioned against "a recurring temptation to feel that some spectacular and costly action could become the miraculous solution to all current difficulties." No sweeping policy or military action (such as a nuclear attack) would bring the victory that Americans desired. He reminded Americans about "the need to maintain balance in and among national programs . . . balance between our essential requirements as a nation and the duties imposed by the nation upon the individual; balance between actions of the moment and the national welfare of the future."[85]

Among the most important areas in which to strike a balance, Eisenhower contended, was the military-industrial complex—America's war-making machine. He intoned, "Only an alert and knowledgeable citizenry can compel the proper meshing of the huge industrial and military machinery of defense with our peaceful methods and goals, so that security and liberty may prosper together." While as president, Eisenhower had enabled, if not created, the threat that he now warned Americans about, he also saw clearly, as Niebuhr had, that American success in technology had bred a dangerous confidence in American power. If Americans didn't outwardly proclaim God was on their side, they illustrated a disturbing lack of humility in the face of a judging God. The American military-industrial complex stood, then, as a material expression of America's all too-comfortable faith in its intentions. Eisenhower reminded Americans that nuclear weapons in American hands were still a danger to the world—"Disarmament, with mutual honor and confidence, is a continuing imperative," he contended. "Together we must learn how to compose differences, not with arms, but with intellect and decent purpose."[86]

To help Americans imagine how they might find balance in their conflicted world, Eisenhower seemed to suggest a theological under-standing of time. In politics, time is measured by elections and the passage of laws; in theology, time is measured by one's actions in relation to an infinite idea of God. Eisenhower told Americans that while they might prepare for war, war would not solve their problems. In this way, he seemed to ask for Americans to forgive him for not using war to seek political ends. "I confess," he said, "that I lay down my official responsibilities in this field with a definite sense of disappoint-ment. As one who has witnessed the horror and the lingering sadness of war—as one who knows that another war could utterly destroy this civilization which has been so slowly and painfully built over thousands of years—I wish I could say tonight that a lasting peace is in sight." It was not, and so Eisenhower advised that Americans had to think the-ologically about their nation—"to be strong in our faith that all nations, under God, will reach the goal of peace with justice." He concluded his final address as president as he had begun his first, praying for his nation: "May we be ever unswerving in devotion to principle, confident but humble with power, diligent in pursuit of the Nation's great goals," and pray "that, in the goodness of time, all peoples will come to live together in a peace guaranteed by the binding force of mutual respect and love."[87]

CHAPTER 3

Civil Religion Redeemed

IKE ENDED HIS PUBLIC SERVICE troubled by the state of the world and praying for his nation; his successor struck a different relationship with God. On a clear January day in 1961, John F. Kennedy proclaimed his faith in an American civil religion. He announced:

> Let the word go forth from this time and place, to friend and foe alike, that the torch has been passed to a new generation of Americans—born in this century, tempered by war, disciplined by a hard and bitter peace, proud of our ancient heritage—and unwilling to witness or permit the slow undoing of those human rights to which this nation has always been committed, and to which we are committed today at home and around the world.
>
> Let every nation know, whether it wishes us well or ill, that we shall pay any price, bear any burden, meet any hardship, support any friend, oppose any foe to assure the survival and the success of liberty.

In this remarkably succinct, evocative section at the beginning of his inaugural address, Kennedy made clear that there existed an American creed that was worth defending. Yet such defense did not foreshadow but rather should prevent "mankind's final war." The endeavor Kennedy called forth was a collective one, requiring national unity and sacrifice to work toward nothing less than "a more fruitful life for mankind." Brimming with confidence, Kennedy declared that "the energy, the faith, the devotion which we bring to this endeavor will light our country and all who serve it—and the glow from that fire can truly light the world." Such confidence was born of the unique position of America in the postwar world. As Kennedy suggested, the nation's ideals were "the same revolutionary beliefs for which our forebears fought" but were carried forward in his day by a nation whose power was unmatched in history. That combination had troubled presidents and ministers alike for the awesome, almost biblical catastrophe that could befall the United States if it mismanaged this historic opportunity. To stave off such tragedy, Kennedy turned, as his postwar predecessors had as well, to God: "With a good conscience our only sure reward, with history the final judge of our deeds, let us go forth to lead the land we love, asking His blessing and His help, but knowing that here on earth God's work must truly be our own."[1]

Kennedy's inaugural was inspiring. Robert Bellah found in it the spark that ignited his interest in an American civil religion. But as much as Kennedy carried forward the promise of the American creed, he also perpetuated its significant ironies. First, the fact that Kennedy invoked God was ironic given the role religion had played during his campaign for office. Just a few months earlier, as a candidate for president he had defended his ability to separate his Catholic faith from his political responsibilities to a large, mostly Protestant audience in Houston, Texas. He declared in no uncertain terms that he believed "in an America where the separation of church and state is absolute—where no Catholic prelate would tell the President . . . how to act, and no Protestant minister would tell his parishioners for whom to vote."[2] But that statement got things absolutely backward: Catholic prelates did tell political leaders how to act, and Protestant ministers most certainly did tell parishioners how to vote.

Thus a second irony of Kennedy's speech was the way it offered an idealized version of both civil religion and American religious freedom.[3] Will Herberg and Reinhold Niebuhr had hit both points in different ways during the 1950s. Herberg, in particular, had pointed out how religion had come to serve politics and the nation in a way that denuded faith of its power to serve God. And Niebuhr had carried on a specifically pointed battle with Billy Graham over the evangelist's obvious attempt to make a certain kind of religion the de facto faith of the nation. The third and final irony of Kennedy's speech, though, was the one he would pass along to his vice-president and successor, Lyndon Johnson. Kennedy asked Americans to be prepared to "pay any price, and bear any burden" to advance the nation's role in world affairs. For Johnson, that burden became synonymous with one word—Vietnam.

As Johnson found out all too well, if civil religion is about anything it is about war and the people who sacrifice and die in it. Johnson not only inherited American involvement in Vietnam from his predecessors, Eisenhower and Kennedy, but he also lived with the death of John Kennedy. The assassination of a president does not instantly create a sacralized legacy, but Kennedy came to be the symbol of America at its most intelligent and optimistic because he died just before a great fall. His death became a civil religious event because in death he had become what no living leader can be—a mythical figure who represented all that was presumed good about his nation. Johnson asked Americans in his first speech after the assassination to continue what Kennedy had begun: "This is our challenge—not to hesitate, not to pause, not to turn about and linger over this evil moment, but to continue on our course so that we may fulfill the destiny that history has set for us."[4] Johnson carried the myth forward and appeared to have shoulders broad enough to carry it far. But in the summer of the 1964, a year after Kennedy's death and a few months before LBJ's landslide victory over Republican Barry Goldwater for the presidency, Johnson began the steady escalation of American involvement in Vietnam.

Johnson might have shared the burden of American interest in Vietnam with his predecessors, but he alone bore responsibility for the course of the war itself.[5] On the day Johnson was elected president, there were a little over 15,000 American troops in Vietnam. In early 1965, the president authorized operation Rolling Thunder, a bombing campaign against North Vietnam designed to disrupt support for guerilla forces harassing South Vietnam's unstable government. On July 28, 1965, Johnson announced at a press conference that he was acceding to the wishes of his military commanders in Vietnam—primarily General William Westmoreland—to increase the number of American troops from 75,000 to 125,000. By the end of 1965, Johnson had accelerated the drafting of Americans into military service and had committed over 180,000 troops to Vietnam. Johnson agonized over the war and its escalation. Near the end of his prepared remarks during the press conference, he made clear that he was well aware of what he was doing: "Let me also add now a personal note. I do not find it easy to send the flower of our youth, our finest young men, into battle. I have spoken to you today of the divisions and the forces and the battalions and the units, but I know them all, every one. I have seen them in a thousand streets, of a hundred towns, in every State in this Union—working and laughing and building, and filled with hope and life. I think I know, too, how their mothers weep and how their families sorrow." Then he added, "This is the most agonizing and the most painful duty of your President." Johnson praised soldierly sacrifice for a cause that sounded greater than the war itself. The United States had to defend South Vietnam from "men who hate," Johnson contended. "We must have the courage to resist," he declared, "or we will see it all, all that we have built, all that we hope to build, all of our dreams for freedom—all, all will be swept away on the flood of conquest."[6]

Johnson' relationship to civil religion illustrated the promise and perils of placing America "under God." In Johnson's first National Prayer Breakfast, he floated the idea that the nation should erect a memorial "to the God who made us all."[7] This memorial would stand with those to George Washington, Thomas Jefferson, and Abraham Lincoln and become yet another symbol of the unity between God and nation that had defined the United States since its founding. Within two years, though, Johnson's tone had changed when he addressed another Prayer Breakfast. In February 1966, a little more than a half year following the decision to send thousands of American combat troops to Vietnam, Johnson ruminated on the need to turn toward God for guidance and solace in a time of war. He quoted Lincoln: "I have been driven to my knees many times by the overwhelming conviction that I had nowhere else to go. My wisdom and that of all about me seem insufficient for the day." The war had begun to produce its death toll, and the president had begun to grapple with his responsibility for those deaths in the face of his own doubts (not to mention those of his advisors and dissenters) about the war. In a letter to Johnson, the mother of a soldier killed in Vietnam said she prayed that God would bless the president and his family and would "guide you in all the terrible decisions you must make." LBJ found this a fitting way to conclude his reflections on the war at that moment—it was a terrible decision that he had to make but one that, at least in early 1966, was still under God.[8]

A very somber president met those gathered for the National Prayer Breakfast in February 1968. He began his brief remarks reflecting on the long, cold nights, the dull and gray days, and the longing he assumed many shared with him for a time when his nation's future looked bright once again. "What our minds know, our spirits often forget," Johnson said. "We weary of the winter and despair of the coming of the spring. We are tempted to turn from the tasks of duty and to lay down the works that are ours to do." He had fully comprehended that the Vietnam War was his; the pledge Kennedy had made to his countrymen had become his successor's inheritance. And under this weight, Johnson told those gathered: "I can—and I do—tell you that in these long nights your President prays." After recalling Franklin Roosevelt's call for unity around the hope of peace, freedom, and security, Johnson closed, "We cannot know what the morrow will bring. We can know that to meet its challenges and to withstand its assaults, America never stands taller than when her people go to their knees." The question that hung in the balance was what America prayed for while on its knees.[9]

If there was a chance America could offer up a collective prayer, only one preacher seemed fit to pray for the nation. Martin Luther King Jr., leader of the American civil rights movement and the recipient of the 1964 Nobel Peace Prize, practiced a different kind of civil religion. His speech at the Lincoln Memorial in 1963—in which he declared his "dream" for the nation—suggested that America had at last begun to address historic wrongs. However, as Johnson became well aware, if there ever was a war that might destroy rather than affirm American civil religion, it was Vietnam. With the demise of Johnson as a moral authority, King stood as an American moral leader whose prophetic, rather than affirmational, civil religion held the promise of saving the nation's soul. He had consistently used a biblical sense of morality to provoke a reckoning with the nation's past. And by 1967 King had determined it was time for him to reckon with Vietnam.

Exactly one year before his death, King finally denounced the Vietnam War. Even though he was the undisputed prophetic voice of his generation, it took King two years after tens of thousands of American troops had been sent into combat to take a strong public stand against Vietnam. But on April 4, 1967, King delivered a jeremiad against the war at Riverside Church in Manhattan. Three thousand people filled the great church and rose to applaud King as he prepared to give his address. In his baritone voice, King began, "I come to this magnificent house of worship tonight because my conscience leaves me no other choice." Echoing other liberal church leaders, King declared, " 'A time comes when silence is betrayal.' That time has come for us in relation to Vietnam."[10]

Previously, King had hesitated to make public his opposition to the war with the kind of strength and conviction that established him as the leader of the civil rights movement. For unlike his call to conscience when exposing the grave injustices of segregation, King's criticism of the war had to target the nation itself. With civil rights, King had curried public support by calling on the nation to be better; at Riverside he castigated the nation because he found its war immoral. King raged against the war, but his fury also engulfed the soul of the nation. "We must speak with all the humility that is appropriate to our limited vision, but we must speak. And we must rejoice as well, for surely this is the first time in our nation's history that a significant number of its religious leaders have chosen to move beyond the prophesying of smooth patriotism to the high grounds of a firm dissent based upon the mandates of conscience and the reading of history."[11] As King intimated, all other wars had received religious blessings—those opposed to war were labeled pacifists, while those who supported war were patriots. Now, at least, a few religious leaders seemed ready to engage Americans in a different kind of religious reckoning, to ask whether American involvement in Vietnam made the United States an immoral nation.

King understood the paradox the war had created for the United States and addressed it directly. "I come to this platform tonight to make a passionate plea to my beloved nation. This speech is not addressed to Hanoi or to the National Liberation Front. It is not addressed to China or to Russia. . . . Tonight," King declared, "I wish to speak . . . to my fellow Americans who, with me, bear the greatest responsibility for ending this conflict that has exacted a heavy price on both continents." He reminded his audience that in 1957, when he helped form the Southern Christian Leadership Conference (SCLC), the motto that group chose was "To save the soul of America." The moral dilemma of Vietnam threatened to "draw men and skills and money like some demoniacal destructive seduction tube" away from all the work yet to be done in civil rights. In a statement that his critics pounced on for its audacity, King argued that a people who abhorred violence in their own nation had allowed their government to become "the greatest purveyor of violence in the world today." King did not make this charge lightly but out of concern for the wellspring of moral authority from which the civil rights movement had come. "Now, it should be incandescently clear," King observed, "that no one who had any concern for the integrity and life of America today can ignore the present war. If America's soul becomes totally poisoned, part of the autopsy must read Vietnam. It can never be saved so long as it destroys the deepest hopes of men the world over. So it is that those of us who are yet determined that America *will* be are led down the path of protest and dissent, working for the health of our land."[12]

King spoke out against the war not because he hated the abstract notion of war or hated the United States but because he took the American promise seriously. When he was a divinity student at Crozer Theological Seminary, King wrote an essay on Jeremiah, calling him the "Rebel Prophet." Jeremiah "seized upon a revolutionary truth," King contended, and stood as "a shining example of the truth that religion should never sanction the status quo." David Chappell, a historian of the civil rights movement, explains that, in this essay, "King sketched out most of the themes he would later emphasize in his political speeches: the nation is in moral crisis; human institutions, including churches and temples, are corrupt; society rejects the prophets who tell the truth[;] . . . and finally, prophetic truth motivates rebellion and renewal."[13] In short, King practiced the tradition of the jeremiad, calling Americans to remember the national covenant between themselves and God—thus the nation had an obligation to do better because it was "under God."

Following his speech, King was "buoyant," but others were not so impressed. The *Washington Post* editorialized that the speech was "not a sober and responsible comment on the war but a reflection of [King's] disappointment at the slow progress of civil rights and the war on poverty." The newspaper captured mainstream opinion, black as well as white, which viewed King's address as an overwrought denunciation of a war he knew little about and as hurting the civil rights movement. In short, his speech alienated friends, occasioned denunciations in the press, and angered his ally in the White House. Reportedly, Johnson barked, "My God, King has given a speech on Vietnam that goes right down the commie line!" Carl Rowan, a black journalist with access to Johnson, said that the president was "flushed with anger" when he read summaries of King's Riverside Church address. King's colleagues in SCLC worried that King's stance would hurt the movement financially and politically. "The tragedy is not that King is going to the peace issue but that he's leaving civil rights," said one of King's close associates. "And how are you going to denounce Lyndon Johnson one day and ask him the next day for money for poverty, schools, housing?" Indeed, King found out just how great a difference there was between the pressure the civil rights movement placed on the nation for racial justice and the pressure that would be required to change the nation's commitment to the war. A Harris poll showed that 73 percent of Americans polled disagreed with his position on the war, and 60 percent believed his opposition to the war would hurt the civil rights movement. Forty-five percent of black respondents also disagreed with King.[14]

So why did King move publicly against the war? There were two reasons: one immediate, a second more existential. The immediate reason occurred on January 14, 1967, when King, on his way to a much-needed respite in Jamaica, leafed through the January issue of *Ramparts* magazine. The issue was devoted to "the Children of Vietnam." King's friend Bernard Lee recounted his reaction: "When he came to the *Ramparts* magazine he stopped. He froze as he looked at the pictures from Vietnam. He saw a picture of a Vietnamese mother holding her dead baby, a baby killed by our military. Then Martin just pushed the plate of food away from him. I looked up and said, 'Doesn't it taste any good?' and he answered, 'Nothing will ever taste any good for me until I do everything I can to end that war.'" In relative seclusion, King had a chance to reflect on his reaction to the war: "I spent a lot of time there in prayerful meditation," he recalled. "I came to the conclusion that I could no longer remain silent about an issue that was destroying the soul of our nation."[15]

King provided a philosophical accounting of his stance against the war in a SCLC retreat in May 1967. He told those gathered that "we have moved from the era of civil rights to the era of human rights, an era where we are called upon to raise certain basic questions about the whole society." When he turned to the issue of his personal opposition to Vietnam, his biographer David Garrow noted that King spoke with great frankness: "I had my own vacillations," he admitted, and then he saw the photographs in *Ramparts*. "Never again will I be silent on an issue that is destroying the soul of our nation and destroying thousands and thousands of little children in Vietnam. . . . When I took up the cross, I recognized its meaning. . . . The cross is something that you bear and ultimately that you die on. The cross may mean the death of your popularity. It may mean the death of a foundation grant. It may cut down your budget a little, but take up your cross, and just bear it. And that's the way I have decided to go."[16]

While it was inevitable that critics would pounce on King's limited grasp of foreign affairs, the preacher's understanding of the nation's soul was dead on. For King, the war became the single greatest obstacle to the nation's realizing any goals commensurate with its ideals. Thus King embodied a glaring paradox of his era: he reflected what civil religion could be when it was prophetic, but when this rebel prophet spoke out against the Vietnam War, relatively few Americans at the time welcomed his stance. What then did King's experience reveal about American civil religion?

King believed the war threw his nation into a theological crisis, meaning that the war challenged Americans to come to terms with what Vietnam was doing to the moral authority of the United States. Of course, King did not consider the nation a church; but he did believe American religious faith had consequences for how the nation acted. Thus the war tested the meaning of the United States as a nation under God. Yet, unlike most of his fellow clergy, King embraced a skeptical theology that shared similarities with Niebuhr's views on human nature. Man was inherently depraved, King believed, and only through inordinate self-sacrifice could genuine social change take place. "King exhorted people to ever greater sacrifice—which alone would give them a measure of power, even if they never lived to see the fruits of their power: creative suffering was the only way."[17] Thus, somewhat like Niebuhr, King did not provide an easy way for the nation to reform itself. In fact, for Americans to admit that the nation had acted immorally would cause as much pain as actually fighting the war. Ultimately, Vietnam illustrated that civil religion was wrapped up in sacrifice. The nation had a choice to make: win the war and lose its soul, or lose the war and save its soul. Such an irony had animated the public theology of Niebuhr. King's prophetic stand against the war exposed the cruelness of that irony.

For Francis Cardinal Spellman, the single most powerful Catholic besides the Pope, there was no irony, there was only victory. Spellman was the American military's vicar and had consistently visited American troops for Christmas since the Korean War. During a visit in 1965, reporters asked what he thought the United States was doing in Vietnam. His reply was infamous: "I fully support everything it does." He then added, "My country, may it always be right. Right or wrong, my country."[18] His Holiness in Rome had another take. Before the General Assembly of the United Nations in October 1965, Pope Paul VI famously declared, "No more war, war never again."[19] Protestant churches in the United States split on the war: conservatives either supported it or went further by denouncing what fundamentalists such as Carl McIntire considered the defeatism of liberals in mainline churches. McIntire declared, "It is the message of the infallible Bible that gives men the right to participate in such conflicts, and to do it with all the realization that God is for them."[20] Leaders of mainline Protestantism, such as John Bennett, Niebuhr, and Harry Emerson Fosdick, argued that successive regimes in South Vietnam had proven to be brutal and authoritarian and thus unworthy of American support. The American public largely stood on the sidelines until the late 1960s. In a poll conducted in late 1964, two-thirds of Americans said "they paid little or no attention to developments in South Vietnam."[21]

However, if religion played a role in the American descent into Vietnam, it did so by underwriting the Manichean view of the Cold War; from Graham to Spellman there existed a unified interpretation that the Cold War was a battle between the forces of light and the forces of darkness. In that sense, then, America was doing God's work by fighting communism in Vietnam. Moreover, American religiosity made it possible to see the Catholic regime that controlled South Vietnam as a bulwark in the quasi-religious war between the God of the Christian West and the God of Communism. Along these lines, a myth grew that Cardinal Spellman had helped get the United States into the Vietnam War through an alliance with South Vietnam's brutal leader, Ngo Dinh Diem. However, apart from Spellman's having almost no influence over American foreign policy, the assumed connection between American religion and American willingness to fight in Vietnam misses an important insight: American churches did not send troops to Vietnam, and

American Christians did not rise up to kill Vietnamese communists. The United States fought in Vietnam because the government sent combat troops to prevent the take-over of South Vietnam by communists supported by North Vietnam. This was not the American Civil War—American presidents did not claim to fight in the name of God.[22]

Religion was relevant to the conflict in another way. As King made clear, the moral foundation of the nation—its ability to claim to be good—was at stake in the prosecution of this war. An editorial John Bennett wrote for *Christianity and Crisis* got to the heart of the theological crisis sparked by Vietnam. Entitled "From Supporter of War in 1941 to Critic in 1966," the article explained, "We believe that the circumstances under which military power is being used in Vietnam are sufficiently different from those under which it was used to defeat Hitler to lead to quite different political and moral judgments concerning the issues raised by this war."[23] In short, Bennett and liberal religious leaders welcomed something short of military victory in Vietnam because they held out hope for something approaching a moral resolution at home. Vietnam threatened the soul of their nation and they didn't want their nation to suffer. Moderate evangelicals certainly felt conflicted about American action in Vietnam, especially as the war grew increasingly intractable, destructive, and unpopular. However, if judged by the response of Graham, the war did not threaten the nation's soul enough for most religious Americans to oppose it. For his part, Graham chose to remain "neutral" on the American war effort, offering his services as counsel to the moral crisis that war precipitated. Such a posture, though, did not prevent Graham from publicly criticizing King's Riverside speech or from rationalizing, "What can people expect me to do? March in protest? Carry a sign? If I do that, then all the doors at the White House and all the avenues to people in high office in this administration are closed to me."[24]

Graham's comment might sound cynical but he was also realistic about his relationship to people in power. Conservative religious leaders represented the majority view among religious Americans, for most assumed that political leaders knew better than they regarding matters of war and national defense. Moreover, there had not been a movement in foreign policy that was comparable to the social gospel in domestic affairs. Since the early years of the Cold War, evangelicals had, by and large, accepted that the "Church of Jesus Christ" (as they often referred to their corporate entity) had "no divine mandate to become officially involved in the approval of economic or political strategies." The vast majority of evangelicals through the late 1960s and early 1970s interpreted this general position as restricting them to "spiritual and moral affairs" not, as in the case of Vietnam, to military strategy and diplomacy. Since there was biblical rationale for war, the fact that the United States was fighting in Vietnam did not in and of itself constitute a moral dilemma for most fundamentalists and many evangelicals. What was a moral abomination was the communist menace American troops were supposedly fighting. Thus, as fundamentalist preacher Carl McIntire put it in 1971, "For a people who believe in God to cringe and retreat in the presence of growing power which repudiates God is an offense. Our 'no-win' policy is a sin against righteousness, the heritage of our nation, the mothers and wives of boys who have sacrificed for political expediency."[25]

Yet, the most popular evangelical preachers, especially Graham, never called the war in Vietnam a holy war. Graham and others well understood the moral complexity of the war; they concluded, however, that they would rather be tougher on communism and Vietnam and softer on America itself than the reverse. However, many evangelicals and fundamentalists also grappled with the fact that for the first time in American history a significant religious movement challenged that patriotic tradition. Although King's prophetic position never became mainstream, the war provoked a sustained opposition not merely to U.S. actions abroad but to the nation as a legitimate source of moral leadership. Liberal religious leaders tried to split the difference between those who viewed America as God's chosen country and those who condemned it as evil by focusing on the war as a particular event that demanded moral analysis. A group that came to be known as Clergy and Laity Concerned about the Vietnam War (CALCAV) found that even this middle-of-the-road position had implications that went well beyond the war.

CALCAV was a religious antiwar coalition that came out of two trends in postwar America: the growing religious involvement in the civil rights movement and the growing popularity of religious pluralism, which made a coalition of Protestants, Catholics, and Jews possible. In summer 1963, following crackdowns by the Diem regime, liberal

American clergy began to express outrage that the United States would support a "regime universally regarded as unjust, undemocratic, and unstable."[26] As the war escalated through 1965 with the introduction of thousands of American combat troops, opponents tried to raise the stakes in the war. In April 1964, A. J. Muste's Fellowship of Reconciliation published an open letter to President Johnson protesting the increased bombing attacks on North Vietnam and the introduction of additional American combat troops in South Vietnam. The letter was signed by twenty-five hundred ministers, priests, and rabbis.

The first coordinated religious protests against the war took shape under the National Coordinating Committee to End the War in Vietnam, which organized the nation's various pacifist sects. The group held coordinated actions on October 15–16, 1965, attracting nearly one hundred thousand people in cities across the United States and around the world to protest the war. Many American pacifists took inspiration from profound religious protests against the war by individuals such as Norman Morrison, Roger LaPorte, and Alice Herz. On November 2, 1965, Morrison, a Quaker, burned himself alive on the steps of the Pentagon. A week later LaPorte of the Catholic Worker movement did the same thing in front of the United Nations building in New York City. But Herz, an eighty-two-year-old peace activist, was the first American to take such dramatic action when in March 1965 she immolated herself on a Detroit street to protest the war.

However, CALCAV was not a pacifist organization, and it positioned itself accordingly. The group took shape almost by accident in October 1965. An ecumenical group of clergy called a news conference to protest the Johnson administration's strong denunciation of war critics. The group held their meeting at the United Nations building in Manhattan. Among the leaders of the group was a young Lutheran minister named Richard John Neuhaus, who with his characteristic dry wit commented, "It concerns us that the President should be amazed by dissent."[27] Neuhaus, Rabbi Abraham Joshua Heschel, and Jesuit priest Daniel Berrigan issued a declaration signed by over one hundred New York City clergy supporting the right to protest the Johnson administration's war in Vietnam. The declaration was signed: Clergy Concerned about Vietnam. Heschel, in response to a question about this group's future plans, stated that it would continue its efforts.

Well aware that they did not speak for the majority of Americans, let alone a majority of their congregants, the group took care early on to steer away from open alliance with groups of the New Left in order to avoid any association with the anti-American rhetoric of radical politics. Nevertheless, many of the members of the group were adamant about the right to dissent and were incredulous when the Johnson administration, the press, and religious conservatives challenged them on this issue. For example, Berrigan's involvement in Clergy Concerned drew the ire of Catholic officials, who disciplined him by sending the Jesuit priest to Latin American. Berrigan returned after protests from "respectable" Catholics (including students at Fordham University) forced the American church to back down, a decision the church probably regretted as Berrigan became one of the most radical religious dissenters during the war.[28]

By the end of 1965 and into early 1966, Clergy Concerned had managed to organize itself into a national body that coordinated local clergy-led groups opposed to the war; it created an executive committee composed of theological liberals. Neuhaus was the youngest, at twenty-nine, and the pastor of Saint John the Evangelist in Bedford-Stuyvesant. Henry Sloan Coffin, as the chaplain at Yale and a veteran of World War II and the CIA (during the Korean War), was the most well known. Bennett was the quiet but prolific intellectual backbone of the group and a strong supporter of the postwar ecumenical movement. Heschel had moved to New York City in 1945 to become a professor of Jewish ethics and mysticism at the Jewish Theological Seminary. And Robert McAfee Brown was the group's link to the West Coast as well as a former student of Niebuhr and Bennett. Historian Mitchell Hall observed that, for this group of men, "Vietnam was an important stage in a lifetime of active concern for making moral choices in the political world."[29]

As coordinator of outreach to local religious groups, Coffin reminded his fellow clergy, "Do not let the hawks monopolize patriotism."[30] Motivating Clergy Concerned was the sense that the war had undermined American ideals and that they, as religious leaders, had a responsibility to respond. The group hoped to encourage the Johnson administration to negotiate a settlement with North Vietnam. Early on they did not advocate civil disobedience or categorical denunciations of the nation. Nonetheless, the executive committee had some problems recruiting clergy from around the country because most knew that their congregations did not support even modest activism against the war.

The relationship between the clergy and the laity over Vietnam proved especially volatile in the Catholic Church. Facing the moral crisis of the war, Catholics contended with two traditions. First, the hierarchical structure of the church dictated that discipline flowed from the officials down to the laity—from the Pope to cardinals to bishops to priests to parishioners. This was nothing like the situation in the Protestant churches, where ministers could be hired and fired and the people who filled the churches did so by choosing the kind of theological statement one wanted to make about God, America, and the world. Thus, during the war, members of the Southern Baptist Church overwhelming supported increasing American military efforts in Vietnam, while members of the Methodist Church utterly rejected that option. For Catholics, the idea of choosing from a menu of choices was anathema to the dogma that made one Catholic: one attended Catholic mass to hear the word of the Lord, not to interpret it in light of personal revelation.

The second tradition that shaped Catholic views was the social position Catholics had occupied for most of American history. As Penelope Adams Moon observes, "America's long history of anti-Catholic sentiment encouraged Catholics to use patriotism as a defense mechanism and to seek consensus as a means of achieving respectability in American society." Loyal Catholics were also loyal Americans. Thus it was not surprising that since officials in the Catholic Church chose to remain relatively quiet on the American war in Vietnam, the Catholic laity did as well.[31]

However, if the church were to change its position, it followed that the laity—millions upon millions of faithful—would change as well. And since the church in Rome did not regard the U.S. government, much less the administration of Johnson, as a source of moral authority, the Catholic Church had the potential to be a substantial moral check on the United States. The Catholic dilemma was this: Catholics were not about to grow anti- or un-American overnight; and the Holy See was not about the encourage them to do so. Moreover, the idea of thousands of Catholics taking to the streets against the American government was not a possibility either—the legacy of anti-Catholicism remained relatively fresh. But Catholics and their church could suggest how their nation fit in a global moral context. If Protestants had founded the United States and therefore considered themselves the keepers of that legacy, Catholics (as John Courtney Murray had argued in the 1950s) had adopted the United States and wanted it to succeed as a moral force in the world. In short, the Catholic Church would much rather make common cause with the United States than oppose it—two great empires of "truth" battling communist "untruth."

The Second Vatican Council complicated this pact. During Vatican II, church officials had given their blessing to the idea of religious pluralism, thus certifying Murray's argument that the United States was not merely a place hospitable to Catholics but perhaps the nation that best enabled Catholics to practice their faith. But the Council had taken another step as well: in the *Decree on the Apostolate of the Laity*, the Council called on the laity to work "as good stewards of the manifold grace of God."[32] Doing good in the world, though, had a variety of implications. For some Catholics, that meant working with the poor; for others it meant opposing the Vietnam War. In general, Vatican II allowed a rich debate regarding the role Catholics played in American life, thereby elevating intellectual debates over the Vietnam War to a level of genuine consequence. Thus, if it mattered when the majority of the Catholic laity supported the war, it also mattered when their church began to debate the morality of the war. For here was a church that had the potential, because of its stature on the world stage and the size of its population within the United States, to bring a prophetic perspective to Vietnam from outside America.

Almost by definition when Catholics took up the papal call to action they offered something other than passive acceptance of the state. There had been precedent for such Catholic action in the United States—in particular, by the Catholic Worker Movement. In 1933, Dorothy Day and Peter Maurin had created this group, which practiced "a literal interpretation of the Christian Gospels with medieval ecclesiastical institutions and modern papal social teaching." The Catholic Worker Movement saw capitalism as a destructive force in modern society that needed to be countered by Christian personalism, or the devotion to personal responsibility, in a world that divorced material concerns from their human consequences. As a result, the Catholic Worker Movement rejected force as a viable response to any human endeavor and so practiced a de facto pacifism. Before Day and Maurin, the American Catholic position on war and peace had been staked out by the Catholic Association for International Peace, an organization that viewed state authority over politics as it viewed papal authority over faith—in absolute terms.[33]

In the specific case of war, the Catholic Church had a longstanding position based on a tradition of just-war teachings. Just-war analysis starts from the position that violence should be avoided but allows that under certain circumstances this position can be superseded. From this position two criteria helped to evaluate the morality of war: *jus ad bellum,* or the right to go war, and *jus in bello,* or limits on the use of force in waging or fighting the war. For American Catholics who considered themselves realists, such as Murray and William V. O'Brien, the Cold War was not an end in itself but a way to provide an "adequate and moral defense of America and the West." Such realists sought first and foremost to preserve Western liberal society without endorsing what they considered to be an overly idealistic internationalism as professed by the Holy See. Given the state of the world in 1960s, Murray and O'Brien rejected the prospect of a world order that could prevent and perhaps even eradicate war. More controversially, realists argued in favor of two types of violence expressly rejected by Rome: limited nuclear war and targeting and killing noncombatants. Murray believed that legitimate governments such as the U.S. government should consider limited nuclear war within reasonable moral bounds; and O'Brien reasoned that modern warfare made it necessary to kill civilians as part of a nation's legitimate claim to self-defense. Modern war had forced the Catholic Church to consider the application of just-war teachings in a new light.[34]

Liberal Catholics such as Justus George Lawler and Gordon Zahn worried that realist logic fell well short of upholding the spirit of Catholic social teaching. Lawler explained, "I would base my own total denial of the morality of any nuclear war not on strict logic, but on the certitude flowing from the converging probabilities created by the history of all recent major wars, by the exorbitant potential of the weapons themselves, by the consequences of the psychological strain induced by more than a decade of living on the edge of a volcano, by the fact that even in limited engagement where our vital interests are not at stake—as in Vietnam—war has [been] prosecuted through immoral means."[35]

Zahn had been a conscientious objector during World War II and had gained considerable intellectual credence for his book *German Catholics and Hitler's Wars*. His point in the book was that the Catholic Church in Germany (and by extension elsewhere) had abandoned its moral responsibility in the world when it failed to resist Hitler's rise to power. But Zahn did not live in Germany in the 1930s; he did live in New England in the 1960s, and his work on Nazi Germany reflected the moral imperative he hoped to apply to American Catholicism. He believed all religious communities operated as societies of faith, not as an arm of state authority, and therefore it was incumbent on such communities to be suspicious of the state in order to check the power it exercised in the name of its people.[36] Zahn put it this way, "It is not simply or even primarily a matter of saving our skins; instead, it is more likely to be a matter of saving our souls. What is being done is being done *in our name*; the more democratic we claim to be in our governmental structure, the great[er the] share of moral culpability each individual will have to bear for his conformity (including his *silent* conformity) to the demands of that government." Even those who didn't share Zahn's pacifism could agree that in light of the Vietnam War "the religious community is the only one of the principal value-forming institutions that is in a position where it could promote or encourage the kind of dissent that is needed today."[37]

Like Zahn, many liberal and radical religious Americans believed the war created a crisis of conscience and so to remain silent about the war was morally dangerous. The war was a moral crisis that demanded a moral response. In early 1967, CALCAV held a two-day meeting that produced a statement written by Robert McAfee Brown; the statement echoed Zahn's imperatives and foreshadowed King's Riverside address:

> A time comes when silence is betrayal. That time has come for us in relation to Vietnam. Our allegiance to our nation is held under a higher allegiance to the God who is sovereign over all nations. . . . Each day we find allegiance to our nation's policy more difficult to reconcile with allegiance to our God. Both the exercise of faith and the expression of the democratic privilege oblige us to make our voice heard . . . and we speak out of a loyalty that refuses to condone in silence a national policy that is leading our world toward

disaster. We are unable to support our nation's policy of military escalation, and we find those to whom we minister caught as we are in confusion and anguish because of it.[38]

In May 1967, CALCAV published *Vietnam: A Crisis of Conscience*, written by Brown, Heschel, and Michael Novak. The book grew out of the belief that policymakers needed encouragement that the public wanted a negotiated settlement of the war. The book sold over fifty thousand copies in a year. In a talk of the same title that Brown gave at a large church in St. Paul, Minnesota, he spoke of the war in expressly moral terms: "At this moment our act of liturgy is a consideration of Vietnam before the tribunal of conscience and before the throne of God." As if to respond to those Catholic realists who had skeptically dismissed what they considered an overly idealistic response by CALCAV, Brown made clear the issue that weighed on his conscience: "We do not differ in our belief that all Vietnamese are children of God[;] . . . [we] do not differ on the dogma that it is wrong to kill civilians." And in a nod to Zahn, Brown noted that he feared the parallels that one could draw between the churches in Germany that did not speak up in time and the churches in the United States at that moment. "The question is not what right have we to be speaking, but what right have we to be silent."[39]

Brown reminded his audience that a debate about Vietnam was already well under way and not merely among radicals or a few clergy but among the "experts" as well. "For me," Brown explained, "the tipping point came in the first Fulbright hearings over a year ago, when I, who had been content to leave the matter to experts, discovered that the experts disagreed, that one could have all the expertise imaginable about Southeast Asia, and still dissent vigorously from our administration policy." J. William Fulbright was the chairman of the Senate Foreign Relations Committee and as such wielded considerable oversight power in foreign affairs. He launched a series of hearings in 1966 that Americans watched on television. The hearings placed the Johnson administration's policy in Vietnam on trial and, like King's dissent on the war, earned the wrath of the president. Fulbright called experts on foreign policy before his committee, including George F. Kennan, the "father" of containment, to critique Johnson's war in Vietnam. In a book that Fulbright wrote that same year entitled *The Arrogance of Power*, he emphasized the wisdom of such expert critiques by suggesting that the war grew out of the misguided moralistic traditions of American foreign policy. Fulbright declared, "Power tends to confuse itself with virtue and a great nation is peculiarly susceptible to the idea that its power is a sign of God's favor, conferring upon it a special responsibility for other nations—to make them richer and happier and wiser, to remake them, that is, in its own shining image. Power confuses itself with virtue and tends also to take itself for omnipotence. Once imbued with the idea of a mission, a great nation easily assumes that it has the means as well as the duty to do God's work. The Lord, after all, surely would not choose you as His agent and then deny you the sword with which to work His will."[40]

His analysis picked up on the themes of hubris and moralizing that Niebuhr had addressed many times before. But now Brown was saying it was time to act on such evaluations: "We must insist that our nation is morally accountable, and morally concerned people must say so. And we must speak and do something about out concern, even at the risk of unpopularity."[41]

In 1967, Clergy Concerned continued to hold out hope that it could channel whatever discontent there might have been among the public into a moral stance that would convince Johnson and his advisors to seek a settlement in the war. Thus, at the most basic level, Brown argued that clergy and their laity had to defend the right to dissent against the nation's war. Remaining silent was tantamount to "idolatry," Brown said, as silence would imply a Spellmanesque line: "My country, right or wrong." CALCAV worked on the assumption that when religious leaders spoke the nation listened. For most of American history, religion provided a kind of moral superstructure to American life. The phrase "under God" made sense only in the pledge to a nation in which religion acted as a kind of cultural glue. And so it must have seemed entirely appropriate for a theologian to appeal to the patriotism of a religiously mixed audience in a Midwestern church. He claimed that he, as a religious American, had an "obligation to continue to point out what the war is doing to us." He feared that if the brutality of the war continued unchallenged, the nation would succumb to a "moral numbness." The *Saturday Evening Post* reported that "at least a million children had been injured . . . and 250,000 had been killed" since the war began.

"One trembles," Brown said, "to think what would be the judgment against our nation" if called to account for such destruction.[42]

Obviously CALCAV made an attempt, as did King and a few Catholic priests and bishops. But would these efforts create a new theological understanding of war as had World War II? Because of World War II it became possible for churches and synagogues to accept targeting and killing civilians and to keep and build nuclear weapons. What had Vietnam done to America's moral understanding of itself? What had the war done to the theology of the Cold War? The war threw Michael Novak, a member of CALCAV who co-authored the book *Vietnam: A Crisis of Conscience*, into a crisis of patriotism: "Many of us who loved our country are sad to see its flag carried in *this* war. We might be as brave as anyone else in other wars, and as eager to leap to the defense of the values dear to our nation. But in regard to this war many have felt, from year to year, increasing shame. It was not in order that our flag might be carried in wars like this that men of the generations before us suffered and died for liberty, for bravery, for justice."[43]

That kind of sentiment was poignantly expressed in a vigil—CALCAV's second mobilization—in Washington, D.C., on February 5–6, 1968. Over two thousand people met at the New York Presbyterian Church, still under the direction of the Rev. George M. Docherty, the minister who had inspired President Eisenhower a decade earlier. They gathered for what they hoped would be a memorial service at Arlington National Cemetery. However, the group was denied the use of the cemetery for that purpose and instead met at the Tomb of the Unknown Soldier. In a brief ceremony led by King, the civil rights leader began, "In this period of absolute silence, let us pray." Rabbi Heschel broke the silence praying aloud: "Eloi, Eloi, lama sabachthani?" ("My God, My God, why have you forsaken me?"). Then Catholic Bishop James P. Shannon concluded the ceremony, "Let us go in peace." The procession covered a half-mile out of the cemetery with each participant holding a small American flag.[44]

Through 1967, CALCAV sought to appeal to middle-of-the-road Americans by steering away from alliances with the diverse antiwar movement and seeking to persuade voters and policymakers that as a religious organization it had the interests of the nation in mind. Hall observes, "To achieve maximum effectiveness, many made a conscious effort to avoid the appearance of radicalism, dressing in coats and ties during public appearances. Indeed, few accepted the radical critique of American society and most were annoyed by leftist sectarianism." And yet, at the same time, many liberal clergy pointedly rejected Cold War myths that saw the world divided in a Manichean struggle that had influenced the course of American foreign policy and made the Vietnam War possible. As the war dragged on through 1968, CALCAV began to support civil disobedience, amnesty for war resisters, and investigations into American war crimes. In a sermon he gave during a three-day protest meeting in Washington, D.C., in February 1969, Neuhaus referred to the Vietnamese as "God's instruments for bring[ing] the American empire to its knees."[45]

Thus CALCAV did not see Vietnam as an international struggle against communist aggression, as did more conservative and reactionary religious leaders and, significantly for CALCAV's wider popularity, most of the public. A Harris poll conducted in December 1967 found that 75 percent of Americans polled believed that antiwar demonstrations only encouraged the communists to fight harder, and 70 percent viewed such demonstrations as acts of disloyalty. This is not to say that the public supported the war—from mid-1967 through September 1970, withdrawal sentiment accelerated from 19 percent to 55 percent. Public-opinion polls recorded a commensurate effect on support for the war and approval of presidential policy in Vietnam. Americans did critique the war, but not in the same terms as CALCAV and those in the wider antiwar movement. The moral crisis that Vietnam sparked begged the question, Who or what judged America?[46]

The April 8, 1966, cover of *Time* magazine was all black with bold red letters that provocatively asked, "Is God Dead?"[47] It became the most notorious cover in *Time*'s storied history. What prompted America's premier newsmagazine to ask that question? Perhaps a statistic from the period provides a clue: a Harris poll found that of the 97 percent of Americans who had recently said they believed in the God, only 27 percent "declared themselves deeply religious." By the mid-1960s, a group of radical theologians advised churches "to accept God's death, and get along without him." This group argued that modern consumer culture had undermined the ability of people to share in a common understanding of transcendence and sacred ritual, thus killing the traditional understanding of God. More mainstream theologians agreed that at the very least modern society no longer accepted God as a force who intervened in the daily lives of individuals. Paul Ramsey, a Princeton theologian at the time, put it this way: "Ours is the first attempt in recorded history to build a culture upon the premise that God is dead."[48]

Ramsey's observation held critical implications for the United States. Just a decade earlier, Americans had begun pledging their allegiance to one nation "under God." What would happen when that God no longer commanded the faith that made the pledge mean something? Was the death-of-God movement the eventual answer to the question Lincoln posed in his Second Inaugural Address? Had modern society finally made Americans give up those divine attributes they ascribed to a "living God"?

Enter Robert Bellah: in the winter of 1967, Bellah contributed an essay to the academic journal *Daedalus* entitled "Civil Religion in America."[49] Bellah was not a theologian but a sociologist, and his essay expressed a qualified optimism about the United States in the midst of a war fraught with moral and political conflict. While he was great admirer of King, Bellah's observations emerged from an intellectual standpoint that was informed by religion but not a product of any one particular faith. Because of his training, Bellah offered a clinical or systematic review of American claims to moral authority. Unlike the politicians who spoke about America as God's nation or the theologians who dismissed such claims, Bellah's rather dispassionate analysis suggested that those on both sides of the Vietnam War shared more common ground with each other than either side might recognize. In a sense, Bellah argued Americans did not need to lose hope during the war—there was a chance they might discover the soul of their nation because they were in danger of losing it.

Bellah wrote his essay in light of the optimism created by the early 1960s, especially the call to national service made by John F. Kennedy and the way in which Kennedy, the nation's first Catholic president, used references to God in his inaugural address to compel Americans to act. Given the controversy surrounding Kennedy's religion, the president did not admonish Americans to be better Catholics or better Christians or even God-fearing people. Rather he employed the widely shared assumption that the United States, as a nation under God, had an obligation to do good. Thus, Bellah argued that Kennedy, like many presidents before him, appealed to the "religious dimension" of American life. "This public religious dimension is expressed in a set of beliefs, symbols, and rituals that I am calling the American civil religion," Bellah explained. The presidential inauguration was one of these rituals that affirmed "the religious legitimation of the highest political authority." The postwar period had seen the development of increasingly overt expressions of civil religion. The Cold War prompted the institutionalization of civil religion, particularly in such acts as adding "under God" to the pledge of allegiance and "In God we trust" to the currency. The apparent willingness of Americans to accept that "ultimate sovereignty has been attributed to God" led not to a theocracy but to a sense that "the will of the people is not itself the criterion of right and wrong. There is a higher criterion in terms of which this will can be judged; it is possible that the people may be wrong." Bellah concluded that Kennedy's appeal to God was not unique but "only the most recent statement of a theme that lies very deep in the American tradition, namely the obligation, both collective and individual, to carry out God's will on earth." Rather than see that mission as either providential or over, Bellah regarded the crisis sparked by the Vietnam War to be one of those critical periods that shaped how Americans understood the religious dimension to their political life.[50]

Bellah was far from the first scholar to observe the religious quality of American life. But he was especially astute at illustrating why civil religion made sense as way to comprehend the American experience in a time of crisis. His argument was fairly straightforward: civil religion was and would continue to be a tangible source for judgment as well as inspiration based on historical experience. Such experiences were not random but were widely considered by generations of Americans to be foundational—they included the Puritan covenant in the new world, the writing of the Declaration of Independence and the Constitution, Lincoln's magnanimity during the Civil War, and the sacrifices made in World War II. Thus, the collective power of such experiences provided a moral standard by which to measure the actions of the United States. He explained that over time Americans had come to accept a common moral purpose of their nation. He described this collective faith as "an understanding of the American experience in the light of ultimate and universal reality . . . [and] at its best [it] is a genuine apprehension of universal and transcendent religious reality as seen in or one could almost say, as revealed through the experience of the American people." Following World War II, that experience changed significantly as Americans encountered and attempted to master the world on terms unprecedented in U.S. history. Bellah too saw the Cold War as a theological crisis, one that made apparent an American civil religion.[51]

Thus while Bellah's essay sprang from "concern with the American Vietnam War," he admitted that he wasn't "fully aware of the new religious phenomenon" that he had observed. "It was a sense of moral crisis in the United States being engaged in a war that had such negative qualities to it that made me [ask], was there anything in our past that would help us avoid this catastrophe we were in."[52] Indeed, in the middle of the Vietnam War Bellah had captured the way that war galvanized a moral understanding of the nation—not merely a moral critique of the nation but an accounting of whether the United States might be a force for good to its own people, let alone to other people around the world. And he came to his insights in quite a Niebuhrian way.

Bellah wrote his essay in late 1966, when he was a professor at Harvard University. That was his second stint at Harvard. His first experience there occurred in the mid-1950s as a graduate student with hopes of accepting an instructorship following the completion of his doctoral work. However, Bellah left Harvard for a research fellowship at the Islamic Institute at McGill University. It was a decision he was forced to make. During the mid-1950s, Harvard, like many other universities, colleges, and schools across the United States, experienced a wave of "loyalty" probes in which faculty and staff had to make clear their pro-American, anticommunist sympathies by helping authorities identify "subversives" on campus. Bellah declined to participate and had to leave Harvard for Canada. But this experience confirmed in Bellah a faith in what he referred to as a chastened, existential, Protestant liberalism. "For all its failures" he explained, "I came to believe that American society needed to be reformed rather than abandoned. In other words, politically I became a liberal, but it was the chastened liberalism of a man with few illusions." From Montreal, Bellah understood that although his nation had forced him into a kind of exile, there was no other nation in which he could place his "hope." Thus Bellah developed an appreciation for the Christian doctrine of sin and its application to national crises, a belief gleaned from the era's two leading theologians, Niebuhr and his colleague at Union Theological Seminary Paul Tillich.[53]

Bellah explained, "I saw that the worst is only a hair's breadth away from the best in any man and any society. I saw that unbroken commitment to any individual or any group is bound to be demonic. . . . The totalism of Communism and the totalism of the 'Free World' are both equally destructive." Like Niebuhr, Bellah feared the excesses of America's "good" intentions. And also like Niebuhr, he believed that "modern Western society, especially American society, in spite of all its problems, is *relatively* less problematic than the developing societies with their enormous difficulties in economic growth and political stability." Thus the Vietnam War did not strike Bellah as a natural extension of American life but as a moral crisis that required the application of "core American values, at least in their most self-critical form."[54]

Bellah's chastened civil religion was born from the theological crisis precipitated by Vietnam. To start, Bellah believed it important to acknowledge the less-than-noble causes the United States had defended on the basis of its nationalistic morality, such as the general design of Manifest Destiny, which ran from the mid-nineteenth century through the 1930s, and, following World War II, the lumping of those "on our side" into a single category of the "free world." The key was to extend the role civil religion played in the struggle for civil rights and to make it work in foreign policy. Yet that would require a sense of judgment that Bellah feared was fading from American life just at the moment when the nation needed a renewed sense of morality. In short, the nation needed God. "But today," he observed in 1967, "as even *Time* has recognized, the meaning of the word *God* is by no means . . . clear or obvious. There is no formal creed in the civil religion," Bellah lamented. Thus, he implored, "it is not [too] soon to consider how [this] deepening theological crisis may affect the future of [civil religion's] articulation."[55]

Vietnam quite simply tested the fundamental existence and operation of an American creed. Bellah declared it the "third time of trial." The first time of trial was "the question of independence," the second was the "issue of slavery"; and each experience brought forth figures and

symbols that contributed to a collective understanding American morality. Such experiences provided landmark statements on the shortcomings
and promise of the United States. Figures such as Washington, Jefferson,
and, most profoundly, Lincoln, reflected on struggles and sacrifices
made by Americans who would not reap the benefits of their efforts.
Following World War II, "every president since Roosevelt," Bellah
observed, "has been groping toward a new pattern of action in the
world, one that would be consonant with our power and our responsibilities."[56] Thus, like previous periods in which civil religion was
revised, the postwar period provided new leaders and symbols. But
which leader and which moment would define this time of trial? In light
of how civil religion operates—how it taps into promise and calls upon
judgment—King seemed the obvious choice as the era's defining figure.
But that was not the case. Instead, Bellah's essay punctuated a moment
in which reforming the nation became an end in itself. King wanted
something deeper than that to be revealed. Bellah, perhaps inadvertently,
discovered that merely renewing faith in the nation was about as far as
this reckoning was going to go. In short, the United States was too big
to fail.

Bellah's notion of a civil religion called attention to the uniqueness
of the American experiment with democracy: American politics had a
meaning that was more than merely the sum of its laws, elections, social
movements, and wars. However, he did not believe that the American
experience made the nation exceptional in a normative way. Other
countries also gained existential understanding of themselves from their
experiences. Bellah had merely applied an approach of identifying
the religious dimension of any society to the specific experiences of
the United States. Thus he argued that while the United States has a
distinctively American civil religion, it does not stand apart from all
other nations or closer to God. In fact, Bellah ended his famous essay
suggesting that the ultimate result of the American war in Vietnam
might be the rise of a global civil religion under which the actions of all
nations struggling to figure out the period of revolution could be both
guided and judged.[57]

Bellah's contemporary Sidney Mead was at once more modest in
his understanding of a national religion and more willing to defend
the exceptional nature of it. In a series of essays stretching from the early

1960s to the early 1970s and collected in a volume entitled *The Nation with the Soul of a Church*, Mead argued that there was not merely a religious dimension to American politics but a "religion of the Republic" from which American politics sprang. Mead explained that "there is and always has been an unresolved tension between the theology that legitimates the constitutional structure of the Republic and the theology generally professed and taught in [the] majority of the religious denominations of the United States." Out of this tension grew a theological struggle between "America's two religions"—denominational faiths and a religion of the Republic both inspiring and judging the actions of the nation.[58]

Much like Bellah, Mead believed there was a religion that developed alongside and in conversation (rather than conflict) with denominational faiths. Religious pluralism existed at the beginning of the republic not simply out of necessity but out of conviction that the new state could not endorse nor be endorsed by any one faith. Thus the founders institutionalized pluralism and made it possible for Americans to be both religious and secular without being hypocritical or overly theoretical. By arguing that there was a historically contingent notion of religious pluralism, Mead by no means dismissed the fact that Protestant churches exerted more influence on American life than did all other religious groups. But that fact had not led inevitably to a national church; rather the persistence of a strong commitment to a Judeo-Christian tradition created a notion of the United States best captured by Lincoln's competing (and ironic) descriptions of America as an "almost chosen people" and "the last best hope for mankind." From the start, then, Americans were religious in general and pluralistic in their ability as a people to practice a multitude of faiths without demanding that one be so dominant that the state would rise and fall according to it.

In his most celebrated essay in the volume, also entitled "The Nation with the Soul of a Church," Mead emphasized that it was not inconsequential that Americans believed they had made a religious covenant with each other to create a new politics that stood under the judgment of God. In short, not only did the United States have a civil religion, but it operated as a moral entity because the nation practiced a prophetic faith. "A nation," Mead concluded, "is 'essentially a spiritual society,' its soul created in the compact of the people." Therefore, when the United States emerged, it did so as a theological society—it possessed a dogma that defined the particular ways in which the people strove toward universality. Mead asked, Do not all religions aspire in a similar way? The United States is an exceptional political experiment because it created a national covenant in concert with (rather than at war against) other religious covenants. Mead seemed to suggest that the United States had been the first nation to pull off the trick of melding sacred and secular influences into a prophetic national faith, "which is to say," Mead explained, "that its ideals and aspirations stand in constant judgment over the passing shenanigans of the people, reminding them of the standards by which their current practices and those of their nation are ever being judged and found wanting." It wasn't surprising that when Mead searched for an expression of this prophetic religion of the republic, he quoted a description of the way American actions in Asia were undermining the sense—both abstract and historical—that the United States was not simply just another nation or empire but the "beacon to all the world" for equality and freedom.[59]

Vietnam, more seriously than any war since the Civil War, focused attention on the covenant at the core of the American soul. As King attempted to demonstrate, the United States was in danger not merely of being immoral but of losing its ability to understand why being moral was significant. The evaluation of the nation by religions had always existed; what made the Vietnam era so crucial was that religious leaders began to have contempt for the faith people had in their nation. King and others who spoke out against the war did so to convince Americans that their misuse of the religion of the republic was undermining their ability to reform the nation. But, as Mead suggested, that covenant among the people of the United States had to be protected from the damage of their government's war in Vietnam. In other words, the war was not a reflection of the American soul, it was a cancer attacking it.

There were laments aplenty about the fate of the American soul in the late 1960s and early 1970s. From King to Robert Kennedy, very few public figures did not call for a moral reckoning in light of the Vietnam War. In the summer of 1972, historian Sydney Ahlstrom observed, "During these very years when fear and hopelessness are corroding the national faith, we have witnessed a renaissance of scholarship about patriotic piety. Is it possible," he asked, "that here we have evidence of a familiar fact—namely, that we often study the history of something only after its demise?" Indeed, one can read essays and books extolling the existence of an American civil religion as eulogies. Ahlstrom added one of his own: a "requiem for patriotic piety." Ahlstrom argued that the "crisis of the present decade finds America's patriotic piety more seriously endangered than ever before," not least, he added, because the interest in civil religion had exposed the nation's contradictions, thus prompting a kind of national nervous breakdown. "Nearly all Americans now have reason to wonder if the 'mystic chords' of memory and affection are still audible. Neither liberal critic nor militant radical can any longer afford simply to attack patrioteers [sic]. Neither can blandly pronounce patriotism's requiem. The bell tolls for them, for the death of patriotism undermines the force of both criticism and protest."[60]

No one seemed to feel this crisis of patriotism more acutely than the winner of the fractious presidential election of 1968, Richard Nixon. Nixon ascended to the office he coveted on January 20, 1969, amid the crisis the American war in Vietnam had wrought. As one of his earliest biographers put it, "Here was a man who believed that human nature, history, common sense, morality, and truth dictated the successful completion of the war; yet after twenty years of trumpeting this message—and finally gaining the presidency, the position from which he could command such a policy—at the decisive hour of his lifetime he could not issue the single order his conscience told him was right: he could not urge the winning of the war."[61] There was no one less equipped to deal with the irony of this situation than Nixon. His paranoia, earnestness, and simplistic faith that America was and would always be one nation under God made him ill-suited to comprehend the dimensions of the tragedy over which he assumed responsibility. Nixon's first inauguration set the tone for the patriotic piety he apparently believed would overwhelm a cynicism that had endangered both the soul of the nation and the God that supposedly blessed it.

Nixon understood the symbolic role of his inaugural address and the potential power of a presidential election to give the nation a new vantage point from which to see itself. And, perhaps not surprisingly, Nixon used religion to help clarify a vision of America, to make sense of the sad state of the nation and to find a path toward redemption. "We find ourselves rich in goods, but ragged in spirit; reaching with magnificent precision for the moon, but [fal]ing into raucous discord on earth," he intoned. "We are caught in war, wanting peace. We are torn by division, wanting unity. We see around us empty lives, wanting fulfillment. We see tasks that need doing, waiting for hands to do them. To a crisis of the spirit, we need an answer of the spirit. And to find that answer, we need only look within ourselves."[62]

Nixon asked Graham to deliver the invocation that began the ceremony. Graham offered what sounded like a jeremiad, calling to God: "Too long we have neglected thy word and ignored thy laws. Too long have we tried to solve our problems without reference to thee. Too long have we tried to live by bread alone. We have sown the wind and are now reaping a whirlwind of crime, division and rebellion." The entire ceremony was apparently designed to appease an angry God, replete with commemorative cards offering prayers of Thanksgiving and music that included devotional hymns as well as the traditional martial music. There was even "a full-scale ecumenical service in the West Auditorium of the State Department—the first of its kind in history." But Nixon didn't want Americans to come to terms with an angry God. Nixon wanted people to "build a great cathedral of the spirit," "to join in a high adventure," to make a destiny rather than be condemned to one. He wanted people "to know that the heart of America is good." Most of all he called on the world to dedicate itself to finding peace. Without irony, Nixon offered a somewhat oblique reference to Vietnam. He used the cadence of a prayer attributed to Saint Francis of Assisi, "Where peace is unknown, make it welcome; where Peace is fragile, make it strong; where peace is temporary, make it permanent." Nixon, a man who had been constantly at war during his political career—with communism, Democrats, and (perhaps most of all) himself—declared himself the leader for peace.[63]

And then he invaded Cambodia. On April 30, 1970, the president spoke to his nation about his "Vietnamization" plan, a plan that would "guarantee the continued success of our withdrawal" by launching attacks on "major enemy sanctuaries on the Cambodian-Vietnam border." "We take this action," Nixon assured Americans, "not for the purpose of expanding the war into Cambodia but for the purpose of ending the war in Vietnam and winning the just peace we all desire." Understanding how contradictory that plan sounded, Nixon broadened the context a bit more, claiming that the stakes were nothing less than survival of Western civilization. "If, when the chips are down, the world's most powerful nation, the United States of America, acts like a pitiful, helpless giant, the forces of totalitarianism and anarchy will threaten free nations and free institutions throughout the world." The United States not only had to prevent that, but it was the only nation that could do so: "It is not our power but our will and character that is [*sic*] being tested tonight."[64]

Nixon believed his strategic invasion of Cambodia would help him achieve his ultimate goal of peace with honor in Vietnam, just as he believed his invocation of God and use of religion would bolster American patriotism and ultimately repair the moral authority of the nation. He was tragically wrong on both counts. His announcement of April 30 set off a cataclysm of protests punctuated by the deaths of students at Kent State University in Ohio and Jackson State College in Mississippi. The war continued another three full years and America's moral authority hit a new nadir. Charles Henderson Jr. argued in 1972 in his book *The Nixon Theology*, "Beyond the literal contradiction involved in promoting himself at once [as] a pacifist and a cold warrior, there is a deeper and more tragic paradox at the heart of his policy. The very idea of winning a just peace in Vietnam after so many years of the most terrible crimes . . . the mere suggestion that we can extract a just peace from such a jungle of injustice is patently absurd."[65]

Henderson concluded that the greatest deficiency in Nixon's "theology" was his inability to recognize the "tragic and the demonic." The president put that deficiency on display in his first major public appearance after the tragic aftermath of his speech on Cambodia. At Graham's invitation, Nixon spoke to thousands of young people who attended the preacher's East Tennessee Crusade on the main campus of the University of Tennessee. Nixon praised this gathering of the nation's youth as a "generation that is not lost[;] . . . it will become the great young generation." It was obviously a crowd favorable to Nixon—"a solid majority on one side rather than the other side," as Nixon put it. His remarks were a scattered offering of "thoughts" on young people, violence, America as a good nation, America as a nation that had done wrong, and about the role of government in meeting the expectations of the time: "I want this Nation to be at peace, and we shall be," Nixon pleaded. "I want the air to be clean, and it will be clean. I want the water to be pure, and it will be pure. I want better education for all Americans, whatever their race or religion or whatever it may be, and an equal opportunity for all, and that shall be." How? Through a spiritual revival: "This nation would not be the great Nation that it is unless those who have led this Nation had each in his own way turned for help beyond himself for these causes that we all want for our young people, a better life, the things that we may not have had ourselves but we want for them." Amid the goodwill Nixon wished for the youth in Tennessee that evening, he failed to mention the young people who had died on two other college campuses and those who would continue to die in Southeast Asia.[66]

Senator George McGovern of North Dakota (Nixon's opponent in the 1972 presidential election) didn't forget. In a searing speech before Congress on September 1, 1970, McGovern implored his colleagues to vote to end the war in Vietnam. Known as the "the amendment to end the war," the McGovern-Hatfield amendment (Senator Mark Hatfield was the co-sponsor) would have forced the United States to end military operations in Vietnam by December 31, 1970, and to pull all troops out by June 1971. McGovern was a veteran of World War II and a decorated bomber pilot who had flown dozens of treacherous missions over Western Europe. He stood, he said, in opposition to the war, in opposition to the concentration of power in the executive branch, and in opposition to the politics that had condemned thousands of Americans to death in Vietnam. "Every Senator in this Chamber is partly responsible for sending 50,000 young Americans to an early grave. . . . This Chamber reeks of blood," the war veteran declared. "Every Senator here is partly responsible for that human wreckage at Walter Reed and Bethesda Naval and all across our land—young men without legs, or arms, or genitals, or faces, or hopes." Responding directly to the kind of rhetoric Nixon had consistently deployed to bolster his war policy, McGovern shot back, "There are not very many of those blasted and broken boys who think this war is a glorious venture. Do not talk to them about bugging out, or national honor, or courage. It does not take any courage at all for a Congressman or a Senator or a President to wrap himself in the flag and say we are staying in Vietnam, because it is not our blood that is being shed." McGovern ended his speech with a plea to his colleagues to do their constitutional duty—to restrain the executive and to be a conscientious body. He returned to his seat in a silent chamber. The senators momentarily stunned, regained their composure and voted down the amendment.[67]

The war ended but not on Nixon's terms. Never admitting that his policies had failed or that the war itself was a tragic mistake, Nixon sought refuge in the theology of Lincoln. Nixon attempted to cast a war of choice in Vietnam as his era's civil war in the hope, apparently, that something profound might emerge from this disaster. In his annual address at the National Prayer Breakfast in February 1972, Nixon ruminated on the meaning of "one nation under God." He concluded that this "charge" made the United States a generous nation—one that sought "liberty and justice for all, not just in America, but throughout the world"—and a nation that had to show humility in face of the work still left to do. "We want nothing from any other nation," Nixon declared. "We want to impose our will on no other nation. We do not want their economic subversion or even submission. We want for them what we have, in their way as we have in our way," he said, attempting (clumsily) to avoid sounding imperial. When he turned at the end of his remarks to an assessment of how the United States was executing its charge, Nixon expressed a revealing ambiguity. He referred to Lincoln's reply to the question of whether "God is on our side." "I am more concerned not whether God is on our side," Lincoln said, "but whether we are on God's side." Nixon asked those gathered to pray not merely for him and the nation but that the United States would, "to the best of our ability, be on God's side." That was as close as Nixon came to admitting some doubt about his nation.[68]

A few months before Nixon's political career came undone, he had a chance to channel Lincoln once again, this time in his own second inaugural address. Somewhat like Lincoln, Nixon addressed the nation as a terribly divisive war was nearing its end. And also a bit like Lincoln, he had to find a way to bind the nation back together. However, Nixon was no Lincoln. In the final third of his relatively brief address, Nixon asked Americans to recommit to the nation, its government, and each other; to look forward to celebrating the nation's two hundredth anniversary.

He recognized that would be a tall order. "Our children have been taught to be ashamed of their country, ashamed of their parents, ashamed of America's record and its role in the world. At every turn we have been beset by those who find everything wrong with America and little that is right," Nixon lamented. "But I am confident that this will not be the judgment of history on these remarkable times in which we are privileged to live." Nixon argued (yet again), "America's record in this century has been unparalleled in the world's history for its responsibility, for its generosity, for its creativity, and for its progress. . . . Let us be proud," Nixon proclaimed, "that in each of the four wars in which we have engaged in this century, including the one we are now bringing to an end, we have fought not for our selfish advantage, but to help others resist aggression." While these were remarkable contentions given the view of the United States in 1973, Nixon made only one reference to God's judgment. After declaring that he had initiated "a structure of peace that can last . . . for generations to come," he told the nation: "We shall answer to God, to history, and to our conscience for the way in which we use these years." Indeed, the nation need not worry about how Vietnam affected its relationship to God, for that war, like all others of the century, had been fought for peace and selfless reasons.[69]

Nixon did not use civil religion prophetically. As historian Martin Marty argued, no president really can. "Presidents could not be presidents," he wrote, "if their main function was to call God down in judgment on his nation's policies." But Bellah nearly howled in disappointment. In an essay he wrote shortly after Nixon's second inaugural, Bellah admitted that if "I had this document before me seven years ago the tenor of that piece [on American civil religion] might have been different." Nixon's "assertion of American goodness without any sense of a need for judgment at all" offended Bellah's intellectual sensibilities. Bellah contended, "If we find, as I think we must, that Nixon's view is hopelessly inadequate to the understanding of the tragic reality of late twentieth-century America, I think we must necessarily conclude that *the* civil religion is similarly inadequate." For Bellah, Nixon's failing as a president was due in large part to his decision to lead a willing population of Americans in a refrain of American goodness and light. Civil religion, as Bellah had argued in 1967, emerged out of recognition of the nation's history and in relation to a sense that God judged that history.

That relationship created a kind of creed that Americans could draw on to help guide their nation, but that relationship was not static; it could change and needed to change when the nation faltered as badly as it did in Vietnam. Bellah made clear that Nixon had not "killed" civil religion as much as he had showed how conflicted it was. The war and Nixon's mishandling of the popular unrest about it forced a transformation of civil religion. Before Vietnam, American civil religion had been primarily about grappling with the spiritual stakes of the Cold War—steeling the American soul for the ideological conflict with communism. After Vietnam, American civil religion would contend with a national soul in shambles.[70]

It remained unclear how a new moral reckoning might still develop. If conservatives simply retrenched around patriotic piety and radicals rejected patriotism in any form, then there was a great swath of intellectual ground between them to plow. But for new ideas to take root they needed to acknowledge the promise of America accepted by the right and to absorb the denunciation of America by the left.

In the early 1970s, as a contemporary debate raged over whether the United States was exceptionally good or exceptionally bad, two relatively young religious leaders set the tone for the next phase in the debate over American civil religion. Interestingly, their religious affiliations suggested ideological tracks quite different from the paths they would blaze. One was Neuhaus, the Lutheran minister who had been a founding member of Clergy Concerned. Neuhaus began his career as a man of the religious left, but as the Vietnam War crawled to an end, he began to shift his focus from the sins of the nation to its "better angels." He considered how his calling as a religious leader might best contribute to salvaging what was left of the nation's civil religion. The other figure was Jim Wallis, a young Christian evangelical, who hoped to lead a movement that would end American illusions about civil religion. Wallis grew up in Michigan, attended Michigan State University at the height of the anti-Vietnam movement, and received theological training at Trinity Evangelical Divinity School near Chicago. While a student at Trinity, he participated in one of the most significant evangelical rallies in recent American history called Explo '72. This youth rally was sponsored by the Campus Crusade for Christ with Graham as the honorary chairman; it attracted eighty thousand students to the Cotton Bowl in

Dallas, Texas. Wallis, no fan of Graham's, helped found the People's Christian Coalition (PCC) in 1971. Wallis and his fellow Trinity students who created the PCC also started a journal that captured their position toward the United States; they called it the *Post-American*.

Neuhaus was born in 1936 in Pembroke, Ontario, to a conservative Lutheran pastor. His family sent him to a Lutheran high school in Nebraska, though, because he was a defiant youth. Neuhaus became a naturalized American citizen when he was sixteen, graduated from Concordia College in Austin, Texas, and completed pastoral training at Concordia Theological Seminary in St. Louis. By 1960 he had followed his father and become an ordained Lutheran minister. Neuhaus started his career in Massena, New York, a small town on the Canadian border. Following a brief stint there, he moved to the opposite side of the state and the opposite end of the demographic spectrum when he assumed the post of pastor at Saint John the Evangelist in Brooklyn, New York. The young Canadian-born minister arrived in 1961 and in short order turned the parish around from a place that was dying to one thriving and deeply involved in the civil rights and Vietnam War protests of the era. It was as pastor of this community that Neuhaus began his journey as a public theologian.[71]

In the early 1970s, he recounted a story of leading one of the first draft-card turn-ins. "More than 500 radical young people gathered in a 'Service of Conscience and Hope,' and more than 200 draft cards were gathered to be returned to the Selective Service." At the end of this service, Neuhaus recalled that he led the group in a "lusty, heartfelt" version of "America the Beautiful." The event made the evening news, with Neuhaus hoping to illustrate that a belief in the promise of America might be prophetic in a dark time. "Unfortunately," he concluded, "that alliance of radical hope and American piety was and is all too rare among those who press for change. The belief that our present situation is unworthy of America is, in some radical circles, outvoted by the dismal confidence that there is no evil not endemic to American power."[72]

As the Vietnam War inched toward its inglorious end, Neuhaus wrote frequently about the dire need for religious leaders and religion in general to play an important role in reconstructing the nation's moral foundation. "In America today," he said in the early 1970s, "there is little vision, and the people perish because we have become repressive and tongue-tied about the religious meanings that motor our social experiment. The answer is not to 'return to religion.' It is rather to become more honest and articulate about the religious dynamics that do in fact shape our public life."[73]

Like many religious intellectuals of the time, Neuhaus internalized the observations of theologian Paul Tillich, who provided a kind of proof for Christianity's relevance to contemporary society. Tillich wrote that since the Christian Church is based on the crucified Christ, an event in history and not a normative claim, there followed three consequences that no Christian could avoid: first, that the Christian Church itself was under the judgment of the event on which it was based (the sacrifice of Jesus); second, that such judgment knew no boundaries and thus erased the "gap between the sacred and secular realm"; and, finally, that "religion conceived as ultimate concern gives substance to culture. And culture is the totality of the forms in which the basic concern of a religion expresses itself. In short religion is the substance of culture; culture is the form of religion." This last point was the most influential and was often the only part of Tillich's proof that made its way into contemporary arguments, for, as Neuhaus believed, the "great strategic error" committed by radical critics of the United States was that they repudiated not only the "existent America . . . but along with it, the symbols that anticipated a future fulfillment of the American experiment." Here Neuhaus had Wallis's evangelical group in mind. Neuhaus rejected the notion of a "post-American" moment in favor of a "historically better" description of a "pre-American" movement. "Historically better, because the American experiment is closely tied to the metaphors of covenant and pilgrimage, the metaphors of testing and experiment. Strategically more effective, because no people can be asked to join an adventure if they are deprived of the symbols of continuity and hope, if they are deprived of the myths which identify the community with which they are able to travel with confidence."[74]

Neuhaus saw that religion played various roles during the war. In a 1970 treatise-like essay on the theological crisis sparked by Vietnam, Neuhaus explained that "religious opposition to the war has more to do with what Robert Bellah has described as the American civil religion than it does with explicitly Jewish or Christians formulations of theology and ethics. The civil religion is, in turn, dependent upon the latter.

The churches and synagogues face the challenge of enabling civil religion to illuminate and guide the course of American power in the Third World." Broadly speaking, even though most religious leaders and congregants either chose not to say much about the war or came out in tepid opposition to it, religion would be vital to repairing the nation after the war. As a founder of Clergy Concerned, Neuhaus had insight into the duality of religion during the war: on the one hand he knew that his group spoke for a distinct minority of religious leaders, but, on the other hand, American churches also chose not to rally to the flag because "too many influential people in American religion had weighed the cause in their several balances and found it wanting." Thus, unlike the case in any previous American war, the presidents who presided over Vietnam, especially Johnson and Nixon, chose to avoid claiming God for the American side. To have made such declarations, Neuhaus noted, would have turned Vietnam into a holy war of such hypocrisy that American civil religion might have truly become unrecoverable. Instead, in a strange way—perhaps ironically—civil religion seemed to offer a way to reform the nation morally.

Neuhaus emphasized that civil religion would be an effective way to address the grave problems brought out by the war because "religious protest against the war [had] widened the gap between the clergy and lay people, between local churches and national headquarters, between denominations and interdenominational leadership, especially that of the National Council of Churches." The vast majority of churchgoers in the country, Neuhaus observed, were "overwhelmingly puzzled, angered, or alienated by religious activism on war and race." Neuhaus predicted that a reaction was coming: "We can expect a new period of pastoral and theological seriousness in American religion, perhaps even something that will look like a conservative renaissance."[75]

Neuhaus believed that Vietnam created a conflict between the government and the nation's civil religion, not between the government and any specific religion, nor between religions themselves. "It is only in this light that one can understand why the last few years have brought the American political process into question so fundamentally— and also why the churches' part in the war protest has alienated so much of their membership." The question after the war would be how the nation's traditional faiths related to America's civil religion. Neuhaus thought moving further leftward would do a grave disservice to the churches because such a move would leave them without a constituency. "It is not enough for the churches to ride along in a legitimating capacity on the bandwagon of radical revolutionary thought because such thought, at least in its present forms, requires the repudiation of the American experience. America hardly needs increased guilt feeling or more reasons for despising itself. It does need a new understanding of itself in a historical dispensation in which its power can be an instrument for creative change. In short, the American civil religion needs to be updated and given a new articulation in order that this country can, not only avoid more Vietnams, but also 'be a blessing to the nations of the earth.' "[76]

Neuhaus wanted America to return "home again." The point was to rebuild the nation's moral sense so that those most concerned and committed to it could believe in it. Neuhaus said he was worried that cynical reactions to patriotism would further distance the era's radical chic—whether they be religious or secular—from their fellow Americans. "We may condescendingly smile at those who agitated for the words 'under God' in the pledge of allegiance, but they are the true believers. And with what would you replace their naïveté? Is America no longer under judgment? And if it is not under judgment, how can it be approved? How then are its legitimating means legitimated? I suggest that the assumption of a prior and approving judgment is a large part of what had held American society together." Neuhaus was almost apocalyptic about the possibility of the American myth being overturned and secularism or nihilism taking its place. "The loss may do a lot for our feelings of sophistication, but it does little for the prospects of social survival."[77]

Thus to stem the tide of both thoughtless patriotism and vacuous radicalism, Neuhaus called for the rise of a Lincolnesque figure who could make sense of this moral calamity. "I believe the best game in town is the interplay between explicit Christianity and America's civil religion," Neuhaus suggested. "Both require careful nurture and constant re-examination. They exist in a symbiotic relationship, each supporting and, to some extent checking the other. Explicit Christianity is not coterminous with American civil religion, nor is the civil religion, left to itself, harmoniously in accord with Christian imperatives."[78]

Wallis rejected American civil religion *because* he was an evangelical Christian. In his first issue of the journal *Post-American*, he declared, "We have unmasked the myth of the American Dream by exposing the reality of the American Nightmare." The issue had a cover photo of a statue of Christ, crowned by thorns, slumped on a throne of stone, and draped by an American flag. The caption under the image read: " . . . and they crucified Him." The "voice of the People's Christian Coalition" had marched not merely against the war and against the support their fellow evangelicals gave the nation, but against America itself. It could be no other way, Wallis wrote. "For the radical nature of the Christian faith to be realized, it must break the chains of American culture and be proclaimed to all peoples." Vietnam, it seemed to Wallis, had exposed the utter corruption of Tillich's proof: "The American captivity of the church has resulted in the disastrous equation of the American way of life with the Christian way of life." The result was that the "church has lost its ethical authority and has become the chaplain of the American nation preaching a harmless folk religion of comfort, convenience, and Presidential prayer breakfasts." The aim of the PCC was to bear radical witness to the nation, to be radical "disciples applying the comprehensive Christian message to all areas of life, culture, and human need— committed to reconciliation, justice, peace, and faith which is distinctly Post-American."[79]

In the next issue of the *Post-American*, Wallis dismantled the idea that America worked well because it possessed two cooperating religions. "There is a church that is captive to the ideology of the system and there is a church that is out to free the captive. There is a church whose god is American, white, capitalist, and violent; whose silent religion and imagined neutrality goes hand and hand with 'nigger' and 'napalm.' There is a church who serves He who comes . . . to call all into question . . . to challenge, resist, and confront Caesar's stronghold." For Wallis, the prophetic relationship between God and the nation no longer held because the church had become no more than a "loyal spiritual adviser to American power and prestige—whose prayer breakfast god is small, exclusive, manipulated by those who would reduce him to a drummer boy marching to the patriotic tunes of the machine."[80]

Wallis and Neuhaus were similar in some ways. Both were the sons of preachers—Wallis's father was the senior elder in a Plymouth

Brethren church. Both were rebels in their youth and attribute their rejection of their father's faith to their own spiritual discoveries. Both were involved in the social movements of the 1960s, though Neuhaus was older and thus more deeply involved in both civil rights and the antiwar organizations, whereas Wallis was slightly younger than Neuhaus and participated in the antiwar demonstrations that hit Michigan State University from 1966 to 1970. And both understood their religiopolitical journeys as "coming home." In his autobiography, Wallis explained that his was "the odyssey of a Midwestern American boy born from the evangelical womb, who lost his faith, took on a secular pilgrimage, and then returned home to the tradition that bore him." But, significantly for Wallis, he did not return to the middle-class, Midwestern evangelism that had defined his boyhood and against which he had rebelled but to the "biblical faith known so well by revivalists and reformers down through the years [that had] the capacity to radically critique and challenge the root assumptions of American wealth and power."[81]

Neuhaus's journey led him to conclude that it was "in resistance" to both the war in Vietnam and the extreme reactions to it "that we must project a new definition of national purpose capable of enlisting American consciousness and conscience in the continuing trek toward the new community for which this 'almost chosen' people, to use Lincoln's happy phrase, was ordained; ordained, if not by God, at least by men prepared to gamble in hope upon divine interventions within history."[82] Wallis's journey began with the realization that the "church and its religion became tied to the nation's destiny. Predictably, we became conformed to an American civil religion that was indeed religious, but hardly biblical. We began to defend America more than the gospel, and made the gospel subservient to the goals of the nation." And so, when he matured into a writer who, like Neuhaus, found an outlet in print journalism, he wrote for a magazine that he and his compatriots called *Post-American* in order "to put forward a Christian faith that broke free of the prevailing American civil religion."[83] Neuhaus thought that, because of Vietnam, the "best game in town" would be negotiating the interplay between Christianity and civil religion. Wallis declared his intention to tear asunder that union because he believed it to be so corrupt. Wallis wanted to redeem Americans; Neuhaus hoped to save a nation. Wallis, the evangelical Christian, focused on the person who had been overwhelmed by the nation; Neuhaus, the mainline Lutheran, worked to make the nation worthy of an individual's faith. While the positions of Wallis and Neuhaus point to a significant theological clash, their conflict was relatively minor in the political sense. The Vietnam War had not destroyed American civil religion; in a curious way, the war made it more significant than ever before.

CHAPTER 4

Civil Religion Reborn

AMERICA IS A COUNTRY MADE BY WAR. The American War for Independence was the first war for the nation, the first war to create national martyrs, and the first war that revealed the contours of an American civil religion. In 1976, the United States prepared to celebrate the two hundredth anniversary of the American Revolution—a struggle that stood as the lodestar among the constellations of national myths. Abraham Lincoln had acknowledged that in his dedication of the cemetery at Gettysburg. And Ulysses S. Grant had marked the occasion of the Revolutionary War's centennial by marching with four thousand troops through Philadelphia in a celebration of military honor and pride. Gerald Ford, president of the United States in 1976, did not march in a military parade. The horror of Vietnam still hung in the air, deflating any comparisons with the war for American independence. Nevertheless, there would be tens of thousands of parades and celebrations during the bicentennial year, the largest being in New York City. The city hosted Operation Sail '76, inviting 224 historic ships (the Tall Ships) to sail around New York Harbor while thousands of people floated in a variety of crafts around them and millions of people stood on shore admiring the display. On the evening of July 4, my family and I and millions of other people watched a massive fireworks display light up the harbor and the New York skyline. As I look back on it now, that celebration seems to stand outside of time.[1]

Reinhold Niebuhr would have understood that reflection. American idealism often hovered apart from the experiences that surrounded it, creating a parallel history of the nation. Niebuhr died in 1971 and thus did not witness the inglorious end of the Vietnam War, the scandal of Watergate, and the resignation of President Richard Nixon. Yet, as Americans considered the nation's two hundredth anniversary in the wake of these disasters, the spirit of Niebuhr's critique of American civil religion became more relevant than ever before. Niebuhr wrote in *The Irony of American History*: "[American] idealism is too oblivious of the ironic perils to which human virtue, wisdom and power are subject. It is too certain that there is a straight path toward the goal of human happiness; too confident of the wisdom and idealism which prompt men and nations toward that goal; and too blind to the curious compounds of good and evil in which the actions of the best men and nations abound."[2] The celebration of America's ideological founding provided yet another moment to reconsider how the nation's history played havoc with its ideals. A common refrain heard from many leaders—political as well as religious—was for the nation to redeem itself through humility, to humble itself before God and by doing so to recall that the United States remained a nation under God's judgment not merely His grace—principles Niebuhr preached but had rarely seen followed in public life.

The mid-1970s seemed to offer such a moment of genuine reflection as American civil religion became contrite. The nation had sinned; its evil ways had led it to a moment of truth. War, political corruption, and social unrest were all of one piece—signs of the impending collapse of America into an ungodly, unholy darkness. If the nation were to be saved, it had to be reborn, and American civil religion offered a way for Americans of diverse religious faiths to share in a born-again experience, which, of course, only evangelical Christians traditionally had. But because this had to be a civil religious experience, the meaning of this national rebirth was hotly contested. At base, the conflict pitted those who believed America could be made "moral" again against those who worked to make it less immoral. This fight began amidst the dusky ending of the Vietnam War.

The National Prayer Breakfast in 1973 provided a snapshot of the contest to redefine civil religion. John Stennis, a senator from Mississippi, asked Mark Hatfield, the junior senator from Oregon, to speak on behalf of the Senate prayer group at the annual breakfast. The year before, the arch-conservative Strom Thurmond had delivered the Senate's message; Hatfield promised to offer a different reading of America's moral state. Hatfield took his seat at the head table between a relatively upbeat President Nixon and the always cheerful Billy Graham.

When he rose to speak, Hatfield faced three thousand people in the Washington Hilton's ballroom, including cabinet officials, military officers, and the Soviet ambassador Anatoly Dobrynin. Hatfield had initially hesitated to accept Stennis's invitation, worrying that the Prayer Breakfast "could serve as another vehicle for enshrining the civil religion of our nation." But ultimately he decided to use the opportunity to address such concerns head-on by calling for the nation to address its "sins."[3]

Hatfield declared, "As we gather at this prayer breakfast let us beware of the real danger of misplaced allegiance if not outright idolatry, to the extent we fail to distinguish between the god of an American civil religion and the God who reveals himself in the Holy Scriptures and in Jesus Christ." While never explicitly saying it, Hatfield's brief speech implied that it was this civil religion that had made the war in Vietnam more palatable to a public too patriotic to comprehend the war's immorality. "Today, our prayer must begin with repentance," he preached. "[As] a people, we must turn in repentance from the sin that scarred our national soul." Much like Martin Luther King Jr., Hatfield believed the war had become far more than a foreign policy fiasco or even a political tragedy; it was a moral catastrophe that threatened to destroy the promise of the nation. The way toward recovery was, in no uncertain terms, by being "born again." "We must continually be transformed by Jesus Christ," Hatfield counseled, "and take his commandments seriously. Let us be Christ's messengers of reconciliation and peace, giving our lives over to the power of his love. Then we can soothe the wounds of war, and renew the face of the earth and all mankind."[4]

The *New York Times* captured the political sting of the speech with the headline: "Nixon Hears War Called a 'Sin.'" And even though Hatfield addressed a crowd of "the most vigorous supporters of the country's participation in the war," he received applause that was "both sustained and energetic." The White House, though, was not pleased. Members of the president's staff were "infuriated," and, evidently, so was Nixon, who placed Hatfield on his list of "enemies." Nixon had his chance to speak, bringing the Prayer Breakfast to a conclusion by praising his recently negotiated cease-fire in Vietnam and reciting the last line of a religious song: "Let there be peace on earth and let it begin with each and every one of us in his own heart." Graham believed that

Hatfield had been so unjust to Nixon that he gently reprimanded him in a letter a few days later. Graham and Hatfield were fellow Baptists and on friendly terms, having known each other since the mid-1950s. But as a close personal counselor to Nixon, Graham apparently felt it his duty to defend the president in the face of Hatfield's "rebuke." "It seems to me that the Breakfast should be a time of praying for and encouraging our political leaders—especially the President," Graham wrote. To Hatfield, Graham's letter confirmed the paradox of being Christian in America. Graham's counsel to Hatfield was simply disingenuous, not because Graham was insincere about the role he wanted religion to play in the nation, but because he believed there was only one way religion should play a role in the nation's affairs—as affirmational rather than prophetic. Hatfield had been hesitant to speak at the breakfast for that reason; he recognized that the politicization of religion had undermined its ability to operate apart from the affairs of the government and the nation. "The Christian must maintain the duality of a pastoral and prophetic witness toward the powerful; indeed," the Oregon senator explained, "I believe this duality necessary in all the mission of the Church."[5]

Yet Hatfield was not speaking from the pulpit; he was speaking to a gathering of America's political elite. He wanted a reconstructed civil religion—not, as he pleaded, simply a return to biblical faith. Thus, like many others throughout American history, he wanted Lincoln's sense of moral balance and irony—a sense that the nation could be good, should be better than it was, and had to face up to the reality that, often, it was neither. In a book that came out during the bicentennial year, appropriately entitled *Between a Rock and Hard Place*, Hatfield pointed to Lincoln's use of religion as an example of the "mature interaction of religious faith and political responsibility." During the Civil War, Lincoln and the Senate had issued three proclamations designating days of "humiliation, fasting, and prayer." Hatfield was especially fond of one such proclamation because it characterized the Civil War as a moral failure, a "punishment inflicted upon us for our presumptuous sins." Seeing Vietnam in a similar light, Hatfield found the appeal in the March 1863 proclamation fitting for his time as well: "'It behooves us, then,' Lincoln declared, 'to humble ourselves before the offended Power, to confess our national sins, and to pray for clemency and forgiveness.'" Here was an alternative to the "pious patriotism of civil religion," Hatfield believed. Lincoln showed that "only through the acknowledgment of our corporate guilt and confession of national sins could the country regain its national purpose and unity."[6] Proclamations of days of humiliation, fasting, and prayer originated with the Puritans and had been used during wars from the Revolution through the Civil War. The Civil War, though, was the last time that the term *humiliation* appeared. Perhaps humility was implied in the proclamations that followed.

Hatfield didn't think so and in December 1973 had offered his own congressional resolution. He asked the Senate to approve a resolution proclaiming April 30, 1974, a National Day of Humiliation, Fasting, and Prayer. In a style reminiscent of the Puritan jeremiad, Hatfield decried the erosion of American faith in its leaders, the dependence on natural resources for energy, and the widespread corruption of the spiritual foundation of the nation. Popular acquiescence to these conditions had created a "moral abyss." And, like the original jeremiad, Hatfield's resolution also offered hope if Americans "recognized their sins" and "repented." The resolution itself captured the brooding atmosphere of the mid-1970s: "Whereas, we have made such an idol out of our pursuit of 'national security' that we have forgotten that only God can be the ultimate guardian of our true livelihood and safety; and Whereas, we have failed to respond, personally and collectively, with sacrifice and uncompromised commitment to the unmet needs of our fellow man, both at home and abroad; as a people, we have become so absorbed with the selfish pursuits of pleasure and profit that we have blinded ourselves to God's standard of justice and righteousness for this society." To recover from such an immoral state required America to fall genuinely "under God." Not too surprisingly, the resolution quickly attracted co-sponsors in the Senate and was passed. However, the House was far more divided about this kind of moral reckoning and buried Hatfield's resolution in committee. President Ford never got a chance to sign it. Hatfield reminded readers in 1976 that, even though his attempt failed officially, "thousands cooperated fully with the spirit of the resolution, abstaining from food, suspending normal activities, and reflecting on our national shortcomings."[7]

Hatfield's resolve might not have reflected the tenor of his time, but his turn toward religion did. From one end of the ideological spectrum to the other and from politicians to preachers, many hoped religion would save the day, for only through religion would the nation find redemption. The collective wisdom seemed to be, make Americans more pious and you'll get better patriots. No other American better exemplified this thinking than the Democratic candidate for president in 1976, Jimmy Carter.

Carter was a one-term governor from Georgia when he decided to run for the Democratic Party's nomination for president. He was one of the new Democrats from the South because he openly embraced the accomplishments of the civil rights movement, a stance he made clear on the day he took office as governor by appointing many African Americans to positions in the state. Carter had grown up in a small, rural community in Georgia but had a fierce intellect and was driven by ambition to succeed in whatever endeavor he chose. He attended the U.S. Naval Academy and ultimately ended up serving as an officer on one the nation's earliest nuclear submarines. The diligence and ambition he demonstrated in his early career in the navy and as a state politician served him well in his bid for the presidency. Carter began his campaign for the Democratic nomination as an unknown candidate. However, he won an early primary in New Hampshire and an early caucus in Iowa by out-traveling and out-stumping his better-known opponents. He also presented himself as a moderate voice of a new South and swept many of the primaries in that region. Given the state of union, it appeared that Americans were ready to believe in an outsider.

Carter had another thing going for him, though: he was openly religious. Carter's faith helped him reach out to people on a personal level, to empathize with them in a way that Nixon never could. Carter's openness about his faith also made him seem moral, good, and trustworthy— character traits no one in 1976 would have ascribed to Nixon. Carter's opponent in the presidential race, Ford, also ran as a candidate to trust, but he had pardoned his discredited predecessor and had to carry the Republican Party forward after the humiliation of Watergate and the drubbing Republicans took in the 1974 midterm elections. Thus, Carter was the "good" candidate. In his book entitled *Why Not the Best?*, published in fall 1975, Carter spoke about his multiple salvation experiences and the effect those had on making him both a better person and a person to whom others could relate. He made faith a central feature of

his campaign because faith had been a central part of his life. He was a
devout Baptist, who prayed on decisions, topics, and problems. He was
a close reader of the Bible and taught Sunday school with his wife,
Rosalynn, at their local Baptist church. Yet he was also a politician with
national ambitions who felt at home in the contemporary world. His
faith was personally significant but also politically useful; he believed the
way to national redemption was through increased personal piety.

In the first half of 1976, the press had locked onto Carter's religion,
labeling him an existentialist Christian because he tempered his old-time
faith with doses of Niebuhr, Karl Barth, Paul Tillich, and Søren
Kierkegaard. In a speech to the Disciples of Christ in Indiana, Carter
"talked of how the nation had fallen short—giving his own disillusionment with it as an example of the learning process." But Carter's religion
also made him hopeful for the nation; he thought redemption possible
because Americans were people of faith. "We've got a good country,
the greatest on earth," he told a gathering of black ministers of the
African Methodist Episcopal Church. "Richard Nixon hasn't hurt our
country; even Vietnam and Cambodia haven't hurt our system of
government. . . . It's still clean and decent, the basis on which we can ask
difficult questions, correct our nation's shortcomings, but we've got to
keep searching." And then he told his Bible class back in Plains, Georgia,
something that was at once profound and too obvious: "America is
learning God is not automatically on its side, and in the eyes of God,
we're no better than anyone else."[8]

In one sense, Carter's piety was refreshing because it was genuine
and it seemed to temper the overwrought patriotism endemic to the
campaign trail. At the same time, Carter's piety was also political and
therefore calculated; as he told one interviewer, "I've never been more
determined to win anything, not because I just want to be president but
because I honestly believe in the bottom of my soul that I can represent
what our people are and what we want to be and what we can be."
Roger Rosenblatt looked askance at the persuasive power of Carter's
piety: "The candidacy of Jimmy Carter seems only to prove that we
prefer grand illusions to petty ones, and that we may be willing to lie to
ourselves more readily than we will accept the lies of others in order to
preserve these illusions." Rosenblatt saw Carter using religion like other
contemporary evangelists, as a kind of popular culture, as a way to speak

about the nation as a moral entity without ever acknowledging the fallacy (even heresy) of that notion. Carter's religion was undoubtedly a political asset in the campaign of 1976. As support from evangelicals in the South and Midwest helped him sweep up delegates to take the Democratic nomination and carry him toward the presidency, Michael Novak observed: "There is a hidden religious power base in American culture, which our secular biases prevent many of us from noticing. Jimmy Carter had found it." Then the question became what to do with it.[9]

Religion was a paradox for Carter. As a devout Baptist, he had no trouble integrating the Bible into his personal life. As a politician, he came to realize, though, that it was not so easy to maintain a subtle approach to religion in public affairs. In October 1976 he made clear to the American Humanist Association that he would be a strong defender of the First Amendment's separation between church and state by promising never to use "political office to force my religious convictions on someone else." But that did not mean he thought faith would not play a role in his politics.

Newsweek declared 1976 the "year of the evangelical." Evangelical Christians seemed to be emerging as a new and potentially powerful voting bloc, and the Democratic candidate for president was a born-again Christian. But the substance of such insight didn't capture the real story. Carter's nomination in the year of America's bicentennial hinted at a transition that was under way. American civil religion underwent a salvation experience, and Jimmy Carter was bearing witness to it.

Before evangelical ministers such as Jerry Falwell, Pat Robertson, and Tim LeHaye commanded widespread attention, Jimmy Carter treated Americans to a revival for political healing. In his acceptance speech at the Democratic National Convention in July 1976, he observed that this would be the year "that we give the government of this country back to the people of this country." Much like Graham at one of his stadium revivals, Carter called on individual Americans to come together under the big tent of the American electoral process and proclaim their faith in the nation, to restore their allegiance to the nation because America (and its government) belonged to and moved through them. "For I believe," he declared, "that we can come through this time of trouble stronger than ever. Like troops who have been in combat, we have been tempered by the fire; we have been disciplined, and we have been educated." Americans had witnessed national sin and would be made stronger as a people once they acknowledged it and returned to their faith. "Guided by lasting and simple moral values," he preached, "we have emerged idealists without illusions, realists who still know the old dreams of justice and liberty, of country and community." Of course, Carter mentioned the various planks in the Democratic platform and made pledges to be a president to all Americans. Ultimately, though, after the planks, the promises, and the promotions, Carter concluded, "My vision of this nation and its future has been deepened and matured during the nineteen months that I have campaigned among you for President. I have never had more faith in America than I do today. We have an America that, in Bob Dylan's phrase, is busy being born, not busy dying." That declaration had a sense of the unbelievable about it. The country was at about its lowest point in self-confidence and trust in public officials since the Civil War. Yet Carter had found more to believe in than ever before. It was fitting, actually, that he chose to use Dylan at this moment, for Dylan had recently abandoned his hard-edged social consciousness in the wake of his own born-again experience. Dylan proclaimed himself saved; Carter promised Americans national salvation once they too were born again.[10]

In the early Cold War, Graham had used American fears of an impending nuclear apocalypse to save individual souls. In the mid-1970s, following the disasters of Vietnam and Watergate, Carter used American doubts about their nation as a way to save the soul of America. Both Graham and Carter were nothing if not sincere about their projects— both believed millions of lives and the life of the nation to be at stake. Both also became symbols for larger cultural transformations taking place. And just as Graham's crusades sparked vigorous debates over the ways religion operated within Cold War America, Carter's nomination was a lightning rod for debates over how religion would help the United States recover from the catastrophes of war and political corruption.

"To be saved, all you must do is raise your hand; to be politically responsible, all you must do is pull the lever." To Jim Wallis, a leader among the Evangelical left in the mid-1970s, the election of 1976 was little more than "cheap grace." Wallis and the journal he helped edit, no longer called the *Post-American* but *Sojourners*, ran a special election issue with the acerbic title "The Seduction of the Church." In the early 1970s, Wallis had made clear his contempt for civil religion. It was a faith that had helped lead the United States into Vietnam and in 1976 was being used by both Carter and Ford to "offer the nation a cheap salvation, a healing without repentance, a reconciliation without justice." In short, he dismissed the patriotic piety of both candidates, even with Carter's obligatory nod to Niebuhr. Wes Michaelson, Wallis's colleague and a former Senate staffer of Hatfield's, warned that the Christian church "must guard against the encroachments of America's perpetual self-justification, which is so blatantly magnified by the rhetoric of presidential campaigns, in order to announce the judgment of God on our land, and proclaim the true hope that is offered through Christ and his kingdom."[11]

Similar sentiments echoed throughout the issue. Gary Wills observed that the sudden discovery of evangelical political power contained ominous portents because, he argued, "it is always dangerous for the gospel to become acceptable." Hatfield called for a Christian politics, rather than a politics practiced and preached by Christians, to free the oppressed, end war, and control rampant commercialism. Pacifist John Howard Yoder advised Christians to consider what was actually at stake in the election. He proposed that "to go to the polls is . . . not . . . a ritual affirmation of moral solidarity with the system. It is one way, one of the weaker and vaguer ways, to speak truth to power." In the end, "our discharge of this civil duty will be more morally serious if we take it less seriously." Michaelson felt the same way about Carter's theology. It was a mess, he argued, of moral hand-wringing and biblical equivocations. At base, Carter's greatest sin, Michaelson believed, was that he offered "to restore faith and confidence in America's goodness by reassuring its people that we are without sin." Michaelson added, "It is hard to think of a notion more profoundly unbiblical."[12]

Wallis and the evangelical left saw in Carter what they despised about civil religion. Carter was in some ways even more dangerous than other religious figures such as Graham because just at the moment when a withering critique of the United States could have been made Carter emerged to undercut the power of that critique. By coupling his pious views on personal Christianity with a moralistic view of the nation and its people, Carter failed to be a force who could critique the nation and cut off other attempts to use religion to champion it. Instead, he became the first incarnation of born-again civil religion. While many evangelicals flocked to Carter, *Sojourners* offered another option: abandon the nation (though not its people).

"Enlightened civil religion will severely tempt the church to join in the nation's bicentennial festivities," Michaelson observed in January 1976. "It will suggest that the church should call forth what is best in America—to return to those ideals which formed the rhetorical basis of the American Revolution. Some have even suggested that 'God has a lot riding on America.'" He didn't, according to *Sojourners*. Speaking for (presumably) all "disciples of Christ," Michaelson asserted, "We have no investment in the destiny of America. Seeing that everything turns out right for this nation, despite its sin, is simply not a task of the Christian church." It was better to work at becoming a prophetic minority of "believers whose very life and witness can unmask the pretensions of this age."[13]

Of course, there is a profound and significant irony to Michaelson's argument. While he, Wallis, and others on the evangelical left condemned Carter because they believed his compromise with civil religion undermined a Christian critique of the nation, their rejection of the nation ultimately undermined the political power of their Christian critique. Moreover, their stance left the political stage open to religious actors who unabashedly embraced the United States as a worthwhile project.

Richard John Neuhaus stepped into that breach. In the mid-1970s, Neuhaus had become a regular contributor to *Worldview*, the journal published by the Carnegie Endowment for Peace. Gathered in the journal's stable of writers were many religious intellectuals who had been on the political left during the civil rights movement and Vietnam War. Following the fall of Saigon and of Nixon, many of these same thinkers began to argue for more religion in the debate over America's fate, rather than less. While aware of the dangers of combining religion and nationalism, Neuhaus reasoned, "Patriotism need be neither vaunting pride nor masochistic shame. It is simply the acknowledgment of responsibility for . . . our time and place as Americans." "Patriotism is the acceptance, for better or for worse," he added, "that we are implicated in, responsible for, inseparable from, what America is and is to be.

'America' is not all we are, but all we are is ineluctably American."
To describe what that meant Neuhaus returned to the familiar language
of the covenant. "The American experiment rests not only upon rational
calculation," he contended, "it invokes a hoped-for destiny." And while
Vietnam had demolished the more optimistic understanding of that
covenant, American patriotism could perhaps offer a sense that the
nation was both "under judgment" and "may yet be a blessing and
not a curse to the nations of the earth."[14]

Not surprisingly, Neuhaus found the prospect of a Carter presidency
to be a watershed for American civil religion. "To put it simply," he
wrote, "the Carter era could signal the end of the public hegemony of
the secular Enlightenment in the Western world." Neuhaus argued that
for a "majority of Americans" any debate over meaning was wrapped up
in "belief systems [that] are inescapably religious." Thus what Carter
seemed to represent was a "remarriage" of the sacred and secular sources
of the American promise. Neuhaus concluded, "Americans are ready to
believe again, and upon President Jimmy Carter may fall the ominous
responsibility to articulate the national faith through a lively union of
public reason and biblical hope."[15]

Neuhaus was correct: the Carter presidency was a watershed for
American civil religion. Few presidents have ruminated about American
civil religion as much as Carter did. His presidency provided a relatively
brief but instructive course in the promise and perils of this national
faith. Carter sought to reaffirm the promise of America while paying
heed to the perils that had recently befallen the nation. To capture the
paradox of his moment, he chose to focus on humility. That wasn't
much of a stretch, as it was abundantly clear that the United States had
been humbled. But how could the president lead a national awakening
through humility? In his inaugural address, Carter counseled, "Let our
recent mistakes bring a resurgent commitment to the basic principles of
our Nation, for we know that if we despise our own government, we
have no future. We recall in special times when we have stood briefly,
but magnificently, united. In those times no prize was beyond our
grasp." Carter's trick, it seemed, was to attempt to acknowledge that
there was reason to have pride in the nation but little reason to express it
just yet. He used a passage from the Bible, from Micah, to set the tone:
"He hath showed thee, O man, what is good; and what doth the

Lord require of thee, but to do justly, and to love mercy, and to walk
humbly with thy Lord." Not a call to arms or action, but perhaps a call
to account for the role America played in the world. To Carter, the
tragedy of Vietnam, as both a war abroad and a war at home, had leveled
whatever was left of the Cold War heroic stance. Here was a nation on
its knees, and, to an evangelical Christian like the new president, that
position could be one of strength because it forced Americans to profess
their faith in each other, in abstract principles on which the nation was
founded, and, he hoped, in the president they just elected.[16]

A week later, Carter returned to that American faith in a speech
extraordinary for its candor and criticism. The occasion was the National
Prayer Breakfast. Carter revealed in the first few minutes of his remarks
that he had wanted to use a different biblical passage in his inaugural
address, from 2 Chronicles 7:14: "If my people, who are called by my
name, shall humble themselves and pray and seek my face and turn from
their wicked ways, then will I hear from Heaven and forgive their sins
and heal their land." Carter admitted that he had dropped this passage
after his staff "rose up in opposition" because it sounded like Carter was
condemning Americans as "wicked." Carter observed that this episode
taught him that there wasn't much chance that the nation would actually
understand the significance of being contrite. "We as individuals—and
we as a nation—insist that we are the strongest and the bravest and the
wisest and the best. And in that attitude, we unconsciously, but in an all-
pervasive way, cover up and fail to acknowledge our mistakes and in the
process forgo an opportunity constantly to search for a better life or a
better country." He admitted that it was easier for individuals to admit
their sin of pride than it was for a nation to do so. And so, he concluded,
"in effect, many of us worship our Nation." Carter's antidote to this
problem was to rededicate the United States as a nation "under God" to
remind Americans that they "are not superior . . . and ought constantly
to search out national and human individual consciousness and strive to
be better." Interestingly, Carter followed this rather pointed critique of
American hubris abroad with a comment about the military personnel he
had met since his inauguration. Perhaps because representatives from the
military traditionally filled the audience of the prayer breakfasts, Carter
thought it important to acknowledge their goodness too. He concluded
his remarks with the observation that it had been the "military people"

who in a "tremendous and startling proportion" had said "God be with you" and "we remember you in our prayers" as he and his wife, Rosalynn, met them in receiving lines. Carter went out of his way to point out that "the symbol of our nation's strength," those "fine people" of the American military, apparently agreed that this nation was indeed under God.[17]

I don't think it was inconsequential that Carter made this odd shift near the end of his remarks. What Carter illustrated, perhaps inadvertently, was that to recover American civil religion in the wake of the Vietnam War would require contending with the complex relationship between war and American civil religion. It would not be enough simply to cease talking about war or promise to be a better nation than the one that fought in Vietnam. In one sense, the United States had sacrificed too much in Vietnam to change the way it defined itself by such sacrifice. In another sense, the bloodshed and destruction that the United States had wreaked abroad complicated the symbolic significance afforded the military. Thus, as much as Carter wanted to distance himself and his nation from the hubris that led to Vietnam, he was also smart and sensitive enough to comprehend that the faith required to rebuild the nation's moral stature came from the same religious wellspring that fed support for the troops in Vietnam.

During the war, most evangelicals had stood by American military efforts. Graham had noted that on visits to Southeast Asia he had seen ample evidence of a "tremendous moral program" for the troops. From earnest chaplains ministering to soldiers in harm's way to the high attendance among servicemen at religious services, evangelical leaders saw the military as immune to the moral decay that they believed endangered many Americans stateside. Stephen Olford, a pastor of the Calvary Baptist Church in New York City, noted that "America may be confused; other nations may have little idea of why we are in Vietnam, but let me say that I did not find one soldier, from the ranks to the generals . . . who was not solidly convinced of our enemy and our cause."[18]

The subtext for such tributes to military service is sacrifice—soldiers are willing to give their lives for their nation. For post-Vietnam America, the idea of self-sacrifice seemed to vanish into the haze of culture wars fought over everything from gender to energy. Carter presided over a nation in the throes of crises but without any unifying reason to make the sacrifices necessary to solve them. Thus what began to emerge during the Carter years was that the United States seemed trapped in a war against everything—poverty, crime, oil dependence, child abuse— and everyone—women against men; homosexuals against heterosexuals; the left versus the right; the religious condemning the secular. Missing from this melee was a struggle that could unify Americans at a moral—if superficial but politically expedient—level. In short, the Cold War had gone missing and gone with it was the sense that Americans were engaged in a moral struggle together.

Carter did not believe the Soviet Union had become harmless or that the nuclear stand-off between the two superpowers had grown innocuous. Rather, as he said in his first major speech on foreign policy, at the University of Notre Dame in May 1977, the rules needed to change. "I believe we can have a foreign policy that is democratic, that is based on fundamental values, and that uses power and influence, which we have, for humane purposes. We can also have a foreign policy that the American people both support and, for a change, know about and understand." He didn't declare the Cold War over but declared America tired of being beholden to it. Carter's logic made some sense: the nation learned a lesson from the experience in Vietnam and in this speech the new president was applying that lesson to foreign affairs. "For too many years, we've been willing to adopt the flawed and erroneous principles and tactics of our adversaries, sometimes abandoning our own values for theirs," he lectured. "We've fought fire with fire, never think- ing that fire is better quenched with water. This approach failed, with Vietnam the best example of its intellectual and moral poverty. But through failure we have now found our way back to our own principles and values, and we have regained our lost confidence." Rather than being about a balance of power or a balance of terror, Carter proclaimed America's new foreign policy to be about human rights because only that kind of foreign policy would be based on the "constant decency in [the nation's] values and on optimism in our historical vision." He told his audience that he wanted a foreign policy that "I hope will make you proud to be Americans."[19]

Carter was trained as an engineer and had worked as an engineer on a nuclear submarine when he was in the navy. He was used to working with proofs. When he entered office, he attempted to create two proofs: first, that the United States was a force for good in the world; and, second, that the Vietnam War and Watergate proved that the country could fail. As president, Carter wanted to resolve the evident contradiction between these two proofs by offering a third proof: that American civil religion would work better without war. In other words, because wars created moral traps, they constantly undermined America's desire to be a force for good. If the United States avoided war and did all it could to help others around the world do the same, then Americans could place their trust in the nation because the nation would represent the best. Rather than building better nuclear weapons, Americans could build better schools; rather than bombing the poor in a far-off land, Americans could eradicate poverty in their own country; and rather than sending off soldiers to sacrifice their lives for a war that undermined the principles of their nation, the president could call on sacrifice to cut dependence on foreign oil; to clean up cities, rivers, and lakes; and to reinvigorate the economy with money that might otherwise be spent for making war. Indeed, the Carter presidency was a quiet period in postwar American history. He kept America out of war.

But he didn't give up entirely on what war meant to Americans. In April 1977, when Carter spoke about his energy policy, he declared that it would take an effort that "will be the 'moral equivalent of war.'" Instead of bringing about the terrible consequences of military conflicts like Vietnam, in this war "we will be uniting our efforts to build and not to destroy." Carter staked a great deal on this new fight but wound up failing to rally Americans, the Congress, or even his own cabinet behind this plan. He learned a lesson from this brief skirmish: energy was simply one front in a much larger war for the soul of the nation. He delivered another speech exactly two years later revisiting the impending energy crisis he had predicted in 1977. Except this time, Carter also began to explore the "moral dimensions of the energy crisis—how the gas shortage highlighted the country's frailties in a world not under its control." The problem was that relatively few Americans tuned in to listen to their commander-in-crisis chasten them. By May 1979, Carter was in a bleak mood, brooding to delegates at a Democratic National Committee meeting about American "paralysis, stagnation, and drift." He believed he understood how to meet the challenges that faced the nation and was willing to be honest with the public if Americans were willing to face and act on reality. The *Washington Post* called the speech a "sermon." The paper could have used a more evocative term—it was a jeremiad.[20]

Carter worked within the American tradition of the jeremiad to rouse his people out of a spiritual stupor by trying to remind them that the nation had sacrificed for great causes in the past and needed to do so again, now! As the world oil market fell under the sway of the Organization of Petroleum Exporting Countries and as the economic fate of the United States became tenuously tied to the machinations of the Middle East, the United States entered a summer of tribulations in 1979. The time had come for Carter to preach hope and resolution rather than to predict doom. He would summon the prophetic power of the jeremiad to shock Americans into action: their decline was imminent unless they stood with their president and began to act like a people who believed they had a destiny as great as their legacy. Yet Carter had come to believe that Vietnam wasn't the problem; Watergate wasn't the problem; even the economy wasn't the problem (though it was depressing). The problem was trust: Carter needed the American people to trust him and listen to him, but that required him to have something to say. The moment of reckoning had come for Carter. He had entered office to rebuild America following the shame of war and political scandal. To rebuild the nation ideologically required repairing a tattered American civil religion. Carter believed that such repair meant reworking civil religion to be less about war and a Manichean view of the world and more about reaffirming the ideals that had little to do with Cold War thinking.[21]

On July 15, 1979, he launched his most purposeful jeremiad. In a nationally televised speech that garnered the largest audience of his presidency, Carter spoke with great urgency: "I want to talk to you right now about a fundamental threat to American democracy." Carter assured Americans that threat had little to do with the idea of America (for that was good and sound) or with American national security (for war was a distraction). "The threat is nearly invisible in ordinary ways. It is a crisis of confidence. It is a crisis that strikes at the heart and soul and spirit of our national will. We can see this crisis in the growing doubt about the meaning of our own lives, in the loss of a unity of purpose for our Nation." The tone of the speech was unmistakably moral, even theological, and for good reason. In preparation for it, Carter had conducted a five-day domestic summit at which the president heard from a broad spectrum of advisors, from governors and economists to religious leaders and sociologists. Among the participants was Robert Bellah, who, as part of the "God Squad," brought religion to bear on the discussion of the nation's problems. Bellah and other religious intellectuals told Carter to speak to Americans about the covenant they had made with a history under God. The president was especially pleased with the advice he received from the God Squad because it gave him the language he wanted to speak about "sin and selfishness and about those national values, like the idea of a covenant, that could push the country out of the crisis it presently faced."[22]

At base, the speech was about faith. "Our people are losing that faith," he declared, "not only in government itself but in their ability as citizens to serve as the ultimate rulers and shapers of our democracy." Carter posed an existential question: How did Americans define themselves and their nation? Was it through the deliberate act of participation in government that Carter suggested or the more abstract notion that America is good and its people good because they are part of the long tradition of Western civilization? And which issues or events provided an answer? For Carter, the crisis that precipitated his speech was the energy problem: "Energy will be the immediate test of our ability to unite this Nation; it can also be the standard around which to rally. On the battlefield of energy we can win for our Nation a new confidence, and we can seize control again of our common destiny."[23] Carter's use of war language was appropriate, for when it seemed freedom was at stake, Americans went to war with a clear understanding of their civil religion. The American Revolution made patriots consider sacrifice for the abstract notion of natural rights that the British had denied them; in the Civil War, Lincoln made clear that the war was fought for a new birth of freedom; in the Second World War, Americans fought and died to defeat the forces that would deny freedom to others (and ultimately them); and the Cold War was seen as a battle between the free world and a world enslaved by a corrupt ideology. Undoubtedly Vietnam had complicated this understanding of war, but not to the extent that Americans were now willing to believe that the "energy problem" created a moral imperative similar to war for freedom. While Americans had spoken about (and continue to speak about) freedom from foreign oil, this is not the same thing as the freedom that was at stake in Second World War or even the Cold War—the context in which Carter's America existed.

Carter's attempt to rework American civil religion made it almost certain that the 1980 presidential election would become a referendum on it. As the nation inched toward that contest, Carter's civil religion responded to a string of crises. After his "Crisis of Confidence" speech, Carter enjoyed an initial bump in public-opinion polls. But by the next summer Carter had failed to consolidate and build on support for a civil religion based on the moral equivalent of war. A gut-level explanation for his failure suggests that Americans don't like to face unpleasant truths about themselves and their nation, but they do like to traffic in grand illusions that, at times, get them mired in tragedies like Vietnam. *Time* magazine put it this way: "[Carter] was a man who also started out riding the country's high hopes (a *Time* Man of the Year in 1976), and who was perhaps most bitterly resented for shrinking those hopes down to the size of a presidency characterized by small people, small talk and small matters. He made Americans feel two things they are not used to feeling, and will not abide. He made them feel puny and he made them feel insecure."[24]

Within a few months of delivering his "Crisis of Confidence" speech, Carter dealt with two foreign policy crises: the taking of American hostages in the U.S. embassy by radical Iranian students in Tehran and the invasion of Afghanistan by the Soviet Union. The two events were a mere six weeks apart in November and December 1979, and they framed the context for Carter's State of the Union address in January 1980. In that speech, Carter declared in less than humble terms that the United States would protect its interests in the Persian Gulf by any means necessary, including military force. The Cold War was apparently back on and "explicit rhetoric of good and evil was once again fashionable." But Carter adopted such rhetoric too late to benefit him. Political analyst Morton Kondracke observed that to Carter's political right emerged "a consistent alternative world view to that of the Democrats, and the public decided to try it. It is a simplistic world view, a John Wayne view, but it is thoroughly American and of obvious appeal: the United States can do anything it wants, if it has the will. . . . Carter and the Democrats told people that the United States was caught by forces beyond its control."[25]

In one sense, Carter's failure confirmed one of Niebuhr's insights: there was no escaping history though Americans never shy away from trying anyway. Perhaps Carter's reading of Niebuhr led him to follow a "theology of fallibility," that the country had committed moral wrongs and had suffered moral wrongs and the right path was to confront rather than to avoid that history. That course of action was not foolhardy; the public never rejected Carter as a person of moral standing.[26]

At the same time that Carter asked Americans to reckon with sin, many of his fellow evangelicals and fundamentalists were doing the same thing. Many had voted for Carter, but by 1980 they had almost completely abandoned their man on the inside. What happened? Jerry Falwell was a case in point. Falwell agreed with many of the details that informed Carter's prognosis of America's sorry state, but he rejected Carter's bedside manner. Humility wasn't required; what Americans needed was, simply and profoundly, faith in God's plan. That plan placed America along the path toward redemption. Falwell would thunder to large crowds, "We pay the price, God will give us what we want."[27] Like Reagan, Falwell dismissed the sincerity with which Carter spoke about American malaise.

Falwell was part of a movement that had its origins in the postwar period but that took off in the late 1970s. Its foundation was a union of conservative Christian evangelicals that grew to incorporate conservative Catholics and Jews. This was the home of the Moral Majority, the Christian Coalition, and eventually evangelicals and Catholics together; unofficially the coalition acquired the name the New Christian Right (NCR). Many of the evangelical leaders came from the South, used television to attract followers and money, built "megachurches," universities, and even theme parks. The best-known members of this group included Falwell, Robertson, LeHaye, Jim Bakker, Jimmy Swagger, and Rex Hubbard. But there was also an intellectual class associated with the NCR that included Neuhaus, Novak, Peter Berger, Will Herberg, Richard Viguerie, and Francis Schaeffer. Even though these men did not agree on solutions to all the problems that plagued America in the 1970s, they did seem consistently to speak together on three issues: first, that a decline in national morality was the key to the nation's problems; second, that to make America moral again required injecting religion into public debates and policy; and, third, the United States was not inconsequential to God—in other words, they argued that as a nation based on Judeo-Christian traditions the United States had to take its covenant with God more seriously than it was or continue to suffer dire consequences.[28] "To think about the American experiment theologically, or to suggest that God is not indifferent to the American experiment, in no way implies that people who are Americans are 'special' in the sense of occupying a superior place in God's concerns and purposes," wrote Neuhaus of this position. "It is by no means the decisive thing, but neither is it a trifling thing, that we Christians in America are *American* Christians. We have a measure of responsibility for this country and its influence in the world." But this influence was larger than that of most other nations because "America impinges upon them all," and therefore these nations too "have more than a passing interest in how the American story within the story of the world is told."[29]

Neuhaus captured the basic position taken by the NCR on how America's Christian heritage related to the Cold War. But he didn't capture the militancy of that vision. To put this position in bald-faced terms, Falwell exhorted in his 1980 polemic, "Listen, America!": "It is right living that has made America the greatest nation on the earth, and with all of her shortcomings and failures, America is without question the greatest nation on the face of God's earth. We as Americans must recommit ourselves to keeping her that way." He concluded, "We are faced with responsibilities. Today, more that at any time in history, America needs men and women of God who have an understanding of the time and are not afraid to stand up for what is right." Falwell issued a call to action, and it was not for the moral equivalent of war, but for war itself.[30]

If Carter's faith led him to believe that war—the Cold War in general and Vietnam in particular—had brought America misery and crisis, Falwell and many in the NCR believed that the Cold War was necessary, Vietnam honorable, and war, in a world beset by sin, unavoidable. In short, Carter's brothers in Christ disagreed with him profoundly on the subject of war. Whereas Carter saw Vietnam as the touchstone for a moral reckoning in the postwar period, the NCR chose World War II, not Vietnam, as its touchstone. While no member of this group had fought in the Second World War or any war for that matter, they considered themselves warriors nonetheless. They rejected pacifism outright because, as Francis Schaeffer argued, pursuing peace was a sham; it led directly to appeasement and, ultimately, to war anyway. Falwell recalled that during World War II Americans were "praying for our boys and thanking God for them and buying war bonds to help pay for the materials and artillery they needed to fight and win and come back." Demonstrations for peace would have mocked the moral seriousness and justness of that cause, and the same applied to the Cold War. Moreover, the outcome of World War II had conferred on the United States the kind of global influence that came with being a just and good power. America, Falwell concluded, "has been great because she has been good."[31]

To the NCR, the Cold War was an extension of the moral lessons of World War II. And that was why, by the late 1970s, Falwell and others on the right made dire predictions about the fate of the nation if it failed to flex its military might. What happened in Korea and Vietnam, Falwell believed, was a loss of will. "We are not committed to victory. We are not committed to greatness. We have lost the will to stay strong and therefore have not won any wars we have fought since 1945." Thus, contra King, most of the bishops of the American Catholic Church, and the first born-again president, the NCR saw Vietnam not as a reminder of the moral limits of the nation or the ambiguities of the Cold War but as a conflict that deserved increased commitment and sacrifice. Rus Walton asked, "What must the nations of the free world think of a country that spends the lives of 58,000 splendid young men and then gives up? Just quits and walks away and says, 'Sorry, fellas, it was all a mistake.'"[32]

Vietnam was, therefore, a good fight done badly. America's leaders, the NCR believed, lost their moral strength and thus the war. But the Cold War, of which Vietnam was only a part, continued. Thus many on the right believed that the Soviet invasion of Afghanistan had reminded Americans—including President Carter—that the nation was indeed still at war. As one historian of the NCR put it, "The [NCR] describe[s] a pattern in which American military might is checked and eventually allowed to be defeated because of the indecision and ineptitude of weak-willed politicians." Carter was only the latest in a line of such ineffectual leaders, a line that began with Truman and his "loss" of China and firing of Douglas McArthur during the Korean War. To understand such a view, we must acknowledge the totalism, or "maximalism," of NCR thought, in which extraordinary measures such as fighting a war were easily justifiable once one saw the world in the "right" terms. With the Second World War as the model for confronting evil on a global scale, the Cold War was then a fight between good and evil as well. If America's leaders were clear about confronting the Soviet threat— "a nation," Falwell declared, "committed to communism and to destroying the American way of life"—Americans and their leader should act like the generation that defeated the Nazis and the Japanese. But instead, Falwell lamented, "we face a decade when it is doubtful if Americans will survive as a free people."[33]

To stave off impending doom, the NCR embraced militarization: it was time for Americans to stop worrying and learn to love the bomb. Indeed, in a truly *Dr. Strangelove* moment, Phyllis Schlafly, a leader of the NCR's march toward national revival, declared that the atomic bomb was "a marvelous gift that was given to our country by a wise God."[34] This odd play on Truman's statement about the bomb took postwar moralizing an additional step in the sense that it implied divine truth in America's ability to obliterate countries at will. The NCR's confidence in American military might trickled down from there, pouring over the military's arsenals and bases around the world, and anointing its men and women in service as nothing less than, as Graham said at West Point in 1972, "beacon lights to guide our nation through this perilous period."[35] In the military, the NCR found exemplars of selflessness and discipline in the midst of a period of unprecedented selfishness and "malaise." The military's devotion to "traditional values" accentuated its role as the front-line defense against the expansion of communism; it was as if the soldiers who were trained to kill communists did so not only in defense of their nation but because they were imbued with values that made them patriots with moral vision.

"In the aftermath of Vietnam," observes Andrew Bacevich, "evangelicals came to see the military as an enclave of virtue, a place of refuge where the sacred remnant of patriotic Americans gathered and preserved American principles from extinction." Likewise, evangelical investment in the military encouraged the "armed forces to see the evangelicals as allies—sharing the same enemies and sharing at least to some degree in a common mission of restoration."[36] Yet this union between the NCR and the military did not remake the Cold War into a holy war any more than Dwight Eisenhower's religious rhetoric and friendship with Graham made the United States into a theocracy. Rather NCR's promotion of the military was a means to a national end—here was a revision of American civil religion in which the country would be made more moral and thus could return to "greatness" by acting more like the troops. The military embodied those Americans who, Falwell said, "love their country, are patriotic, and are willing to sacrifice for her."[37] Thus the troops operated as a lodestar in the fight to "redeem" America because on the battlefield, the NCR imagined, morality was clear.

Thus, as the Christian left condemned the nation to save individual souls, the Christian right sacralized the nation to save the soul of America. The NCR consistently railed against political leaders as incompetent, immoral, ungodly, and weak, but just as consistently hoped that elections would bring a new generation of politicians to power who would save the nation. It was further irony that in its extreme condemnation of communists for worshiping the state, the NCR supported the greatest buildup of the American state's military force in the nation's history. But that position came from a hero who seemed heaven-sent to the NCR. In the election of 1980, evangelical Christians could have again chosen Carter, one of their own, but instead turned out in huge numbers for Ronald Reagan, a divorced, infrequent churchgoer who regarded the United States as nearly divine—or at least a "city upon a hill." The NCR had found the man to redeem America. He was also the most astute tactician of American civil religion.

Reagan quoted from the Bible, proclaimed a deep faith in God, believed that the United States was a nation "under God," and even claimed to have had born-again experiences. Yet he was no born-again Christian; he wasn't even especially religious. "Reagan was an Emersonian," John Diggins concluded; "he had an Emersonian sense of the becoming and unfolding of all things, a cosmic assurance that Americans could always count on a 'bright dawn ahead,' that time is boundless and the world endless." In this way he was the opposite of his predecessor. Carter's acts of contrition and his appeal to humility came from his devotion to a prophetic religion. Reagan's optimism and promises to revive America came from an equally devout faith, but one that renounced the limits that religion traditionally imposed on human ambitions. To put it the terms of the time: America went to bed sick with malaise but awoke revived by a new morning of optimism.[38]

The fact that Reagan offered a rhetorical alternative to Carter was not such a surprise; after all, the alternatives were either to go further into an analysis of evil and despair or to simply dismiss the "gloom and doom" of an "environment of exhaustion." If the left wanted to crucify the nation on its cross of hubris, Reagan wanted to crucify the critics on their own cross of doubt, contrition, and guilt. But, of course, Reagan didn't merely reject malaise. He "sacralized the nation" by employing a trick that has since become legendary: he separated the disastrous actions of the state from the nearly divine nature of the American promise. Unlike Carter, who attempted to make the state a check on the excesses of the nation, Reagan unleashed American civil religion so that Americans might come to believe in the promise of America as much and as deeply as he did.[39]

Reagan had been practicing this faith for a while. In between his time as governor of California and president of the United States, roughly from 1975 through 1979, Reagan had a radio program. He wrote scripts and delivered them on-air through hundreds of radio stations, allowed them to be reprinted in hundreds of newspapers, and was heard (and read) by probably millions of Americans.[40]

So, for example, in September 1976, in the midst of the bicentennial year, Reagan told his listeners, "Sometimes I think we need to remind ourselves of what it is we're trying to preserve in this country." He spoke about the wisdom of foreigners who viewed America with pride even at its darkest or weakest moments. He recounted an editorial published by the *London Daily Mail* around July 4, 1976, by Ferdinand Mount, a member of the British elite and a politically conservative writer and editor. Mount chastised his countrymen and fellow Europeans for enjoying the humbling of America: "For all its terrible faults," Mount wrote, "American is still the last, best hope of mankind, because it spells out so vividly the kind of happiness which most people actually want, regardless of what they are told they ought to want." Such a statement undoubtedly captured Reagan's heart, not so much because it sounded patriotic or even nationalistic but because it sounded unbounded. It was the individual soul, unburdened by history, God, and (especially) the impositions of the state that found its purest expression in the American promise. "It is the only nation founded solely on a moral dream," Mount wrote. "A part of our own future is tied up in it and the greatest of all the gifts the Americans have given us is hope." Reagan concluded his broadcast: "Thank you Mr. Mount—we needed that." Indeed, Reagan hoped to inspire the United States in much the same way—emotionally, simplistically, effectively—as Mount had inspired Reagan.[41]

Reagan had a paradoxical understanding of the United States. The nation's greatest asset, he believed, was the way its system "freed the individual genius of man." But he also constantly denounced the state produced by that system. This seeming contradiction, though, became an effective one-two punch: while Reagan praised the nation for reflecting the best in the American people, he could blame the state when things went wrong (as in Vietnam). This approach worked brilliantly in his first campaign for president, when he ran against Carter. In one of Reagan's most effective political jabs, he'd wittily remark: "A recession is when your neighbor loses his job. A depression is when you lose yours. And recovery is when Jimmy Carter loses his."[42]

Carter sought to use the state to reform the nation, to rebuild the trust of Americans in the nation, and, ultimately, to redeem the nation following the tragedies of the late 1960s and early 1970s. For him, civil religion required popular supplication to the authority of God, for only by restraining the excesses of patriotism could Americans build a moral nation. The state had to play a role in this kind of civil religion. For Reagan, the state forced Americans to prostrate themselves before the false god of public policy. Carter wanted public policy to make the nation moral. Reagan believed that the only stumbling block to American greatness was public policy that could do nothing else but constrain individual freedom. At base, the difference between Carter and Reagan came down to sin. Carter believed that people could improve with guidance, but that just as Christians needed to find Jesus in order to inspire them to be moral, Americans needed the state to help them make manifest their desire to improve as a nation. Reagan certainly believed people could be bad, and nations and ideas could be evil; but he was unburdened by the notion of original sin. He waved away the belief that people are constrained by forces external to the individual, that human nature cannot break free completely from the legacy of the biblical fall from God's grace. The state and public policy were thus terrible manifestations (and even reflections) of the belief that the individual does not have the authority and power to remake his or her world. In Carter's view, people needed the state and its policies to help them recognize their limits. Nonsense, Reagan preached, the only thing one needed to know about limits was that there weren't any.

In his first inaugural address, Reagan illustrated how his interpretation of American civil religion would be an ideological counterweight to Carter's national theology of humility. "I do not believe in a fate that will fall on us no matter what we do," Reagan said. "We have every right to dream heroic dreams." While acknowledging that economic problems plagued Americans, Reagan did not characterize the situation as some kind of hope-crushing national pathology. Rather, he famously declared, the problem was not the economy or trust or some national malaise: "In this present crisis . . . government is the problem." The obligation of government was to get out of the way to allow Americans to realize a promise that the nation embodied because it enshrined individualism. "If we look to the answer as to why for so many years we achieved so much, prospered as no other people on Earth," Reagan explained, "it was because here in this land we unleashed the energy and individual genius of man to a greater extent than has ever been done before. Freedom and the dignity of the individual have been more available and assured here than in any other place on Earth. The price for this freedom at times has been high, but we have never been unwilling to pay that price."[43]

Reagan understood the polemical value of speaking about sacrifice for the nation. But he chose not to resort to it. Following a section in which he paid homage to the "Founding Fathers," immortalized by monuments on the Washington Mall, he recognized "those monuments to heroism" in Arlington Cemetery and, in particular, the grave of a Martin Treptow, a soldier who had died in the First World War. Reagan referred to a passage in the diary Treptow had carried until he died in battle: "America must win this war. Therefore I will work, I will save, I will sacrifice, I will endure, I will fight cheerfully and do my utmost, as if the issue of the whole struggle depended on me alone." His story was ripe for a call to national sacrifice. And yet Reagan employed it to make the opposite point: "The crisis we are facing today does not require of us the kind of sacrifice that Martin Treptow and so many thousands of others were called upon to make. It does require, however, our best effort and our willingness to believe in ourselves and to believe in our capacity to perform great deeds, to believe that together with God's help we can and will resolve the problems which now confront us." "And after all," Reagan concluded his address, "why shouldn't we believe that? We are Americans." Here was a hint of what was to come in the Reagan presidency. Carter faced the legacies of the Vietnam War and the Cold War by reworking American civil religion to avoid military conflict because that led to moral quandaries. Yet he ended up declaring war on many other things (the economy, energy, and American self-indulgence), and ultimately he couldn't avoid reigniting the Cold War over the Soviet invasion of Afghanistan. His counterparts in the evangelical right, of course, had no qualms about militarizing American civil religion for their political and moral agendas. The Christian left simply concluded that any war involving the United States was doomed to moral failure. For his part, Reagan wanted to do something about the connection between American civil religion and war. But to the surprise of many, especially his supporters on the right, he sought to go much further than Carter by illustrating that war was unnecessary in any form—cold, nuclear, even ideological. Reagan would deploy civil religion to counter the militancy of the right and the radicalism of the left. And in his doing so American civil religion was reborn.[44]

Only two months after his inauguration, Reagan had a religious experience. On March 30, 1981, John Hinckley Jr. attempted to assassinate the president. The shooting severely wounded two people, and one bullet ricocheted off the presidential limousine and lodged near the president's heart. Reagan was rushed to George Washington University hospital for emergency surgery. He made a remarkable recovery, and his rather optimistic response captivated Americans, making the president a heroic figure for the first few months of his administration.

The president had almost died, and that experience apparently affected his political vision. He wrote in his diary, "Whatever happens now, I owe my life to God and will try to serve him in every way I can." Rather remarkably for a cold warrior, that meant working to defang the Soviet Union and to deflate the dangerous, near-apocalyptic tensions of the Cold War. Perhaps it took the realization that he had almost perished

to reawaken a particular sense of humanity that had led him in the days
following Hiroshima and Nagasaki to join the "Ban the Bomb" movement. The Reagan of the early 1980s was a complicated political character. While never comfortable with the awesome destructive potential
of nuclear weapons, Reagan also found the unilateral position of the
nuclear "freeze" movement unacceptable, in no small part because that
position made no attempt to reconcile the ideological conditions that
made the cold war a reality. Instead, as Diggins persuasively argued,
"Reagan's sensibility partook of the tragic vision of liberalism, the conviction that the cold war presented the world with no possibility of a
morally good choice. Had Reagan been a true religious fundamentalist,
he would have had no cause to agonize about such a situation, since his
diplomatic decisions would have been guided by divine grace. That
he did so agonize puts Ronald Reagan in the company of Abraham
Lincoln."[45]

Indeed, like Lincoln, Reagan developed an American civil religion
that would allow him to counter the religiosity of those who saw either
divine blessings or wrathful judgment in American history. And, also like
Lincoln, Reagan understood that the moral dilemmas of American history could not be resolved if he applied only rational analysis: he needed
to construct an interpretation of American destiny that could transcend
the malaise of the 1970s and the hard-line response of the 1980s. Two
speeches made less than a year apart illustrated Reagan's attempt.

On March 8, 1983, President Reagan gave an address to the annual
convention of the National Association of Evangelicals (NAE), in
Orlando, Florida. The speech became known as the "evil empire"
speech because Reagan declared that the communists who controlled
the Soviet Union were the "focus of evil in the modern world." Reagan
decided to speak to the NAE for a few reasons, among them to counter
the nuclear-freeze movement, which had existed since 1945 but had
grown stronger in the wake of Vietnam and the near-disaster at Three-
Mile Island, a nuclear power plant in eastern Pennsylvania. The freeze
movement was substantial, and, with the support of millions of people
around the world, it posed a direct rhetorical and political challenge to
Reagan's policy of "peace through strength." But foreign policy has
traditionally worked to the advantage of a shrewd president, and for
Reagan a "moral" foreign policy became a means to an end for his first

administration. Reagan and his advisors intended to demonize communism and thus remind Americans that in comparison with the Soviet Union they had much of which to be proud.

Thus, in the first part of his speech, Reagan focused on the two characteristics he believed distinguished the "goodness" of America from the evil of communism—religion and freedom. He thanked his evangelical audience for their support, prayerful as well as political. "We need your help," the president confessed, "to keep us ever-mindful of the ideas and the principles that brought us into the public arena in the first place . . . The basis of those ideals and principles is a commitment to freedom and personal liberty that itself is grounded in the much deeper realization that freedom prospers only where the blessings of God are avidly sought and humbly accepted." He continued that he believed "the American experiment in democracy rests on this insight." Here was the crux of Reagan's civil religion: America's God was one that endowed the nation with freedom and personal liberty (rather than humility or sacrifice or love). For Reagan, God's grace in American history was found in the declaration that all men are endowed with certain inalienable rights by their creator. Reagan called this "discovery . . . the great triumph of our Founding Fathers." Indeed, Reagan pointed out that Thomas Jefferson said, "The God who gave us life, gave us liberty at the same time." And what did Americans do with this God-given freedom and liberty? Liberating themselves from the British empire was only a first step. Once they were no longer ruled by tyrants, then what? Reagan answered by appropriating Tocqueville: "That shrewdest of all observers of American democracy, Alexis de Tocqueville, put it eloquently after he had gone on a search for the secret of America's greatness and genius—and he said: 'Not until I went into the churches of America and heard her pulpits aflame with righteousness did I understand the greatness and the genius of America. America is good. And if America ever ceases to be good, America will cease to be great.'"[46]

Reagan rather smartly argued that the genius of America was the freedom its citizens had to thank their own personal God they lived in a nation that ensured their right to practice their religion. It's a circular argument that doesn't make clear which came first, American first principles or a God to whom Americans owe allegiance. However, that didn't matter to Reagan because he praised the Founders and

Tocqueville for something very specific: Americans enjoy freedom from tyranny because of God-given rights, those rights ensure life and liberty. To do what? To what end? To go into the churches of America and hear from its pulpits, in righteous exhortations, that America is good and therefore great. But why is America good? Because Americans have freedom, granted by God, not necessarily to judge but to affirm the actions of their nation through their individual religions. They are not commanded by a tyrant to love their country; no ideology or a state church sanctifies the nation; religion does not validate politics in America. Rather, Americans do this by their own free will and, as Reagan emphasized in his speech, by building a nation on the exceptional combination of transcendent ideals in regard to God and natural rights. "Reagan looked to religion less as a source of divine guidance," Diggins concluded, "than as a bulwark against the power of the state."[47]

On the face of it, Reagan's speech was heartening to Christian evangelicals because the president so clearly attacked the idea of secularism and spoke so glowingly of the role religion played in American life. But the point of the speech was not to stump for school prayer or even against secularism in America but to articulate how the Cold War remained the defining moral dilemma of the age. Distractions from the left and also the right had to be put in their proper perspective, Reagan believed. He did not necessarily disagree with either but offered a different emphasis: he wanted recognition that the evil that existed in the world resided not in the nuclear arsenal of the United States or among liberal secularists, but in the Kremlin. Moreover, unlike Carter in his speech to Catholics at Notre Dame, in which he attempted to reduce Cold War tensions through an appeal to reason over ideology, Reagan actually declared an end to the Cold War in his speech to Christian evangelicals. Calling on the spiritual energy of American civil religion, Reagan testified, "I believe that communism is another sad, bizarre chapter in human history whose last pages even now are being written. I believe this because the source of our strength in the quest for human freedom is not material, but spiritual. And because it knows no limitation, it must terrify and ultimately triumph over those who would enslave their fellow man." Reagan exhorted his audience, "Yes, change your world." He then quoted Thomas Paine, his favorite American patriot, saying, "We have it in our power to begin the world over again." Reagan the radical intended to shake up a world that had come to know a cold war deadlock that threatened the existence of the future. To Reagan, the future was clear: because communism had violated what he considered the natural tendency toward individual freedom, the Soviet Union could not withstand the challenge posed by the morality of the American promise. Thus, while war was out of the question, the moral equivalent of war was not.[48]

Reagan's speech provoked a predictable rebuke. Observers across the political spectrum criticized Reagan's use of religious language as a pseudo-theological argument for what many saw as nothing more than an attempt to rally support for a military buildup. A political cartoon captured the general sense of outrage: Tony Auth depicted Reagan as a strident crusader; with a bayonet attached to a cross in one hand and a sword in the other, he shouts, "Onward Christian Soldiers!" In the cartoon, Reagan attempts to appeal to a crowd that is led by religious leaders—a preacher, a nun, and a Catholic bishop stand in front of a throng of people who are marching as part of the nuclear-freeze movement. In the heart of the "evil empire," Soviet leaders regarded the speech as "an obstacle, not a spur, to negotiation." The speech also failed to move the leadership of the NAE to endorse publicly Reagan's foreign policy. And yet, what seemed at first as a senseless and unnecessary provocation by the president, became a prelude to Reagan's most ambitious scheme. Over the next four years, Reagan proposed to abolish the nuclear arsenals of the two superpowers, he reversed his opinion of the Soviet Union as evil, and he declared the Cold War over.[49]

That turn of events had everything to do with faith, but not religion. In his evil empire speech, Reagan had asked his audience to "pray for the salvation of all those who live in the totalitarian darkness—pray they will discover the joy of God." Such an appeal clearly resounded with overtones of sanctimonious piety and even crusade-like zeal. Yet, Reagan's cause was nondenominational and had more to do with his sacralized version of freedom than with God's judgment. He wanted to rescue the people under communism from a system that denied them the freedom to believe in God. He didn't need to profess his own faith in a God, only that he believed passionately that people should have the freedom to believe. Graham, preacher to successive presidents, told Reagan in the early 1980s that his recent experiences in the Soviet Union made it clear that the people in the Soviet Union wanted such freedom. Such information confirmed for Reagan that the Cold War was a conflict not between people as much as between ideas. And ideas were not like religious doctrine; they were much more fluid and competitive. A people could decide to choose how to organize around an idea, as clearly both Americans and Russians had. But that also meant that people could change their minds and decide to organize around a new idea. The key for Reagan was that in its most essential form humanity had the freedom to choose how to organize, and thus any idea that curtailed that freedom too much violated his view of human nature. Of course, to Reagan the greatest violator of this doctrine was communism because it ultimately restricted people to a single choice. Reagan's civil religion, rather than his faith in democracy, Christianity, or even the American state, led him to believe that the Cold War could end without going to war because ultimately people want to be freed in order to choose how they live rather than to kill people in order to decide how others should live.[50]

Less than a year after the notorious evil empire speech, Reagan made a televised address to the nation on January 16, 1984. The fact that his speech kicked off a presidential-election year was important, as the public continued to have concerns regarding the potential ramifications of Reagan's hard-line rhetoric toward the Soviets. Moreover, the nuclear-freeze movement continued to garner support, and the American public remained as conflicted and anxious about the role of nuclear weapons as they had been since the early years of the Cold War. Reagan, therefore, had politically expedient reasons to change his tone regarding the Cold War. But his speech did not represent a dramatic change in policy as much as a change in emphasis. After all, Carter was the policy wonk, hoping to construct a better world out of more effective, efficient, and moral policies on energy, war, nuclear arsenals, the Middle East. Reagan appealed to sensibilities that were at once simple and profound. The beginning of Reagan's address reminded Americans why he had pushed a policy of peace through strength: "History teaches that wars begin when governments believe the price of aggression is cheap," he lectured. "To keep the peace, we and our allies must be strong enough to convince any potential aggressor that war could bring not benefit, only disaster. So when we neglected our defenses, the risks of serious confrontation grew." Taking a page out of his 1980 campaign, Reagan argued that Americans and their nation were better off in 1984 than they were four years earlier. "We are safer now," Reagan said, "but to say that our restored deterrence has made the world safer is not to say that it's safe enough. . . . Nuclear arsenals are far too high, and our working relationship with the Soviet Union is not what it must be." In short, the president acknowledged the fears Americans had during his first term and then turned to what he did best—dream.[51]

"As I've said before," Reagan told his global audience, "my dream is to see the day when nuclear weapons will be banished from the face of the earth." For Reagan believed that "a nuclear conflict could well be mankind's last." And therefore, "priority number one" of the next Reagan administration, the president explained, was "reducing the risk of war . . . especially nuclear war." The best way to do that, of course, was to eliminate all nuclear weapons. "Indeed," Reagan told his audience, "I support a zero option for all nuclear arms." But wasn't this the man who had increased military spending and had exacerbated tensions in the Cold War by calling the Soviet Union an evil empire? Here was Reagan inviting the Soviets to dream of a nuclear-free world with him, as he had invited Americans to dream of a revitalized nation four years earlier. "The people of our two countries share with all of mankind the dream of eliminating the risk of nuclear war. It's not an impossible dream, because eliminating these risks are so clearly a vital interest for all of us." Without the common threat nuclear weapons posed, people could enjoy their common interest in freedom.[52]

Reagan brought home this point in one of his most famous parables. He asked people to imagine a casual, chance meeting between a Russian couple and an American couple—he called them Ivan and Anya and Jim and Sally. What would they share? Reagan asked. "Common interests have to do with the things of everyday life for people everywhere," he explained. The exchange would not mimic a summit on arms control or a debate over ideology but would be a conversation about hobbies, jobs, and kids. Common people unhindered by restrictions that occupy the business of states don't choose war, Reagan declared. "People want to raise their children in a world without fear and without war. . . . Their common interests cross all borders." We were all alike, Reagan concluded; perhaps it was time that governments acted on that wisdom.[53]

The American public responded to Reagan's invitation to dream. The president's poll numbers on foreign policy rose to above 50 percent, staying above that mark for the rest of his presidency.[54] A year later, in March 1985, Mikhail Gorbachev ascended to the top of the Soviet leadership and not too long after that Reagan's dream of a nuclear-free world and an end to the Cold War began to seem increasingly realistic. And yet we also know that for many the Reagan era was not one of dreams but of nightmares. The slogan of freedom had also been used to justify war in Vietnam. Likewise, in Reagan's era, freedom took on nearly criminal implications as it was used to cover up a strategy in the Third World that led to brutality on a scale that mocked the noble dreams of the president.

By one historian's account, the war in Nicaragua between the communist Sandinistas and the American-backed Contras took thirty thousand civilian lives, "the overwhelming majority at the hands of the Contras." "They were a bunch of killers," one advisor to the Joint Chiefs said about the Contras. They "slaughtered people like hogs," another observer claimed. And the atrocities—the murders, mutilations, tortures, and rapes—happened with the knowledge (if not the approval) of the CIA. Historian Greg Grandin concludes, "An enormous chasm existed between the idealism used by Reagan to justify support for the Contras and the actions his charges took on the ground."[55]

And yet the soldiers fighting the war in Nicaragua (and El Salvador and Colombia and Guatemala) were not American soldiers. While making that point does nothing to alleviate the ethical obligations the United States had in the region, it does reflect Reagan's relationship to war. Just as Reagan believed Americans at home need not sacrifice, the president also avoided asking Americans to sacrifice abroad. Members of Reagan's administration disagreed with their president's tack. Alexander Haig (Reagan's first, short-lived secretary of state) and William P. Clark (national security advisor) advocated a hard line toward communism in Latin America, which included taking out Cuba's communist dictator, Fidel Castro, once and for all. But Reagan was not interested in fighting any war other than his ideological and largely rhetorical cold war. He wanted to avoid anything that reminded Americans of Vietnam or that threatened to place restrictions on his ability to portray the United States as the leader of the free world.

Reagan ensured that another country's nightmare would not disrupt the dream he had sold Americans. The idea of sacrificing for the nation had been rendered defunct by Carter's failed presidency, Reagan believed. "In the early '80s," political essayist Peter Beinart writes, "Americans didn't want to be told to sacrifice; between Vietnam and stagflation they had been sacrificing more than enough." When it came time to invade another country, Reagan chose Grenada; his neoconservative advisors wanted most of Central America. In such schemes, Haig was joined by conservative and neoconservative intellectuals William F. Buckley, Norman Podhoretz, and Irving Kristol, all of them endorsing the use of force, including American combat troops, to "reverse the totalitarian drift in Central America." When Haig propounded his support for turning Cuba "into a fucking parking lot," Reagan and his political advisors understood that rants of such true believers could not overwhelm the faith that Reagan was taking great pains to cultivate. Haig left office in 1982, replaced by George Schultz, a statesman for his time, Beinart notes, who "didn't see America's back as perpetually against the wall" and thus counseled caution and patience because in the struggle against global communism time was the side of the United States.[56]

The public had already taken sides, and Reagan knew it. In March 1982, the public responded to Haig's war chants by telling a Harris poll that a significant majority of Americans disapproved of any aggressive foreign policy in El Salvador. By 1984, pollsters had stopped asking about El Salvador as Reagan and his advisors began to speak in generalities about Central America to avoid creating an easy association between El Salvador and Vietnam. Nicaragua was a different story however. From the beginning of his two terms in office, Reagan made Nicaragua a primary foreign-policy interest, only covertly. Grandin observes that the United States "relearned, after the disaster of direct involvement in Vietnam, to farm out its imperial violence."[57]

Vietnam hadn't eradicated the American claim to moral leadership as much as it had driven such leadership underground. That meant the Reagan administration took moral positions on foreign affairs but avoided using American combat troops to enforce those positions. Conservative columnist Charles Krauthammer caught the cloaked boldness of the administration's position: unlike his immediate predecessor, who introduced his doctrine with great fanfare even though he couldn't enforce it, "President Reagan saw fit to bury his doctrine in his 1985 State of the Union address beneath the balanced budget amendment, school prayer and the line-item veto. That he decided to make his a footnote is as much a tribute to Mr. Reagan's prudence as to his modesty." Though perhaps understated, the Reagan Doctrine had radical implications. It proclaimed, according to Krauthammer, nothing less than "overt and unashamed American support for anti-Communist revolution." That position appealed to conservatives like Krauthammer for two basic reasons: first, it brushed aside the legacy of Vietnam by recommitting U.S. support to "all armed resistance to Communism"; and, second, it announced American willingness to act alone, even if that meant violating international law and the sovereignty of other nations. As Krauthammer concluded, "The West, of late, has taken to hiding behind parchment barriers as an excuse for inaction when oppressed democrats beg for help. The Reagan Doctrine, while still hiding a bit, announces an end to inaction."[58]

The high-minded promotion of freedom fighters often led to direct support for anticommunist forces, who simply killed hundreds of thousands of people. Central America was a moral abyss, not a moral touchstone or even a moral quandary. Most Americans not only rejected the use of combat troops in foreign wars but also strongly disliked hearing about their nation acting thuggishly and supporting thugs. So, the consensus that seemed to reign within the White House regarding the morality of supporting "freedom fighters" in Central America did not represent the views of most Americans. Thus rather than deploy troops to Nicaragua, the Reagan administration had to launch an offensive on the home front to convince skeptical (and slightly cynical) Americans that there was still a cause worth fighting for, just without American soldiers.

The domestic debate over Reagan's Central American policies provoked a face-off between coalitions of convenience. On the right, neoconservatives such as Jeane Kirkpatrick, Kristol, and Novak made common cause with "militants from the carnivalesque right," such as the World Anti-Communist League and Moonies from the Nicaraguan Freedom Fund. Unifying this hodgepodge was a fighting faith, but not one worth dying for. Robertson captured the ideological radicalism of this faith as well as its practical limits: "It is our responsibility to assist victim nations in their attempts to overthrow their Communist captors and to roll back Soviet expansion. Wherever indigenous freedom fighters volunteer to fight and die to establish liberty and democracy, we must come to their aid with money and guns." Indeed, America would send aid—often illegally—but would leave the fighting and dying to those glorified "indigenous freedom fighters."[59]

Reagan's policies toward Central America provoked an understandably severe reaction from the left. However, unlike Nixon, Reagan did not make opposing him easy. Thus even though a majority of Americans told pollsters they didn't like war and they didn't like nuclear weapons, they also didn't like communism or the sense that it might be expanding. Thus the collection of groups who opposed Reagan on the left faced a paradox: while they often viewed Reagan as a bombastic militarist who wanted to send the arms race into space, they were stymied in their attacks on the president by the fact that, like the public, he too didn't like war, nuclear weapons, and communism. So, in one sense, the left had real issues on which to oppose Reagan; Central America and the increase in nuclear weapons were genuine concerns that could be addressed. But, in another sense, the left had a problem in regard to American civil religion. Reagan had captured the middle-high ground in which civil religion resides by using the Cold War as a moral cause but avoiding the deployment of American combat troops and offering an alternative to the nuclear-freeze position in 1985. What then was the left's angle on civil religion?

If Reagan saw America as a city upon a hill, Wallis viewed the nation as wallowing in the same moral swamp as the Soviet Union. "A totalitarian spirit fuels the engines of both Wall Street and the Kremlin," Wallis argued. "Both American and Soviet powers have acted to create and maintain client regimes in other countries that exercise control through means of repression, terror, and torture." They were, in the politically charged language of the time, morally equivalent. The alternative was clear, according to Wallis. "The gospel is biased in favor of the poor and oppressed. It presents a call to the church—that body that is most dynamic when it is most a minority living in radical contradiction to the values of the world by its proclamation and demonstration of a whole new order called the kingdom of God." God's kingdom had to stand in opposition to the Pax Americana to be true to an allegiance that went beyond the nation and its inherent will to expand, make war, dominate, and destroy.[60]

Wallis's vision reflected a broader repositioning of American churches in the 1970s and 1980s. In the Chicago Declaration of Evangelical Social Concern, drafted in 1973, a document supported by many mainstream (as well as radical) evangelicals, the prevailing logic was that because "God requires justice," evangelicals had to "demonstrate repentance in a Christian discipleship that confronts the social and political injustice of our nation." This position meant attacking the axis of civil religion and war. "We must challenge the misplaced trust of the nation in economic and military might—a proud trust that promotes a national pathology of war and violence which victimizes our neighbors at home and abroad. We must resist the temptation to make the nation and its institutions objects of near-religious loyalty." Such a categorical rejection of the nation as a force for good in the world led to categorical opposition to Reagan's actions against communism in Central America and, especially, to the longstanding American policy on nuclear weapons. By the late 1970s evangelical leaders advocated the total abolition of nuclear weapons, and even Graham had a change of heart, asking his supporters to reconsider their support for U.S. strategic policy. In an interview with Wallis in 1979, Graham said, "The present arms race is a terrifying thing, and it is almost impossible to overestimate its potential for disaster. . . . Is a nuclear holocaust inevitable if the arms race is not stopped? Frankly, the answer is almost certainly yes." Graham, no radical, spoke for many evangelicals who told a Gallup poll that they favored "an immediate verifiable freeze on the testing, production, and deployment of nuclear weapons." However, around the same percentage also told pollsters that they approved of the way Reagan handled the nuclear-arms situation.[61]

In post-Vietnam America, many churches felt it imperative to stake a position publicly on issues of war and peace that seemed to contradict their historical views. The Catholic Church was perhaps the most surprising exemplar of that trend. Historian Mary Hanna points out that "American bishops loyally supported every war in our history. . . . World War I produced only one American Catholic conscientious objector; World War II, about 200, nearly all of them followers of Dorothy Day's Catholic Worker movement." But by the late 1960s

"American Catholic attitudes had changed dramatically, [registering] the greatest percentage increase in conscientious objection . . . in this formerly more supportive religious group." By the 1970s, the American Catholic leadership followed, proving that the post-Vietnam church was no longer Francis Cardinal Spellman's church.[62]

This change began in earnest with the pronouncements and spirit that emanated from the Ecumenical Council called by Pope John XXIII, known as Vatican II. The council gave all Catholics a "license to act," to involve themselves vigorously in social-justice action, to join groups promoting civil rights, antipoverty, and antiwar positions. The conscientious-objector issue, though, caused problems for the Catholic hierarchy in the United States. Draft boards refused Catholic men who claimed such status on the grounds that the church did not have a tradition of pacifism. To respond, the National Conference of Catholic Bishops turned to the just-war tradition. Renewed interest in and study of this medieval doctrine had implications for the contemporary position of the Catholic Church toward the United States. From 1968 to 1971, the American Catholic hierarchy turned away from supporting the American war effort, declaring Vietnam an unjust war and demanding its end in a resolution issued in November 1971. According to leaders of the church interviewed by Hanna in 1973, this letter was a "declaration of independence" from supporting the nation's position on war and peace. "Church leaders would now be much readier than they had been in the past to challenge political decisions they believed morally wrong." The issues that emerged most prominently included Vietnam, abortion, and the American policies on stockpiling and possible use of nuclear weapons. In fact, in the post-Vietnam period Catholics linked war, abortion, and nuclear weapons together through the church's broad understanding of a right to life.[63]

In May 1983, in their pastoral letter entitled "The Challenge of Peace" the National Conference of Catholic Bishops declared its opposition to nuclear weapons. "In simple terms," the bishops explained, "we are saying that good ends (defending one's country, protecting freedom, etc.) cannot justify immoral means (the use of weapons which indiscriminately threaten whole societies)." Rather than accept the rosy view of "morning in America," the bishops warned, "we fear that our world and nation are headed in the wrong direction. More weapons with greater destructive potential are produced every day. More and more nations are seeking to become nuclear powers." And with a direct jab at what many people viewed as the dangerous brinkmanship of the Reagan administration, the bishops concluded, "In our quest for more and more security we fear we are actually becoming less and less secure."[64]

The pastoral letter had gone through three substantial versions before the Conference officially issued it. The process that produced the final product included a good deal of debate between the more pacifist wing of the Catholic Church and those bishops who adhered to an interpretation of just-war theory that, traditionally, counseled deferring to state authority in matters of war and peace. A committee of bishops and their advisors worked on the letter for over a year, during which the group held hearings, issued drafts, and invited officials from the Reagan administration to contribute testimony. In the end, though, the Conference knew the letter would "prove highly controversial, not least because [it] would almost certainly voice major criticisms of U.S. defense policy in the past and probably even more of the hawkish . . . Reagan administration." In other words, the American Catholic bishops, who overwhelmingly voted in favor of the 1983 letter, wanted to strike a prophetic stand toward their nation.[65]

In this way, the letter was very much a reflection of the struggle that came to define American civil religion in the wake of Vietnam. The American Catholic Church had a pacifist faction within it—best represented by Day and Gordon Zahn—but that faction had exerted little influence over the church hierarchy. In the 1970s, though, the wars in Central America, the Supreme Court's decision in *Roe v. Wade,* and the abject and existential terror many people felt living with a nuclear stand-off emboldened Catholic leaders to go beyond decrying the immorality of the Vietnam War and to influence the agenda of the nation. Father J. Bryan Hehir, the Catholic priest who served as the key architect of "The Challenge of Peace," approached the issue of nuclear weapons from within a broad understanding of what Pope John Paul II had termed "the consistent ethic of life." That position embraced ending the threat of nuclear war, opposing abortion and the death penalty, and fighting against the kind of oppression and poverty that pervaded the developing world. Hehir attempted to find a point of collaboration between the pacifists, who had carried the day during the Vietnam War, and the just-war advocates, who argued that nuclear deterrence was not an end in itself but a means to prevent Soviet expansion at the price of democratic freedom. Hehir was sensitive to the criticism by conservative Catholics and observers outside the church that the letter presaged a move toward outright pacifism or the adoption of a position in direct conflict with that of the U.S. government. This was the era during which liberation theology inspired many Catholics to imagine the church as a vanguard institution standing with the poor of Central America to resist and perhaps even topple oppressive regimes. The religious and secular left in the United States lumped the Reagan administration in with regimes tagged as global oppressors. And so a letter that came out boldly against American defense policy might also be seen as another version of the left's condemnation of the United States as an immoral nation.[66]

Buckley prominently promoted that concern by dedicating almost an entire issue of the *National Review* in April 1983 to Novak's essay "Moral Clarity in the Nuclear Age." Where Hehir and the Conference found a need to strike a series of balances between various moral positions (what one author described as ethical pluralism), Novak decided that the bishops had authority only in the spiritual affairs of the faithful. In other words, such authority did not necessarily extend in absolute terms to interpreting the affairs of state through "tactical and strategic judgment." A bold contention in its own right, Novak's assertion led him to declare that "the God of the Last Judgment will not be satisfied by a claim that a Christian followed the general authority of his bishop or of anyone else; each will be judged by what he or she did in the light of his or her own concrete moral reasoning in particular cases." Novak spoke for those Catholics who opposed the bishops' conclusions regarding the immorality of nuclear deterrence. And in this case, Novak and other like-minded Catholics were in agreement with the Reagan administration.[67]

While Novak provided a rationale for Catholics to contest the position of their church in the United States, his argument had larger implications. He rejected the drift of the bishops' letter. It failed to take a strong enough stand against the idea of moral equivalence between the Americans and Soviets. The two powers were not equal in moral terms, Novak asserted; the Soviet Union was still beholden to an ideology that "rejects 'bourgeois formalism,' including promises and signed agreements." Indeed, before Reagan uttered the phrase, Novak suggested a policy of "trust but verify." Furthermore, if the bishops had come to their position out of a sense of solidarity with the less-fortunate of the world, Novak suggested that abandoning a viable policy of nuclear deterrence would be more costly financially because the United States and its allies would be required to build up more expensive conventional forces. But the bottom-line defense Novak presented was pure civil religion: "To abandon deterrence," he warned, "is to neglect the duty to defend the innocent, to preserve the Constitution and the Republic, and to keep safe the very idea of political liberty. No President by his oath of office can so act, nor can a moral people." Indeed, the sanctity of the American promise had to be protected, even at the price of endangering the material existence of the entire population.[68]

And yet, Ronald Reagan rejected such logic. He believed that relying on a policy of "mutually assured destruction" was precisely not a policy that would keep a moral people safe. Even though Reagan had presided over huge increases in military spending during the first few years of his presidency, by 1983 he had his finger on a different kind of trigger—he wanted to launch talks to reduce, not intensify, the nuclear stand-off. The year of the bishops' letter, 1983, registered a spike in public fear of nuclear weapons and popular support for some kind of freeze in the arms race. The House of Representatives went so far as to pass a resolution endorsing a mutual freeze on the production of nuclear arms.[69] And on November 20, 1983, the president watched a television movie called *The Day After*, which aired across the United States. The next day Reagan told aides that he found it "very effective" and that it left him "greatly depressed." Indeed, the White House was inundated with phone calls in response to the dramatization of a nuclear attack on the United States launched after a skirmish along the border between East and West Germany had escalated into the use of tactical nuclear weapons. A vast majority of callers said they agreed with Reagan's intention to reduce nuclear weapons. The film had captured the popular view of the nuclear threat; Novak offered the other side—a glimpse at the neocon mindset that saw the Cold War in almost millennial terms. Some of Reagan's generals and a growing number of hard-right ideologues saw nuclear war as either winnable or as a necessary risk to take in the defense of "first principles." Diggins noted, "The neocons believed that anything less than full nuclear might poised to strike would be appeasement; Reagan believed anything more would be Armageddon."[70] Reagan won the argument and helped end the Cold War.

One of the lasting ironies of the period from the end of the Vietnam War to the end of the Cold War was that Reagan began it by chastising politicians he held responsible for "losing" the war in Southeast Asia, and he ended it by avoiding the mistakes and assumptions that led to Vietnam in the first place. Reagan's target, it turned out, was not communism or the Soviet Union, but the elimination of nuclear weapons. Gorbachev's reforms led to the dissolution of the Soviet era, not Reagan's military policies. The irony of this assessment is that Reagan recognized that fact; his critics on the left and the right did not. The left believed that the Cold War ended despite Reagan's worst intentions. The right, led by the emerging neocon core, believed that American might—ideological as well as military—had buried the Soviets. Disagreeing with his opponents on the left, Reagan rejected any moral equivalence between the Soviet Union and the United States. But he qualified that position and by doing so revealed a difference with the right: he rejected the idea that the Cold War was a Manichean struggle. To Reagan, winning the Cold War meant simply living the American dream—not vanquishing evil within or outside the nation.[71]

Reagan helped rebuild an American civil religion. He did so in two ways: first, he unabashedly promoted pride in the United States as a moral nation; and, second, he avoided entangling the United States directly in the moral morass of a difficult war. Reagan simultaneously dismissed the judgment of the Vietnam War while he internalized and implemented its lessons. Carter had done just the opposite: because he accepted the judgment of Vietnam, he built his public policies around his acknowledgment of United States as a "fallen" nation. Carter viewed civil religion as prophetic—the nation needed a way to find its true self, to be reborn in the wake of tragedy. Reagan saw civil religion as affirmative, best expressed through his appropriation of Winthrop's image of a "city upon a hill." Reagan used that image in his first presidential address, and he returned to it in his last.

"I've spoken of the shining city all my political life," he told Americans, "but I don't know if I ever quite communicated what I saw when I said it." His explanation did not add clarity or profundity. Reagan's vision was, he said, of a "proud city built on rocks stronger than oceans, windswept, God-blessed, and teeming with people of all kinds living in harmony and peace." Of course, it didn't matter what Reagan actually meant when he used this metaphor because by the time he left office he had answered definitively the question he posed to Americans in the 1980 campaign—were they better off today than they were before he took office. By 1989 he could claim that not only was the country better off but he had helped make the world better off. However, Reagan saw the implications of that success in decidedly unadventurous, even symbolic terms. "After 200 years, two centuries, [the nation] still stands strong and true on the granite ridge, and her glow has held steady no matter what storm. And she's still a beacon, still a magnet for all who must have freedom, for all the pilgrims from all the lost places who are hurtling through the darkness, toward home." Not exactly a call to arms to spread freedom actively around the world.[72]

Reagan's civil religion was a bridge between the Vietnam War and something new. Rather than even attempt to define the nation through war, he declared victory when Americans began to have pride in the nation again. But he also recognized that there was a battle between those who were part of this "new patriotism" and those for whom "well-grounded patriotism is no longer in style." Reagan had inaugurated his revival of civil religion amidst and in response to the culture wars. During the 1980s, the Cold War still dictated the terms and dimensions of American civil religion: Americans viewed the nation through the lens of the Cold War, clarifying whether the nation was a moral or immoral force in the world. As Reagan left office he warned that the greatest threat to the American "spirit" was not a disastrous war but a kind of national apathy, a willingness to "forget what we did . . . [and] who we are." His advice was quite simply to ritualize affirmation of the nation, to forsake prophetic judgment of the nation, and to look nowhere else but to the nation.[73]

CHAPTER 5

Civil Religion at Bay

ON AUGUST 27, 1987, George H. W. Bush held an outdoor news conference at O'Hare airport in Chicago. At the time, Bush was still Ronald Reagan's vice president. But he was also running for the Republican nomination for president. At a campaign stop in Chicago, a reporter for the *American Atheist News* named Robert Sherman asked Bush how he intended "to win the votes of the Americans who are atheists." Bush responded a bit sarcastically that he guessed he was "pretty weak in the atheist community." After all, he pointed out, "faith in God is important to me." Sherman asked somewhat incredulously, "Surely you recognize the equal citizenship and patriotism of Americans who are atheists?" Bush responded, "No, I don't know that atheists should be considered as citizens, nor should they be considered patriots. This is one nation under God." When Sherman pressed Bush on his views of the constitutional separation of church and state, the vice president explained that he supported the constitutional principle but wasn't "very high on atheists."[1]

The old adage that there are no atheists in foxholes took on an enlarged meaning in the Cold War. Successive presidents from Harry Truman to George H. W. Bush had made clear the nation as a whole had to be vigilant in its defense of ideals. For his part, Bush saw himself as a soldier in the two great moral battles of the twentieth century, first as a navy pilot in World War II and then as a public servant in the Cold War. In short, he had risked his life for and had devoted his life to his nation.[2] The conflation of God and nation in Bush's mind did not contradict the legal necessity of separating church from state because he did not ask Americans to worship in any particular way. He did, though, ask all Americans to have faith in their nation, a faith, as he explained when commemorating Loyalty Day in 1989, that demanded "more than civic pride; it also requires constant loyalty to the principles upon which our country was founded." Bush spoke of "fidelity" to the nation's principles and the need to remember and emulate the "sacrifices" that the founders had made to secure "the God-given rights and freedom of the American people." To Bush, America's veterans had "demonstrated exceptional devotion to their country." Loyalty Day gave "all Americans an opportunity to reaffirm their allegiance to the United States."[3]

Bush was a product of war, and he understood the fundamental meaning of the United States through war. And so legalisms like the one Sherman raised only annoyed Bush's sense of duty that he believed all Americans owed the nation. In the presidential campaign of 1988, he located that duty specifically in the flag and the pledge of allegiance. As the Republican candidate for president, Bush rhetorically berated Michael Dukakis, his Democratic opponent, for a decision the Massachusetts governor made to ban compulsory flag salutes in public schools. While Dukakis's position on the pledge had been perfectly legal and in keeping with constitutional decisions by the U.S. Supreme Court, the Democrat still found his opponent making hay of an action he had taken a decade earlier. Bush asked at any opportunity, "What is it about the American flag that upsets this man so much?" The flag certainly made Bush happy, as he celebrated his candidacy with flags at rallies and in advertisements and led crowds who gathered on the campaign trail in vigorous recitations of the pledge. *Time* reporters covering Bush rallies concluded sardonically, "Five weeks after the Republican convention, the public can be certain of two things about George Bush: he loves the flag and he believes in pledging allegiance to it every morning."[4] Democrats ultimately came to rue this insight as Bush thumped their candidate by "out-flagging" Dukakis on the patriotism issue.

If Bush's love of the flag and the pledge appeared cynical (because it was partisan) during the campaign, as president his return to the flag suggested there might be something deeper. In the summer of 1989, the U.S. Supreme Court handed down an unexpected decision in favor of a citizen's right to burn the American flag. The court decided 5–4 in *Texas v. Johnson* that the "Texas venerated objects law had been unconstitutionally applied to deprive [Gregory Lee] Johnson of his First Amendment rights." The immediate reaction according to polls and statements made by a variety of public officials indicated many Americans opposed the Court's ruling and supported some kind of constitutional amendment to overturn it. Republicans in Congress acted swiftly by drafting language for a proposed amendment. President Bush, though, stole the moment: in a speech he delivered on June 30, 1989, at the unveiling of the Iwo Jima World War II memorial at Arlington National Cemetery, he declared to more than forty-five hundred spectators, including many veterans, "What the flag embodies is too sacred to be abused." Surrounded by an army of flags, the Marine Corps Band, and a chorus of singers who led the gathering in "The Star-Spangled Banner," Bush pushed the symbolism of the flag once again into public debate.

For Bush, the flag represented sacrifice: dwarfed by the massive statue commemorating a battle that cost nearly seven thousand American lives and over twenty thousand Japanese lives, he pronounced, "[The flag] reminds Americans how much they have been given and how much they have to give. Our flag represents freedom and the unity of our nation. And our flag flies in peace, thanks to the sacrifices of so many Americans." Speaking at the end of the Cold War, Bush defended his reverence for a symbol that sustained unity during an era that for him was almost sacred. He acknowledged that the flag was "merely fabric," but contended, "To the heart, the flag represents and reflects the fabric of our nation—our dreams, our destiny, our very fiber as a people. And when we consider the importance of the colors to this nation, we do not question the right of men to speak freely. For it is this very symbol, with its stripes and stars, that has guaranteed and nurtured those precious rights—for those who've championed the cause of civil rights here at home, to those who fought for democracy abroad."[5]

Bush was not the first president to make political and ideological use of the flag and the pledge of allegiance. His immediate predecessor, Reagan, had gone to great lengths to inject both into national politics. At a Flag Day ceremony in 1985 Reagan admitted, "I always get a chill up and down my spine when I say that Pledge of Allegiance." In his own campaign stops for Bush in 1988 he also hammered Dukakis and the Democrats by using the pledge and the flag as symbols that separated true patriots from the post-Vietnam generation, who were suspicious of overt expressions of patriotism. Reagan never tired of publicly proclaiming his belief that the nation was indeed "under God." Thus Bush had an ally in his old boss when he took a hard line toward "unbelievers."[6]

But unbelievers in what? Not any traditional religion, but civil religion. Reagan and Bush both treated the notion that the United States was a nation "under God" as if religion were a natural resource. It provided unlimited virtue for Americans, warding off the detrimental effects that came from living with the remnants of unbelief dredged up by the Vietnam experience. But neither showed any intention of acting as if the nation was under God's judgment. Reagan had made that clear during his eight years in office. He took Jimmy Carter's born-again civil religion and turned it on its head, remaking civil religion into itself a born-again experience. Carter had sought to use civil religion as an authentic religious experience that guided Americans through repentance in order to be born again as better citizens. Reagan led Americans in an enthusiastic embrace of the nation itself guided by the assumption that God didn't need Americans to repent, he needed them to be better Americans—free of sin and full of hope. Bush practiced a similar civil religion, going so far as to lay his life on the line for America. The least he thought other Americans could do was pledge to the nation's flag.

The controversy that swirled around the flag and the pledge was an old one. Historian Richard Ellis has written perceptively about the contested meanings of both, observing that such patriotic reverence has revealed the way civil religion creates an illusion of consensus among Americans. "Civil religion obscures the very real conflict between a religious conception of American national identity and a secular, civic conception of national identity," he argues.[7] And while Ellis's focus on the symbols of American civil religion illustrates the dangers of imbuing the flag and the pledge with sacred meaning, I think he simplifies how civil religion operates. After all, in the debate between Carter and Reagan over versions of civil religion, who was secular and who religious? And who could better claim to represent a religious conception of the nation, Jim Wallis or Richard John Neuhaus?

Thus when looking at the seemingly false reverence Bush and Reagan had for the symbols of civil religion, we should remember how postwar civil religion took shape. First, it is significant that the United States was in an almost constant state of war from 1942 through 1992. Second, the Protestant churches that had dominated discussion about the nation's moral authority had begun to lose their prominence. The combination of these two trends made the construction of new kind of

American civil religion increasingly imperative. In the absence of a single dominant faith, civil religion grew in significance as a nondenominational way to create a "high" moral ground between a variety of religious and secular views of the nation. The struggle, then, was not between religious and secular views of the nation but over who could muster an effective strategy to dominate a moral discourse about the meaning of the nation. Carter had failed in his attempt to use a biblical sense of judgment. Reagan successfully revived pride in the nation by creating the illusion of a martial state. But Bush faced the prospect of defining civil religion in the absence of any viable war. And that situation had not existed since the early days of World War II, when Bush had entered public service.[8]

"The Republicans, post-Reagan, adhere to a literalist faith in the power of elemental national symbols," observed Sidney Blumenthal in the *New Yorker*. "They brandish them as if by this ritual they could indefinitely prolong the 1980s." A vacuum had emerged as the Cold War ended. Euphoria over its conclusion could not match the existential satisfaction of the Cold War itself. Gone was the moral necessity of standing against communism; the complicated emotion of fear in the face of nuclear war; and the organizing, totalizing logic of strategic planning against another superpower. In place of the war to end all wars rose the culture wars—partisan sniping over offensive art, vulgar musicians, and flag burning. Blumenthal concluded, "The flag amendment [was] a substitute for an agenda, a proxy for political discourse. Through it, the president arouses and mobilizes the country, but to no larger purpose."[9]

In 1988, Princeton sociologist Robert Wuthnow offered an incisive assessment of the role religion had played since World War II in articulating that higher purpose in American life. His book *The Restructuring of American Religion* appeared just at the moment that Americans seemed to become aware of religious involvement in politics.[10] The Christian right, or religious right, had shown itself to be a formidable force in the rise and demise of Carter. Reagan often appeared to understand and play to the power evangelicals and fundamentalists even though he was not among either group theologically; and issues from abortion to support for Israel were kept at the center of American public debate by groups such as the Moral Majority and its successors, the Christian Coalition and Focus on the Family. Wuthnow's argument was intellectually significant because it explained why the religious right seemed more involved in politics than ever before. Even though religion had always played a prominent role in the governing and defining of the nation, it seemed that fundamental changes had occurred by the 1980s.

Wuthnow observed that when Vietnam and Watergate made discussions of public morality a central feature of the public square, "the wall between private morality and public institutions began to break down." Thus, once "morality and politics were being discussed in the same breath, evangelicals found it only natural to condone political activities that appeared to uphold standards of morality." This insight pushed many to engage in politics. And while politics in isolation was still considered a dirty business among many on the religious right, "it was entirely proper to speak on issues of morality." Wuthnow noted that conservative evangelicals promoted their agendas as patriotic piety, wrapping themselves and their positions quite literally in the flag. As Jerry Falwell preached, "Our task is not to Christianize America, it's to bring about a moral and conservative revolution."[11]

Using studies that had empirically measured the role religion played in politics, Wuthnow reported on the changing landscape of American electoral politics. For example, he pointed out that in 1976 church attendance did not serve as an indicator of political participation. But in the 1980s conservative religious folk were much more likely than liberals to be politically active. Thus, media coverage of religion in politics during the 1980s would be disproportionately about conservatives.[12] Moreover, the public image that emerged was one of deep divisions between conservatives and liberals in regard to political issues rather than theological concerns. In other words, the debate over religion in American life was not about how one discerned God's plan for Americans or whether God was even relevant to such a debate; rather, it was about who would get to decide how to assess the moral nature of the nation. It was the difference between theology and civil religion. If theology was the issue, battles among religions in America would have collapsed under the weight of highly detailed bickering. Instead, civil religion was at stake; religious leaders focused on the nation and the state of its soul. As Wuthnow observed, "There is a deeper level of understanding at issue in public discourse—a level of implicit and explicit claims about the character of the nation itself, the propriety of its actions, and the nature of its place in history and in the world. These constitute an extremely important dimension of public life, for they provide the assumptions on which the nation is legitimated."[13]

The Cold War had provided an ideological grid of sorts that had helped guide the debate over the nation. The late 1980s offered a moment of opportunity to create a new grid. To describe the way the debate over civil religion proceeded in the late 1980s, Wuthnow picked a metaphor with contemporary relevance—the pledge of allegiance. He claimed that conservatives of the religious right saw America as "one nation under God," and liberals such as the National Council of Churches, Wallis's Sojourner's Movement, and a contingent of Catholic bishops aspired to ensure "liberty and justice for all." Wuthnow noted, though, that these "competing interpretations of civil religion actually converge at a number of points. They agree with one another in asserting the importance of religious values to the political process; both assume the existence and importance of transcendent values in relation to which the nation may be judged; they agree on the relevance of certain biblical principles, such as compassion, equity, and liberty (while disagreeing on the priorities given to the principles); and they in fact draw on a common heritage of Judeo-Christian symbols and stories." In a nation that could draw on exclusively religious or secular traditions to assess itself, only civil religion provided a hybrid of both and in doing so offered something to both sides and provided an alternative to exclusionary arguments.[14]

In the late 1980s, even a hardened sectarian like Pat Robertson was no match for the power of civil religion. Robertson ran for president and offered himself, quite literally, as a Godsend to the American people. But the electorate rejected him. His campaign stalled against Bush in part because most Americans had faith in American civil religion, not in Robertson's preaching. Even Robertson could see this: during his campaign he believed it necessary to step down from his ministry—formally giving up the title of reverend—in order to be seen by Americans as a viable candidate for president.[15]

Bush defeated Robertson in the primaries and then Dukakis in the general election to become president, yet his mandate was ambiguous. It was clear that he would be America's first post–Cold War president—a man shaped by war ascended to the nation's highest office in an era of relative peace. There was a tinge of irony, therefore, when in the late summer of 1989 Bush announced that the "gravest domestic threat facing our nation today" was not communism or nuclear weapons but, the new president intoned, "drugs."[16] Within a few months of making this assessment, Bush launched Operation Just Cause, sending an American force of nearly thirty thousand troops into the relatively small, strategically significant nation of Panama. Bush told the public that he took this action "to safeguard the lives of Americans, to defend democracy in Panama, to combat drug trafficking and to protect the integrity of the Panama Canal Treaty."[17] Rather incredibly, the entire operation took a little more than three weeks. The target of the American invasion was Panamanian dictator Manuel Noriega, a former American ally who U.S. forces seized on charges of drug trafficking. When Noriega surrendered to American military officials, the Bush administration congratulated itself for scoring a successful regime change. More important, though, American casualties were incredibly low: Americans lost fewer than thirty personnel. Panamanian troops lost a little more than two hundred men, but civilian deaths rose into the low thousands. American popular opinion stood at over 70 percent in favor of the invasion, indicating that approval of war continued to be influenced by the legacy of Vietnam.[18]

But was the operation "just" or just good enough to keep the attention of Americans? Historian Michael Sherry observed around this time that Panama wasn't war to Americans—it was an "operation." Americans didn't want another war, not after Vietnam and the long slog through the Cold War. Instead, Americans got the war on drugs, on AIDS, on cancer, on almost everything but actual enemies. "The search for war's moral equivalent privileged the arena of war itself," Sherry argued. "It posited something good in war[,] to be extracted from it and applied to other endeavors. It presumed that Americans found purpose only in war, that their state functioned effectively only in a warlike mode, and that the nation knew triumph only in warfare, with World War II still their model in that regard."[19] Their first post–Cold War president understood the metaphorical power of war. Yet Bush wrestled not with the morality of war—the fighting and dying—as much as with the moral vacuum that seemed to exist in its absence. All presidents claim to understand that asking a nation to go to war is the gravest demand that they can make. Bush possessed the greatest peacetime military force in the history of the world. His nation stood victorious—or at least it was still standing—after a fifty-year showdown with the Soviet Union. He had ordered American troops into battle in Panama, but that was about as third-rate a theater of operation as someone with Bush's military experience could conceive. Thus Panama could not begin to put to rest the question that hung in the balance: After the Cold War, what was America?

Joshua Muravchik provided an answer that became emblematic of a new generation of idealistic thinkers. In a book written just after the invasion of Panama but before the Gulf War, Muravchik argued that there was nothing ambiguous about the end of the Cold War: "America has won the cold war," he declared, "not on the strength of its arms and the skill of its diplomats, but by virtue of the power of the democratic ideas on which the American system is based and the failure of the Communist idea." Thus, Muravchik pointed out that American ideals rather than American might had brought victory in the Cold War, and therefore in the aftermath of this long struggle the United States had an unprecedented opportunity to lead in the world: "America is a great force for good . . . and what is good for democracy is good for America." Thus the United States had to transition from being the greatest bulwark against communism (a position that had gotten Americans in trouble sometimes, especially in Vietnam) to being the greatest promoter of democracy. The rule Muravchik incorporated into his vision had become popular in the immediate aftermath of the Cold War: "the more democratic the world becomes, the more likely it is to be both peaceful and friendly to America." Yet the specter of Vietnam continued to have an effect, for Muravchik was careful to note that encouraging democracy was not the same thing as "initiating aggressive war for the purpose of imposing democracy. Neither international law nor world opinion would accept that," he acknowledged. "Nor would the American public long agree to shed its blood for so selfless a cause."[20]

Maintaining some caution when considering war had come to be called the "Vietnam Syndrome." Undoubtedly such wariness was well earned. But another significant aspect was the general malaise that infected the American sense of national morality as a consequence of fighting in Vietnam. Americans had learned not only that they didn't want to repeat the military disaster of Vietnam but that their nation had done some bad things despite its seemingly noble intentions. That was why even the most patriotic declarations—from Reagan's "morning in America" to Bush's flag-burning amendment—seemed affected by the moral implications of war. Indeed, Abraham Lincoln's bequest lingered in the aftermath of another morally complicated conflict.

Still, as president, Bush needed to develop a way to express American greatness in order to reap some reward from presiding over the end of the Cold War. In other words, Bush wanted to capitalize on the end of the Cold War in order to sweep away the Vietnam Syndrome. Yet, as Richard Haass, a top advisor to Bush, remarked, "I wrote memos, suggested presidential speeches, but Bush wasn't comfortable with grand doctrine. His anti-grandness gene kicked in."[21] Perhaps it makes sense that Bush responded to the end of the Cold War with some modesty; after all he had seen how genuine grand strategies develop—under the imperative of grand threats from the Nazis and the Soviets. The absence of a terrifying menace, not surprisingly, made it difficult for Bush, who was known more as a skilled bureaucrat than as an imaginative policy-maker, to rise to the occasion.

However, war came again to America. A little more than two years after Bush took office and in the same year as the Soviet Union collapsed, the United States went to war in the Persian Gulf. And while this war was in no way comparable to the two wars that defined Bush's life, he saw it as nothing less than an era-defining conflict. He was determined that the Gulf War (as it came to be called) would inaugurate an era no longer beholden to the moral legacy of Vietnam.

On August 2, 1990, Saddam Hussein, perhaps the single deadliest tyrant in the Middle East at that moment, launched an invasion of Kuwait. Hussein wanted Kuwaiti wealth and tried to extract it by force, killing and torturing those who got in his way; Kuwait was in for a nightmare occupation. On the morning of August 8, in an address to the nation, Bush returned to a traditional American posture. Speaking on live television and radio from the Oval Office, Bush asserted, "In the life of a nation we're called upon to define who we are and what we believe. Sometimes these choices are not easy. But today as President, I ask for your support in a decision I've made to stand up for what's right and condemn what's wrong, all in the cause of peace." The president explained that he had ordered American troops to Saudi Arabia to defend that nation from Hussein's threat. With the Vietnam Syndrome clearly in mind, Bush explained, "America does not seek conflict, nor do we seek to chart the destiny of other nations. But America will stand by her friends. The mission of our troops is wholly defensive. Hopefully, they will not be needed long. They will not initiate hostilities, but they will defend themselves, the Kingdom of Saudi Arabia, and other friends in the Persian Gulf."[22]

Bush's initial response to the invasion of Kuwait combined a kind of old-fashioned resolve against international bullies with his characteristic aversion to grand pronouncements. For example, when asked by reporters whether he would implement measures allowed under Chapter VII of the United Nations Charter to restore peace in the Middle East by removing Hussein from power, Bush reasoned, "I would like to see him withdraw his troops and the restoration of the legal government in Kuwait to the rightful place."[23] As if to emphasize that this situation would not elicit the American cowboy ethic, Bush began a series of discussions with partners in the United Nations (U.N.), Europe, and, most surprisingly, the Soviet Union. For the first time since the Korean War, the United States asked the U.N. to authorize military action, if necessary, to restore Kuwait's sovereignty. On November 29, 1990, the U.N. set a date for Iraq's withdrawal from Kuwait: January 15, 1991. As Bush and his administration orchestrated a multinational coalition to join the fight against Iraq's invasion, the president also ordered the deployment of over two hundred thousand American troops to Saudi Arabia as part of what came to be called Desert Shield. Bush explained at a press conference that he had authorized the troop increase to defend "the better world that we all have hoped to build in the wake of the Cold War."[24]

By mid-November 1990, President Bush had sent four hundred thousand U.S. troops to the Persian Gulf to "encourage" Saddam to evacuate Kuwait and return to Baghdad. It became clear that this mission was unlike any American military operation since Vietnam. The press repeatedly asked the president about what seemed to be a transition from a defensive mission—to protect Saudi Arabia—to an offensive position capable of allowing U.S. troops to fight a ground war against Iraq's million-man army. The response from congressional leaders also reflected anxiety about such operations. In a letter to Bush signed by Senate Majority Leader George Mitchell; the chair of the Senate Foreign

Relations Committee, Claiborne Pell; and the chair of the Senate Armed
Services Committee, Sam Nunn, the senators wanted to know whether
the president would explain why the nation had moved to an offensive
"posture." While the three congressional veterans were quick to add that
"the Congress and the nation stand behind our troops in the Gulf," they
also contended that "in face of the troop buildup, the President owes
the people of the nation a clear description of our goals in the region, the
potential costs of achieving those goals, and the purposes we intend to
achieve there."[25]

In light of such questions and in response to an emerging antiwar
movement in the United States, Bush moved to a rhetorical posture
consistent with his ideological foundation. On November 22 he spoke
to troops stationed at Dhahran, Saudi Arabia. Within the first few minutes of his prepared remarks, Bush employed the "Munich analogy" by
referring to the "folly of appeasement." He told the troops, "There are
times when any nation that values its own freedom must confront
aggression." "We will not appease this aggressor," he promised. Then,
referring to World War II, he compared Saddam to Adolf Hitler:
Saddam was the kind of dictator the world had not seen for "seventy
years" because he had "gassed his own people" and unleashed "chemical
weapons of mass destruction." The president warned, "Every day that
passes brings Saddam one step closer to realizing his goal of a nuclear
weapons arsenal." To Bush, it was imperative for the world to stop
Saddam; and America had to take up its role as leader of that world. Bush
flexed American moral authority in a way that was unimaginable even a
few years before. The rebuilding of American civil religion would go
through the Persian Gulf and in the process redeem America's conduct
in its last major war.[26]

Redemption was clearly on the president's mind when he went out
of his way to make clear how this operation was different from Vietnam.
He told the troops that "you have launched what history will judge as
one of the most important deployments of allied military power since
1945."[27] Moreover, the operation had the blessing of the United Nations.
Bush had built his rationale for moral war: first, the target was another
Hitler, who, unlike the original Hitler, would be stopped before he caused
too much havoc, and, second, the United States had marshaled forces
through the U.N., an institution that stood among the most noble results of

World War II. By late November, the U.N. authorized the use of force to "restore international peace and security" to the Persian Gulf.[28] Bush used that occasion to address concerns. Bush emphasized the brutal nature of the Iraqi occupation of Kuwait. He was careful to describe American intentions in almost humanitarian terms: he understood that Kuwait was not a democracy and that liberation of Kuwait from the Iraqis would not mean freedom for all the people of Kuwait. If Bush purposefully employed the Munich analogy to make his case in the Gulf, he also knew that he could not avoid the Vietnam analogy. "In our country, I know that there are fears about another Vietnam," he said. "Let me assure you, should military action be required, this will not be another Vietnam. This will not be a protracted, drawn-out war." He promised "not to permit our troops to have their hands tied behind their backs." And he pledged, "There will not be any murky ending." At the end of the president's prepared remarks, he made an appeal to Saddam to enter into discussions leading to Iraq's unconditional exit from Kuwait. Yet after Bush's presentation of an argument that made the crisis sound like a choice between freedom and appeasement, it grew increasingly difficult to imagine how the United States would not go to war.[29]

As Elizabeth Drew observed in a long essay in the *New Yorker*, Bush had performed a nifty trick of diplomacy that had effectively weakened the Vietnam Syndrome. Many in Congress hesitated to vote to give the president authorization to use force against Iraq in part because they had vowed "never again" to repeat mistakes that led to the nightmare in Vietnam. However, Bush had used the U.N. and through it had gotten an ultimatum against Saddam backed by a coalition of over twenty other nations. This was not Vietnam; Congress was not voting to stop another Vietnam; and Bush's diplomacy had rendered Congress largely irrelevant anyway. The only victory scored by voting against the authorization of force was if the war went badly—very badly. It did not.[30]

The success of the war was not a foregone conclusion however. Conservative pundits such as Charles Krauthammer and William Safire defended Bush's comparison of Saddam to Hitler, but conservative presidential hopeful Patrick Buchanan barked, "Before we send thousands of American soldiers to their deaths, let's make damn sure America's vital interests are threatened." Democratic senator from New York Daniel Patrick Moynihan was outraged that Bush, by unilaterally moving thousands of troops into the region before anyone publicly questioned his rationale, had basically treated the situation in the Gulf as if the Americans were still fighting the Cold War. Michael Walzer, an expert on the just-war theory and a critic of the Vietnam War, reasoned that a war against Iraq would be just but dangerous because the United States would not fight for itself but for the political survival of another nation.[31]

At base, the most serious question was whether Kuwait's sovereignty was worth dying for. Colin Powell, chairman of the Joint Chiefs of Staff, harbored serious doubts about the moral stakes of this venture.[32] Were the deaths of American soldiers a valid price to pay for Kuwaiti freedom? Alex Molnar didn't think so. Molnar was the founder of the Military Families Support Network and the father of a twenty-one-year-old marine being shipped off to the Gulf. In an op-ed published in the *New York Times* and picked up by other papers around the country, Molnar raised the specter that the American buildup in the Gulf was for little more than oil. "Is the American 'way of life' that you say my son is risking his life for the continued 'right' of Americans to consume twenty-five to thirty percent of the world's oil?" It was a charge Bush understood acutely and that he addressed by elevating his rhetoric so that the coalition he had amassed against Saddam was second only to the Allied forces in World War II. Molnar understood why the war would be defended on quasi-theological grounds but left readers pondering the following encounter: "As my wife and I sat in a little cafe outside our son's base last week, trying to eat, fighting back to tears, a young marine struck up a conversation with us. As we parted he wished us well and said, 'May God forgive us for what we are about to do.'"[33] Indeed, nothing haunted Bush more than the notion that this war would be perceived as unjust, unbecoming a noble nation like his—an endeavor of evil. If he was to avoid such a fate, the war had to be quick and relatively painless. It had to be the *un*war but inspire all the patriotic fervor of a real one.

By January 12, 1991, Bush had congressional approval to go to war. Following an extended debate and much hand-wringing, Congress passed a joint resolution authorizing the president to use force against Iraq. On the evening of January 16, Bush once again spoke to the American people from the Oval Office about the Persian Gulf crisis. This time he announced that the air war against Iraq's forces in Kuwait and against targets in Iraq had begun. "Tonight," the president said in a solemn address, "the battle has been joined." Responding to the most common criticism that the United States had not waited long enough, Bush declared four times in four consecutive paragraphs that "while the world waited" Saddam did unbearably terrible things to the people of Kuwait. The bottom line, Bush asserted, was that "while the world prayed for peace, Saddam prepared for war." He repeated to the American public that "this will not be another Vietnam." But more than that, he declared that "we have before us the opportunity to forge for ourselves and for future generations a new world order—a world where [the] rule of law, not the law of the jungle, governs . . . the conduct of nations." To put this in Niebuhrian terms, this war would allow a moral man to create a moral society. A tall order, especially for a president not comfortable making sweeping pronouncements.[34]

The closest Bush came to explaining his conception of a new world order was in his State of the Union address in the middle of the Gulf War. On January 29, 1991, he entreated a Joint Session of Congress and the American people to consider that "what is at stake is more than one small country; it is a big ideal; a new world order, where diverse nations are drawn together in common cause to achieve the universal aspirations of mankind—peace and security, freedom and the rule of law. Such is a world worthy of our struggle and worthy of our children's future." Bush was clearly proud of his international coalition, but such an assembly reflected a larger ambition of internationalizing American ideals. The president seemed to suggest that a world where the U.N. could function in concert with an American civil religion should give the world hope that good was starting to triumph over evil. "If we can selflessly confront evil for the sake of good in a land so far away, then surely we can make this land all that it should be. If anyone tells you that America's best days are behind her, they're looking the wrong way."[35] Bush hoped to bury the Vietnam Syndrome. Overcoming the military failure of Vietnam paled in comparison to dealing with the malaise that had darkened the ability of Americans to imagine their destiny. In the Gulf War, Bush would use a victory to reawaken that imagination just as surely as Vietnam had subdued it.

A month later, Bush had his victory. On February 27, he announced that "Kuwait is liberated." Bush had a chance to make the kind of statement that had eluded all his predecessors since Truman: "No one can claim this victory as its own," Bush intoned, "for it's not only a victory for Kuwait but a victory for all the coalition partners. This is a victory for the United Nations, for all mankind, for the rule of law and for what is right."[36] Bush had his good war.

On March 6, Bush delivered his first postwar speech. He thanked all the officials involved in the operation, from his own administration to the coalition leaders. Bush gushed, "Above all, I thank those whose unfailing love and support sustained our courageous men and women: I thank the American people." For Bush, the ability to speak about the public's "love" for the troops meant, as he remarked shortly after the war ended, "By God, we've kicked the Vietnam Syndrome once and for all." The victory was over a phantom as much as a tyrant. Bush spoke of developing his new world order in the same way as he had assembled and successfully shepherded the coalition against Saddam. "The Gulf War put this new world to its first test. And my fellow Americans, we passed that test." The last section of his speech was an appeal to Americans to use the patriotism generated during the war as way to permanently kick the lingering malaise of older, more pessimistic times. "If we can selflessly confront evil for the sake of good in a land so far away, then surely we can make this land all that it should be. In the time since then, the brave men and women of Desert Storm accomplished more than even they may realize. They set out to confront an enemy abroad, and in the process, they transformed a nation at home." Bush attributed to the troops "confidence and quiet pride" and asked people to "think about their sense of duty, about all they taught us, about our value, about ourselves." Clearly this was a moment Bush hoped to relish and build on; he wanted a celebration for the returning troops to commence immediately and to culminate on July 4th as a day to honor the troops— perhaps it could be a public burial for the Vietnam Syndrome, that infectious malady that had weakened the American spirit. Bush declared, "We're coming home now—proud. Confident—heads high. . . . We are Americans."[37]

Bush hoped to turn victory in the Gulf War into a larger existential leap for Americans. However, in his last State of the Union address, in January 1992, he seemed caught between honoring a quickly fading era and creating a new American future. He admitted that he felt he had not yet fully appreciated the watershed moment over which he had presided.

"There were times when I was so busy managing progress and helping to lead change that I didn't always show the joy that was in my heart. But the biggest thing that has happened in the world in my life, in our lives, is this: By the grace of God, America won the cold war." America might not have fought a great war, but Bush had a war that made America feel good. The war had revealed, yet again, that people could express their faith in the nation. Bush declared, "Now we can look homeward even more and move to set right what needs to be set right."[38]

The problem was that when Americans looked "homeward," they didn't see the same thing. Like Bush, most Americans had grown dependent on war to act as an organizing principle in their lives. Without it, their minds substituted self-interest for national duty and whatever joy that had been in their hearts was mixed with anxiety.

The Gulf War failed to prove transformational. Bush had hoped the successful prosecution of the war would answer calls to atone for the sins of Vietnam, though he never fully understood why a nation that had sacrificed in World War II and led a noble cause in the Cold War had to bear the burden of a good war gone wrong. The notion that the Gulf War would somehow remake America pervaded the buildup to the war and its aftermath. In the month that it began, Krauthammer wrote, "War is an exercise in surprise, and the real surprise of this one may be that it was not about Kuwait, not about Iraq, not even about the future of the Middle East, however much all of these will be shaped by the outcome. It may turn out to have been a war about America." Much like Bush, Krauthammer believed that the way to disperse the bad spirits that had hung over American patriotism since Vietnam was success in another war. He imagined that a "dazzling" American victory would inaugurate a "new, post-gulf America . . . its self-image, sense of history, and even its political discourse transformed." A few months earlier, Krauthammer had contended in a widely read essay in *Foreign Affairs* that Iraq had "inadvertently revealed the unipolar structure of today's world" with its invasion of Kuwait. Bush had illustrated this unipolarity with his swift response to the Gulf crisis: "American preeminence is based on the fact that it is the only country with the military, diplomatic, political, and economic assets to be a decisive player in any conflict in whatever part of the world it chooses to involve itself." True enough, but such unipolarity did not speak to the moral aspect of America's self-image. What the war in the Gulf promised, Krauthammer suggested, was the recovery of American self-confidence that it could turn history for the better. "That was the legacy of the last good war, World War II, a legacy lost in the jungles of Vietnam."[39]

The idea of "Erasing the Vietnam Nightmare," was the cover story for *Newsweek* the week of February 3, 1991. The generals who led the fight in the Gulf, including Powell and Stormin' Norman Schwarzkopf, had risen through the military ranks in the gloomy years that followed America's "only" lost war. However, they and fellow military officials did not plan Desert Storm as a violent catharsis. All involved, though especially Powell, reminded civilian officials that "this war [was] certain to lead to its own irredeemable horrors."[40] And much like the military, with its wariness about going to war in the Gulf, protesters who joined a relatively large and quickly mobilized antiwar movement struck the *New Republic*'s Jacob Weisberg as a group that would oppose any war "as long as they look at all American intervention through the lens of Vietnam."[41]

William Bennett argued that antiwar protesters and those members of Congress who voted against authorizing the use of force in the Gulf feared more than another military debacle: they doubted the nature of America's soul. In the *National Review*, he suggested that the victory in Desert Storm would not merely bury the memory of the loss in Vietnam but reset assumptions about America itself. "We are already seeing a healthy reassessment of our fundamental institutions," he contended. "The military, so unjustly maligned by the elites these past 25 years, is the war's big winner." And mainline churches? They revealed, yet again according to Bennett, that "on matters of profound moral importance, they have virtually nothing useful, significant, or specifically religious to say." The press also came under Bennett's scrutiny for badgering the Bush administration with questions that illustrated either a woeful lack of savvy when covering a war (he noted that many reporters never missed an opportunity to ask about troop movements) or, more serious to Bennett, a kind of fatalist expectation that the war would go badly and so it was up to press "to protect [Americans] from their own worst instincts" (such as supporting the troops). But those troops, Bennett asserted, were "teaching us a civics lesson. . . . A commercial republic needs to be reminded about the importance of things like duty, honor, virtue, and the hitching up of one's purposes to larger purposes beyond the self."[42]

Bush certainly thought religion mattered. Michael Barone noted that the president sought the advice of "at least four religious leaders" including perennial presidential favorite Billy Graham in the days leading up to the decision to begin the bombing campaign. According to Bush confidants, the president and first lady prayed nightly and "aloud for the safety of the American forces and for [a] quick, decisive U.S. victory in the gulf."[43] Bush believed he had right on his side—he followed his own "just-war" doctrine. "Those familiar with the president's thinking say that he hews to the classical doctrine of a 'just war' based on a belief that deadly force is sometimes a tragic, but moral, necessity." Bush combined a view of providential design and unipolarity to create his moral vision. He claimed to be born again, at least by the 1988 campaign, and to believe that God's will was not a complete mystery—for instance, he thought there was a reason his life had been spared during World War II. Bush grew downright righteous when he read reports of Iraqi atrocities in Kuwait. In an exchange with the presiding bishop of the Episcopal Church, Edmond Browning, Bush listened to his own pastor argue that the president should give Saddam more time. Bush shot back, asking Browning whether he had read the Amnesty International report on the occupation of Kuwait. Then, growing visibly angry, Bush barked, "What is the morality of not doing anything?" America had to do something, Bush demanded, for it was the "only nation strong enough to stand up to evil."[44] The president knew that Vietnam had shocked many churches into taking positions that were at least suspicious of American military policy and operations and that during the Gulf War such suspicion was apparent again. Even the presiding bishop of his own church remained "unconvinced" by Bush's moral argument.[45]

The war also raised a broader question that addressed both Bush's traditional use of the just-war doctrine and his hope for a new world order. Pacifist and influential theologian John Howard Yoder believed the question was not whether a war was just or not but whether the system Bush employed (let's call it moral unipolarity) could "foster restraint." In short, could Bush's moral vision "say no to a particular war?" The role churches played in the debate over the Gulf War turned on a discussion involving civil religion that had emerged early in

Cold War. Yoder's question suggested that there were two competing realms of moral thought about the war: the first was Bush's system of beliefs that he used to take action; the second was the larger system of judgment under which Bush's actions would fall. In other words, who or what would judge the actions that flowed from Bush's moral vision? Yoder wrote in the *Christian Century* that he saw the moral debate over Bush's actions "as a test of whether the entire just war mode of moral discourse is adequate to guide the responsible citizenship of people who claim that their first moral obligation is to the God whom Jesus taught them to praise and obey, and their second to the neighbor, *including the enemy*, whom Jesus taught them to love."[46]

On that point, conservative Catholic intellectual George Weigel responded in a way consonant with Cold War civil religion: "Much of the formal religious leadership of the country, and particularly the leadership of [the] oldline Protestant [churches] and the Roman Catholic Church, abdicated its teaching responsibilities and showed itself incapable of providing the kind of public moral leadership it had traditionally exercised in American society." The role of civil religion in the Gulf War came down to this question: Would religious leaders and their churches counsel the operation of civil religion (in effect, guide it) or would they oppose it? There was considerable opposition to a moral rationale for war; as the *New York Times* reported in February 1991, leaders of more than "20 major Protestant and Orthodox Christian denominations, joined by 15 Roman Catholic bishops, have reaffirmed their opposition to the war and called for a cease-fire." The National Council of Churches (NCC), an organization that claimed to represent over forty million Christians in the United States, declared that the Gulf War was "a war that should have been avoided" and a war "that cannot be reconciled" with the Gospels. However, much like the situation that prevailed in the early Cold War and Vietnam, religious leaders such as Richard Land of the Southern Baptist Convention speculated that most congregations were overwhelmingly against the stance that the NCC had taken.[47]

For Weigel, the point wasn't that these groups had sound religious grounds to oppose the Gulf War, but the spirit in which they expressed their opposition. "The deepest taproot of the politics of the religious left is its profound skepticism about the American experiment. A racist, imperialist, militarist, and, laterally, sexist America cannot act for good ends in the world. That is the orthodoxy in the NCC and in a depressingly large part of the Catholic episcopate." But the figure that Weigel paid special attention to was Wallis, editor of *Sojourners* and the ideological opposite of Weigel's friend Neuhaus. Wallis helped organize a peace pilgrimage to the Middle East in the buildup to the war and generated opposition to the Bush administration's moral claim to war. All this work only illustrated to Weigel that Wallis was "firmly lodged in the camp of those who blame America first and early." Since the mid-1970s, Wallis deeply distrusted moral claims made in the name of the nation. And while he was not the most eloquent or sophisticated exponent of Christian witness in America, he had built himself and his movement into a touchstone of anti-civil religion rhetoric.

The Gulf War was different, Weigel asserted. The Bush administration had built a coalition of support and worked through the U.N. precisely because it was cognizant of the Vietnam Syndrome. And yet, Weigel observed, "the leaders of the oldline Protestantism and American Catholicism cannot bring themselves to say that here is a situation in which the use of proportionate and discriminate armed force is morally justifiable." Neuhaus contributed to the attack in a long op-ed piece in the *Wall Street Journal* that both defended Bush's application of just-war theory to the Gulf and dismissed religious leaders who disagreed with the impending action there. Neuhaus explained, "The council's condemnation of allied action in the Gulf was entirely predictable. The council and the bureaucracies of its chief member churches were thoroughly 'radicalized,' as it used to be said, in the Vietnam era." From that time forward, mainline Protestants and a few Catholic bishops became functional pacifists. Neuhaus pointed out, though, that few of these leaders possessed the intellectual rigor to subscribe to philosophical pacifism. Rather, "in their view, justice is typically on the side of whatever force is hostile to the U.S., whether in Latin America, Africa, Asia or the Middle East."[48]

Neuhaus had captured a conflict at the heart of this debate—what was the proper relationship between religious intellectuals and the nation? Stanley Hauerwas had an answer. As a Protestant theologian with strong preferences for Yoder's views on pacifism, Hauerwas was a somewhat unlikely figure to be a rising star in the debate over religion in America. But he did more than merely express pacifist views; like Neuhaus, he thought civil religion was indeed a game, only he believed its success was destroying Christianity. Hauerwas sat on the editorial board of the conservative religious journal *First Things*. Neuhaus was the founding editor of the journal and, by 1991, had converted to Catholicism and been ordained a priest. In a letter to the journal Hauerwas took issue with the position Neuhaus had expressed in the *Wall Street Journal*.[49] Cleary this was a debate the two theologians had engaged in previously.

While Hauerwas argued that Neuhaus had mischaracterized pacifism, a broader issue surrounded this exchange. Hauerwas challenged Neuhaus on the legacy of Reinhold Niebuhr. It had been a few years since Niebuhr's ideas had played a role in public debates. He died in 1971 a staunch opponent of the Vietnam War amidst profound doubts about the legitimate prosecution of the war by the United States. But during the Gulf War, Niebuhr's thought—especially his critique of pacifism during World War II—was used to defend the war. In other words, Niebuhr became an intellectual crutch for those employing World War II analogies. For religious intellectuals such as Weigel and Neuhaus, it was time to stand up to the Hitler of the 1990s and decry pacifism in a way that echoed Niebuhr's stand in the mid-1930s. And yet, as Niebuhr surely would have pointed out, his thought had limited application in 1991—after all he made his arguments about pacifism at a time when the real Hitler threatened millions of people.[50]

The key to understanding why both Hauerwas and Neuhaus called on Niebuhr can be reduced to one word: "we." Niebuhr employed the universal "we" in one of his most famous essays, when he declared that the Christian church was not pacifist in the face of Hitler—why "we" needed to defend Western civilization in the midst of the great totalitarian threats of the 1930s and 1940s. Niebuhr played the part of a great public theologian in a time of grave crisis. Hauerwas and Neuhaus had emerged by the last decade of the twentieth century as candidates to succeed Niebuhr. In his *Wall Street Journal* essay, Neuhaus had used a construction that resembled Niebuhr's exclamation against pacifism; Hauerwas pounced on it. "The crucial question is," Hauerwas argued, "who is the 'us'? Your rhetoric," he told Neuhaus, "mixes 'we Christians' with 'we Americans' in a way that I think compromises our ability as Christians to be a people with habits necessary to help our non-Christian fellow citizens realize that the story of righteousness they associate with being Americans is deeply problematic."[51]

For Hauerwas, the "we" or "us" in the debate over the application of Christian doctrine starts and largely ends with those who profess devotion to the church, not with those who are needed by the nation to help make sense of secular actions with religious language. To make this point plainly, Hauerwas told Neuhaus, "You continue to presume that Christian ethics is to be written in a manner that makes it accessible to those in power. . . . In contrast, I assume that Christian ethics is to be written first and foremost for Christians in the church, some of whom may find themselves in political office." According to Hauerwas, Niebuhr and now Neuhaus grew too close to those in power and by doing so compromised the power of the one who sat in judgment over them all. Hauerwas challenged Neuhaus and his allies: "Consider . . . the difference between your [Neuhaus's] application of the [just-war] theory and its use to inform penitential practice by Christians for the examination of conscience. The latter use requires the presumption that when Christians kill[,] their souls are in jeopardy. In contrast, your use of the theory does not presume that salvation is at stake or that the church exists as part of that salvation. All you assume is the nation-state in a system of nation-states." Hauerwas lumped Neuhaus in with his general critique of Niebuhr—neither spoke as Christian theologians but as American theologians who were Christian. The distinction was crucial.[52]

And Neuhaus dismissed it: since "at least the second century, millions upon millions of Christians have thought . . . it to be their moral duty to engage in warfare. Many of them have been esteemed by the church as exemplars of Christian virtue, and some have been canonized as saints." When Hauerwas suggested that Christians called to follow Jesus could not "imagine being other than nonviolent," Neuhaus asked whether those Christians who had gone to war—who could "imagine" reasons for doing so—were anything but faithful followers of Christ. "Perhaps what you are really saying," he told Hauerwas, "[is] that they are not Christians, in which case you would seem to be excommunicating the overwhelming majority of those who, past and present, thought themselves to be Christians." It was a rather severe barb to throw at his

First Things colleague, but, then, Neuhaus got to the question that hung over their exchange—did they even conceive of their roles as public theologians in ways that were remotely compatible? Neuhaus mused, "I know you now disown the title 'sectarian,' but it does seem that sectarian is the right word for those who affirm a church that has slight relationship to the empirical reality that is the church through time." Indeed, Neuhaus brought up a favorite construction of Hauerwas's, that Christians have always been "alien citizens"—"people for whom 'any foreign country is a homeland, and any homeland a foreign country.'" Neuhaus said he accepted that understanding but wondered how Hauerwas conceived of being "a good citizen" of America "when you speak of our nation, you put 'our' in quotes. Why is that? Are you suggesting that one can be a citizen without a nation, as you sometimes seem to suggest that one can be a Christian without a church?"[53]

By the early 1990s, Neuhaus had developed an intellectual trinity of sorts: himself, his church, and his nation. This trinity had started on the left and had drifted rightward politically over time toward an anti-anti-Americanism. Neuhaus had presented a clear alternative to Wallis in the late 1970s, and by the 1990s it seemed that Hauerwas had become the next sparring partner. Wallis had offered a fairly consistent reading of America's sins stemming from the nation's behavior in Vietnam through to its consumerist ethos of the 1980s. Hauerwas, though, pushed Neuhaus to articulate a different kind of understanding of the relationship between a theologian and the nation. Whereas it was relatively easy for Neuhaus to dismiss Wallis because Wallis stood opposed to almost everything Neuhaus was, Hauerwas considered himself a conservative theologian like Neuhaus. And for this reason Hauerwas tested Neuhaus's public theology from the inside. That was why Neuhaus took particular exception to Hauerwas's argument that a Christian ethics is first and foremost for Christians and not necessarily accessible to all Americans unless those Americans follow Christ. In response to this challenge, Neuhaus spoke about a notion fundamental to American civil religion— that America was a nation under God. As such, this view "assures a certain correspondence, albeit disordered by sin, between His will and human reason and the laws of nature. As a result, ethics grounded in and thoroughly compatible with Christian faith is 'accessible' also to non-Christians. It is, in other words, a public ethic."[54]

In his popular 1984 book, *The Naked Public Square*, Neuhaus had offered a form of public Christianity that avoided the liberal polemics of Wallis and the antilogic of the Christian right. Neuhaus's project was this: he believed that "those forces in American religion that are best able to articulate an American future that holds together prophecy and patriotism, love and criticism, will . . . play the dominant role in giving moral definition to the nation." He was not willing to accept that the ethics of his church could not be made useful as a public theology. Hauerwas wanted Neuhaus to forgo this project in favor of imagining that a nation under God is a contradiction in terms—only Christians live under God. Neuhaus sought to broaden the understanding of God as a "transcendent point of reference" to the nation as a whole and thereby minister to the nation as an entity with moral implications.[55]

The choice was stark: Hauerwas wanted to counsel Christians to be better Christians and by being better Christians they would make America a better place. Neuhaus wanted to counsel the nation to be a better nation by insisting it accept an ethics based on Christianity that was accessible to all and true because it was Christian. Both offered alternatives to the American civil religion that Bush had hoped to construct in the wake of the Cold War and through the success of the Gulf War. Since the end of World War II, no public theologian, including Niebuhr, had much hope of competing with the faith Americans had in their nation. But, much to Bush's dismay, he presided over both the end of the Cold War and the end of the civil religion that had been forged within it. Sidney Blumenthal observed in the *New Yorker* that, "between 1988 and 1992, the idea of decline moved from a controversy among intellectuals to conventional wisdom among the masses."[56] That was the vacuum Hauerwas and Neuhaus (among others) would seek to fill.

A little over a year after America welcomed home its troops from the Gulf, a Gallup poll reported that 84 percent of the people surveyed were dissatisfied with the state of the nation.[57] A reporter for the *New York Times* sensed such popular conflict in the celebrations for the returning troops: "Many Americans could not find triumph in the conquest of a nation with the gross national product of Kentucky."[58] Bush seemed to have little idea what to do without a war—cold, hot, or otherwise. As historian Sherry pointed out, "War is a bad healer."[59]

But what had to be healed? The moment of bitter truth for Bush appeared in the late summer and fall of 1992—during the final stages of his campaign for reelection. Things had not gone well for the president. Even though he had led the nation to a victory in the first major war since Vietnam, he had also been chastised for failing to act boldly during the Russian coup that toppled Mikhail Gorbachev; he came in for a scathing rebuke from the conservative wing of his party for agreeing to raise taxes; the religious right had little use for him; and he had to run against a collection of candidates who, frankly, wouldn't have been in politics much less presidential campaigns during the Cold War. The conservative firebrand Buchanan thundered about America's decline; business tycoon Ross Perot preached fiscal prophecies; and Bill Clinton, governor of Arkansas and the first presidential contender to have been born after World War II, acted as if Bush had been a failure in foreign affairs and had betrayed his party in domestic policy. It had become popular at the time to mock Bush's inability to do the "vision thing." His administration favored the "status quo plus." In the election of 1992, that position didn't cut it. Bush lost to Clinton, though Clinton didn't pull a majority of the votes. Bush lost with the lowest vote total of any sitting president since William Howard Taft and a lower percentage of the popular vote than Herbert Hoover got in his loss to Franklin D. Roosevelt.[60]

In the wake of this embarrassing electoral defeat, Bush gave one of his final speeches as president at West Point Military Academy. West Point has served for many presidents and public figures as a place to unveil significant military policies and to discuss the challenges of war. On January 5, 1993, Bush used his visit to make a statement about public service. He spoke about the seriousness with which he took his role as commander in chief, especially when he deliberated sending Americans to fight and sacrifice. The president continued his promotion of a new world order, in which the United States would take a leading role in encouraging the growth of democracy and the enforcement of the rule of law—sometimes through military force. His voiced cracked when he spoke about marines who had taken terrified Iraqi soldiers as prisoners, attempting to calm their fears by saying, "It's okay. You're all right now. We're Americans." And he pointed to a scene in Somalia where a young marine wept as he carried an emaciated child. "There can be no doubt about it," Bush declared, "the All Volunteer Force is one of the true success stories of modern day America." Indeed, in the military, Bush saw the elements that made a good society: "duty, honor, country." These were the ideals that he hoped would organically take hold in the optimistic aftermath of the Cold War or be reaffirmed by the resounding success of the Gulf War. He now knew he was wrong. His time had passed.[61]

He ended his address with a story probably told many times but certainly more poignantly in January 1993. He explained that a little over fifty years ago, in June 1942, he began his service to the United States. It was commencement day at Andover, the exclusive private school Bush attended, and it was his eighteenth birthday. Henry Stimson, the secretary of war, addressed the graduates, advising them to finish their schooling (presumably college as well) "before going off to fight for one's country." Bush told the cadets, "I didn't take his advice. . . . When commencement ended, I went to Boston and enlisted in the Navy as a seaman 2nd class. And I never regretted it." In the fifty years that had passed, the world had changed dramatically for the better, Bush said. The fight had been won and now, as he said, it was time for him to get on with life.[62]

For another fight had emerged. It wasn't a real war, but that didn't stop partisans from calling it such. At the 1992 Republican National Convention, the one that nominated Bush for a second term, the fiercest partisan in this new war took the podium on the first night. Patrick Buchanan unleashed a stinging rebuke to contemporary America. "Friends," he implored his half-stunned, half-crazed convention audience, "this election is about more than who gets what. It is about who we are. It is about what we believe and what we stand for as Americans." In fact, as became clear from this speech, the election wasn't really about the Republican candidate, Bush. It was about a new war that Bush had almost no part in. "There is a religious war going [on] in this country. It is a cultural war, as critical to the kind of nation we shall be as the Cold War itself. For this war is for the soul of America." Buchanan's list of threats grew to legendary proportions. "The agenda of Clinton & Clinton," Buchanan thundered, "would impose on America: abortion on demand, a litmus test for the Supreme Court, homosexual rights, discrimination against religious schools, women in combat units."

If that agenda became law, Buchanan warned, could we still call this nation "God's country?" Hell no![63]

It is safe to conclude that Bush did not find the culture wars a worthy coda to the Cold War, but as he found out, there was little possibility of escaping this euphemism. As the president who presided over the end of the Cold War, Bush had an interesting job, one that was, at once, enviable and impossible: he could help lead a moral accounting of America's Cold War. His nation had been "victorious," but what did it win? Many Americans had "paid any price and bore any burden," but to what end and at what cost? Democracy had triumphed over communism, but what did that tell us about history, ideology, even politics?[64]

Ralph Reed witnessed Buchanan's speech and observed bluntly that the Republicans were once "united by Communism and now they're not." Reed was the young leader of the Christian Coalition, a group that formed out the two million supporters of Robertson's failed 1988 presidential bid. This was a formidable group because it had ideological coherence, religious fervor, and political experience. Reed explained the opportunity that presented itself to the Christian Coalition: "The old dichotomies of liberal-conservative, internationalist-isolationist, dove-hawk are breaking apart. There are some ideological categories being formed that don't have any history in [the] politics of the Cold War." And with insight that seemed astute beyond his years, Reed concluded, "The end[s] of wars don't bring stability. They bring chaos and recriminations. Postwar eras are periods of an enormous realigning of political lines."[65]

The "culture wars" seemed to mock the idea of civil religion. By the early 1990s, scholars, including Robert Bellah, gave up arguing that civil religion might adequately describe a set of values held in common by a large swath of Americans. It became apparent that the Cold War had created such moral anxiety that Americans were willing to accept a certain level of moral consensus—for example, that America was a better nation than the Soviet Union. However, as Bush found out, even a successful war could not quash a debate about the United States as a moral nation, a debate that had begun in the aftermath of Vietnam and had been barely suppressed through the final decades of the Cold War. The question became, What would fill the void left by the Cold War?

James Davison Hunter's 1991 book, *Before the Shooting Begins,* had introduced the term *culture wars* into the American lexicon. Hunter argued that at the center of contemporary debates about culture were a series of "public issues concerned . . . with the body. Controversies about abortion, sexual harassment, pornography, 'vulgar' art or music, sex education, condom distribution, homosexuality, AIDS policy, or euthanasia and the 'right to die' all trace back to the human body." At stake, though, was not merely the question of whether teens should receive condoms in sex-education class, but whether such an act indicated the progress or decline of society as a whole. The timing of his book was crucial. In the wake of the Cold War, America seemed to fall apart. Americans couldn't agree on anything. Hunter asked rhetorically, "Is it not impossible to speak to someone who does not share the same moral language?" The implications of such an impasse were ominous; Hunter added that Americans might need to recall that "the last time this country 'debated' the issues of human life, personhood, liberty, and the rights of citizenship all together, the result was the bloodiest war ever to take place on this continent, the Civil War." After all, Hunter contended, *"culture wars always precede shooting wars."*[66]

That might be the case, but, as John Woodbridge wrote in the evangelical magazine *Christianity Today*, "the vast majority of Americans are not hostile toward evangelicals and are not ready to shoot anybody." Woodbridge and other observers such as sociologist Rhys Williams pointed out at the time that most Americans thought they held moral principles, but ultimately their views were so complex that they didn't divide neatly along a single axis. As Williams noted, "Many Americans continue to want their society and their politics infused with moral commitment," but those same Americans did "not care much about—or care for—politics." Williams suggested the reason using the term *war* seemed so apt for this period was not because Americans were ready to kill each other or anyone else, for that matter, but because war had consistently helped clarify an American civil religion. Generations of Americans understood their faith in the nation by the sacrifices made by other generations (and perhaps their own) in war. And so Williams thought it unsurprising that partisans in cultural debates would resort to war-talk (in addition to God-speak) in order to rally people to their causes.[67]

Among the first debates to enter the culture wars concerned preparations for the five hundredth anniversary of Columbus's discovery of America. In the years just prior to 1992, groups all over the country began planning celebrations, memorials, and, inevitably, inquisitions. An editorial in *First Things* illustrated the battle lines. The NCC, an organization that had in the early part of the Cold War blessed America's atomic bombing of Japan and its decision to proceed with a nuclear face-off against the Soviet Union, declared that the Quincentenary of Columbus's first voyage to the New World was not a time for celebration but for "reflection and repentance."[68] The editors of *First Things* found the NCC's "jeremiad" another reminder of the muddled responses to the crimes that critics of the United States had tallied over time. The point of such moralistic accounting was, according to the editors, "to vilify the American experience."[69]

Neuhaus and his conservative allies contended that there existed a "new class" of intellectuals who channeled self-loathing criticism of the nation that gave them privileged perches from which to whine. A classic description of this group came from Moynihan, who, in a memo to his then boss President Richard Nixon, contended, "There is a struggle going on in this country of the kind the Germans used to call a *Kulturkampf*. The adversary culture which dominates almost all channels of information transfer and opinion formation has never been stronger, and as best as I can tell it has come near [to] silencing the representatives of traditional America."[70]

At almost the same time as the Columbus fiasco was the "flap" over a federally funded program to develop "National History Standards." In 1992, the National Council on Education Standards asked Gary Nash, a historian at UCLA, to coordinate the creation of National History Standards. The project enlisted organizations impressive in number and scope. Secondary school teachers as well as Nash's colleagues at the university level participated in the writing of three books that would serve as general guidelines for K–12 administrators and teachers in the construction of curriculum. Nash explained, "All the national standards had one thing in common: to provide students with a more comprehensive, challenging, and thought-provoking education in the nation's public schools." They had one other thing in common: they were all overwhelmingly rejected.[71]

The National Standards project became engulfed in a firestorm of punditry and polemics. Rush Limbaugh hated them, Lynne Cheney (head of the National Endowment for the Humanities—a sponsor of the project) hated them; and, most damning, the U.S. Senate voted 99 to 1 to condemn them. Nash pointed out that the guiding principle for the project was to bring the latest scholarship to bear on what American children learned. "With this criterion in mind," he explained, "the many organizations participating in building the standards applauded the attention given to previously neglected segments of human history. In the case of U.S. history, this focus meant incorporating standards that reflect the rich and sober scholarship of recent decades on women, ethnic and racial groups, labor, and popular culture. In a country priding itself on having a government of, for, and by the people, it was thought that a history of, for, and by the people might befit a democracy." To the project's critics, though, "the more inclusive approach to recovering the past smacked of grimness and gloominess."[72] As one historian wrote at the time, "The charge, fair or not, is that the National History Standards have deliberately focused on what has been violent or unjust or depraved about the American experience, at the expense of most of what has been good about it. We are portrayed, or so the critics argue, as a nation of victims—and victimizers."[73]

During this time, even the "good war" came under scrutiny. In 1994, the Smithsonian planned an exhibit to mark the fiftieth anniversary of the atomic bombing of Japan. While that event had sparked some debate in its immediate aftermath, since the early 1950s (or after the Soviets had detonated their bomb) moral qualms about dropping the bomb had become isolated in academia. Most Americans understood it as a justified action that ended the Second World War and saved Japanese as well as American lives. The exhibit, called "The Crossroads: The End of World War II, the Atomic Bomb, and the Onset of the Cold War," laid out the stakes this way: "The atomic bombing[s] of Hiroshima on August 6, 1945, and of Nagasaki three days later, were the first and—thus far—the only use of nuclear weapons in anger. Although mankind has lived with war and violence throughout its history, the atomic bombings announced the arrival of a new and qualitatively different peril, one that still threatens humanity: sudden, mass and indiscriminate destruction from a single weapon." Like the National History

Standards, the *Enola Gay* exhibit, as it came to be called, hoped to address what it acknowledged to be a difficult subject by enlisting scholars and the latest research. "The primary goal of this exhibition," the curators explained, "will be to encourage visitors to undertake a thoughtful and balanced re-examination of these events in the light of the political and military factors leading to the decision to drop the bomb, the human suffering experienced by the people of Hiroshima and Nagasaki and the long-term implications of the events of August 6 and 9, 1945." The bottom line was that the exhibit would refrain from outwardly celebrating the war as a moral triumph and, instead, complicate the memory of the war's end by offering a theory that perhaps the atomic bombing of the Japan had not been necessary.[74]

America's foremost Cold War historian, John Lewis Gaddis, observed in 1996 that "these two episodes [the controversies surrounding Columbus Day celebrations and the Enola Gay exhibit] have in common a tendency to treat the American experience—whether throughout the entire sweep of American history or with respect to the specific decision to use the bomb—in ways that reject American exceptionalism and tilt toward a kind of 'moral equivalency.'" But a moral equivalency between the United States and what? To make this point, Gaddis pointed to a debate held at the Oxford Union in 1984 that pitted Marxist historian E. P. Thompson against American Secretary of Defense Casper Weinberger. The site of famous academic gamesmanship, the Union posed a challenge only college-seminar participants could love or find relevant: "Resolved, there is no moral difference between the foreign policies of the U.S. and the U.S.S.R." The outcome of such a debate promised to change few minds about the nature of the subject obviously under critique—the United States. However, playing such a game reflected a profound, existential crisis created as the Cold War came to an end. Whereas the horrors of World War II had been explained in the context of fighting a war for the struggle and survival of civilization itself, the end of the Cold War brought no such clear resolution. Many terrible things had been done by both sides; so where did that leave the United States? Thompson described the United States and the Soviet Union as "two terrorist states [with] born-again Christians on the one side and still-born Marxists on the other." Weinberger dismissed Thompson's posturing, telling the audience that the debate between him and Thompson was immaterial compared with the debate of ideas between the United States and the Soviet Union: "It's about freedom," he declared. "Individual, personal, human freedom, and whether we and our children will be allowed to exercise it." The American secretary of defense won the debate by a vote of 271 to 240.[75]

During the Cold War, the point about freedom mattered in large part because the struggle was over the ideas that the two superpowers represented. Following the Cold War, those ideas came under scrutiny for what they led to and what they justified. Had the American promise of freedom delivered the world from a superpower showdown by being better than Soviet ideas in absolute terms? Or had one set of ideals been used to mask naked ambition and the atrocities that were the products of those ambitions?

Gaddis raised these questions to needle his academic colleagues by offering a "moral" assessment of the Cold War. He made clear that the understanding of the Cold War had entered a new phase: it was no longer beholden to the schools of international-relations theory or great power politics but to a larger moral project. In short, the Cold War had entered its mythological phase. Gaddis claimed that when considering the moral dimension of the Cold War, he was most interested in the "relationship between national security and national ideal . . . the question of how the nation could defend itself against what appeared to be mortal peril without compromising those deeply rooted values that had caused the nation to exist in the first place." Contending with that question, of course, has been among the most common uses for American civil religion, as civil religion assumes that the United States consistently tests its ability to live up to its guiding ideals. Yet, as Gaddis noted, the Cold War was a special situation because it was a sixty-year period of sustained, constant testing of the nation's ability to exercise power in light of professed ideals. In the parlance of Bellah's original notion of civil religion, the United States had never experienced a "time of trial" like this.[76]

The Cold War taught Americans a great deal about themselves, not all of it entirely positive. Gaddis suggested that there were good moments—the Truman administration and Reagan's return to idealism—and bad ones—Vietnam, Carter, and the Iran-Contra affair. The problem that plagued the United States throughout the Cold War, Gaddis explained, was attempting to square ends with means: "To what extent . . . was it necessary to sacrifice what one was attempting to defend, in the course of defending it?" In other words, because the United States had to use its considerable power to contain a mortal threat, Americans had to understand that their nation had to do evil things, but with good intentions.[77]

Thus, Gaddis argued, American policy toward the Soviets grew into something more than merely opposing or containing the Soviet Union. The Cold War went well beyond a conflict over national interests and grew into a struggle over ideas. In the end, U.S. opposition to the Soviet Union forced a much larger debate over the fate of the world and the arc of history. In simple terms, the American victory in the Cold War was an existential victory for the world and its history—better ideas had won out.

One way Gaddis made that point was to consider the Cold War in cultural terms: "Why did American culture, to say nothing of the American example in organizing politics or markets or the protection of human rights, spread as widely as it did during the second half of the twentieth century?" "For whatever reason," Gaddis offered, "the American model took root more readily in other parts of the world than did that of its major Cold War adversary, the Soviet Union—this despite the fact that Marxism-Leninism was, from the start, an internationalist ideology that deliberately sought transplantation." Indeed one could assume that without trying too hard—as it did in Vietnam—the American model would have prevailed in the Cold War no matter what because the United States represented something more universally desired than any other alternative.[78]

Yet, we know that Americans did terrible things—such as in Vietnam—and that the nation had to account for them in light of the moral idealism that it professed. Gaddis pointed to Niebuhr and the school of hardened realists, such as George F. Kennan and Arthur Schlesinger, who liked to grapple with moral conundrums such as dropping the atomic bomb. But using Niebuhr to rationalize doing evil for a greater good missed a vital paradox of Niebuhr.[79] Niebuhr distrusted both the ability of any nation—including the United States—to do good, while he also had faith that the West would, ultimately, do better than the alternatives to it, including the Soviet Union. The problem of using Niebuhr to assess the moral success of the United States was that Niebuhr made his sharpest and most quoted observations at the end of World War II and at the beginning of the Cold War, when it was conceivable to imagine that something he understood as Western civilization was in genuine peril. One might argue, as many have, that in the period following the Cold War, the aspect of Niebuhr's insight that was most relevant was not his hand-wringing about doing evil for a greater good but his scathing indictment of American hubris, materialism, and policymaking devoid of historical understanding. Judge Americans on what they had wrought, Niebuhr counseled, not on their ability to feel bad about their actions.[80]

Clinton's administration proposed to do just that. George Bush worked from the premise that because the soul of the nation was good—the bulwark against tyranny during his lifetime—even atrocities committed by the nation could be cast in the context of a good nation having to do bad things in order to make the world better. But such reasoning worked only under the imperatives of an actual war. Clinton had to offer a different set of assumptions: he argued that America could do better in the world because it no longer operated in a period of moral ambiguity caused by war. In a speech delivered to an audience in Milwaukee a month before the general election in 1992, Clinton laid into Bush for practicing a foreign policy devoid of ideals and locked in a Cold War mentality, "when foreign policy was the exclusive preserve of a few aristocrats." Those days were over, Clinton declared, and we now lived in "a world where freedom, not tyranny, is on the march, the cynical calculus of pure power politics simply does not compute. It is ill-suited to a new era in which ideas and information are broadcast around the globe before ambassadors can read their cables. Simple reliance on old balance-of-power strategies cannot bring the same practical success as a foreign policy that draws more generously from American democratic experience and ideals and lights fires in the hearts of millions of freedom-loving people around the world."[81]

Clinton was born a year after Bush came home from war. He went to college in the middle of the Vietnam War and was shaped more by denunciations of war than by sacrifices for it. Like his predecessors, he believed that America had a unique role to play in history, but for the first time since Franklin Roosevelt that understanding didn't seem to require a martial attitude. Clinton imagined the world in terms that Francis Fukuyama had made famous: liberalism was the future, and its expansion defined America's existential purpose.[82] On these terms, America need not be an "enforcer" but an "enabler" or "enlarger" of the blessings promised by liberalism. No action better captured the irony and possibilities of change than Clinton's attempt to enlarge the blessings of the ideals that Bush held dear—duty, honor, country—to homosexuals. One of Clinton's first bold moves as commander in chief was to end the military's ban on gay men and women serving their nation openly.

Clinton's move to lift that ban fit perfectly into the culture wars. Here was an issue that should have made sense to a nation imbued by a martial spirit: all able-bodied people should be allowed to serve as themselves. And yet by simply acknowledging, not even expanding, the rights of homosexuals to serve their nation, Clinton created a firestorm of criticism. At issue was not merely the culture-war debate over homosexuality but the intersection of the culture wars with real war. While civil religion as a mythic source of common values and moral judgment no longer seemed viable, the civil religion born of war and war's demands continued to be crucial to American life. Rather than disproving the existence and significance of American civil religion, the age of fracture (as one historian has called it) illustrated that the source of civil religion was America's relationship to war.[83]

Seven months after taking office, Clinton announced the new understanding regarding homosexuals serving in the military. He delivered his speech at the National Defense University at Fort McNair to an audience of military personnel who were not receptive to any change in policy toward gays serving openly. In light of their objections, an agreement had been reached before Clinton gave his speech to create a policy that came to be known as "don't ask, don't tell": homosexuals could serve in the armed forces but were not suppose to make it known to their superiors that they were homosexual. He called it "an honorable compromise that advances the cause of people who are called to serve our country by their patriotism, the cause of our national security, and our national interest in resolving an issue that has divided our military and our Nation and diverted out attention from other matters for too long."[84]

Although Clinton defended the compromise by pointing out that both Congress and the public opposed lifting the ban, Richard Mohr, a writer for the libertarian journal *Reason*, still condemned Clinton for failing to call on the moral authority of his office to define it as "an issue of human rights . . . to be settled by appeal to morality and resolved in a principled manner." Instead, Clinton made a different appeal that attempted to avoid the cultural wars altogether. He said near the end of his speech that he respected the fact that the military was a "conservative institution" whose purpose was "to conserve the fighting spirit of our troops, to conserve the resources and capacity of our troops, to conserve the military lessons acquired during our Nation's existence, to conserve our very security, and yes, to conserve the liberties of the American people." Clinton recognized the military would be the repository of faith in the abstract notion of the nation in a time when the ideals of that nation were anything but clear.[85]

The fact that Clinton became a central player in the culture wars was not surprising; he was destined to play a leading role merely because he grew into adulthood in the age that served as the touchstone for those wars—the 1960s. Yet Clinton didn't want that role. Like all other presidents he wanted to unite the nation through ideals that cut across age, class, gender, race, and sexuality. And he understood that presiding in an era without the Cold War would demand a new moral and mythical structure for the nation. The Cold War had illustrated that civil religion relied on war to expose the soul of the nation. Domestic issues simply didn't cut it. As the example of Martin Luther King Jr. illustrated, war can make and break mythical heroes. Bush might have lost the 1992 election because of domestic issues, but he once held a 90 percent approval rating—largely because for a brief moment he seemed to be commander in chief more than president. Thus it was supremely ironic that Clinton decided to take on, at the very beginning of his presidency, the issue of gays in the military. By doing so, he injected the divisive culture wars into the one institution that, out of all other institutions at that moment, still had some relation to civil religion. For the military had come to see itself and was seen by a significant portion of the American public as the last bastion of the nation's morals: it defended the nation because it defended the nation's soul with guns.

Thomas Ricks wrote an essay for the *Atlantic* in July 1997 that came close to providing a "state of the military" for civilians. In a paragraph that captured a sense of the age, Ricks observed, "There is widespread agreement that over the past few decades American society has become more fragmented, more individualistic, and less disciplined, with institutions such as church, family, and school wielding less influence. Whatever the implications of these changes, they put society at odds with the classic military values of sacrifice, unity, self-discipline, and considering the interests of the group before those of the individual." Amidst the cacophony of voices all undermining each other in the culture wars, the military seemed almost to rise above the din. I say "almost" because the military also developed a distinctive view on the "collapse" of American culture. William Lind, a military analyst who exerted a good deal of influence over the ideological composition of the Marine Corps at this time, explained, "Starting in the mid-1960s, we have thrown away the values, morals, and standards that define traditional Western culture." The "New Class" of cultural elites, "who hate Judeo-Christian culture" but push "an agenda of moral relativism, militant secularism, and sexual and social 'liberation,'" were to blame. While Buchanan and other culture warriors argued along similar lines, this one was especially disconcerting because the author identified a new threat for the marines: "The next real war we fight is likely to be on American soil."[86]

That shocking statement made the most sense in the context of military life. To provide a "boots-on-the-ground" perspective, Ricks spent time with young soldiers who had returned to their civilian lives following the eleven-week boot camp on Parris Island. To a man, these new marines felt "alienated" from their old lives and, "at various times," Ricks wrote, "each of these new Marines seemed to experience a moment of private loathing of public America." They felt a great lack of "common ground" with their friends; saw civilian life as "nasty" and rather "pointless"; and all pined to return to the source of their new lives—having become marines, they felt as though they "had joined a cult or religion." And they had, in a way. Most soldiers come to feel a great divide between military life (and death) and the civilian world; we should be worried if there isn't such a difference. But Ricks had described these men and, later in the essay, their officers and commanders in terms that one could have applied to seventeenth-century Puritans. The military was indeed transforming into something resembling a religion, one that honored the nation rather than a deity. Civil religion didn't die in the 1990s; it moved to the military.[87]

It wasn't enough for the people in the military to recognize a religious dimension in itself, the public it served had to as well. The public that had once defamed the military, that had run away from service in it and had decried atrocities committed by it, had grown to admire the military more than any other institution in American life. According to Gallup poll data collected in the years following the Vietnam War, the public's trust in the military had gone steadily upward, spiking at 85 percent in the immediate wake of the Gulf War. That was also the moment when Bush's approval rating hit the stratosphere. However, unlike that president and the presidency in general, opinion of the military never dropped below 60 percent after that. In 1997, the year Rick's essay appeared, the military "bottomed out" at 60 percent. Confidence in the presidency that year stood at 44 percent; confidence in banks, at 40 percent; in Congress, at 21 percent.[88]

In an era that might be characterized both by the process of fracturing and by a sense of self-loathing and self-aggrandizement, the military seemed to combine both aspects of the civil religious divide observed by Wuthnow. In short, the military saw itself protecting a nation "under God," while it also attempted to promote "liberty and justice for all." The first part could be seen in the open identification many in the military had with conservative values and faith. The second part was more than apparent in the work the military was called on to do all over the world.[89]

The military's existential purpose was put to the test in the Clinton presidency. While America did not engage in any large-scale war, it did send the military far and wide, to deliver food and water to Somalia, a desperate African country ravaged by civil war; to drop millions of tons of bombs in the Balkans to stop a genocide; and to prevent the complete breakdown of Haiti's social structure. For an administration that did not have much experience with the American military, the Clintonites came to use American force a great deal more than might have been expected in a time of "peace."

And that made Colin Powell uneasy. When Clinton was elected, Powell served eight months in his administration as chairman of the Joint Chiefs. Powell was the most significant military official in the nation at a moment when the military far surpassed the commander in chief in trust and popularity. But Powell was more than merely a soldier; as a veteran of the Vietnam War, his personal and professional history reflected an ideal many Americans had wanted to believe about the nation. He stood as the personification of the American dream—a black man born in Harlem and raised in the Bronx who rose to great heights nobly serving his nation. Yet Powell disagreed with Clinton's approach to homosexuals serving in the military and the new president's tough talk on foreign affairs. To Powell, both issues illustrated Clinton's lack of understanding of moral authority. This new team didn't seem to know anything about what actually happened when American troops hit foreign soil or American bombers unloaded their ordinance—people died. Powell was certain that Clinton couldn't comprehend that reality; if he had, the new president would not have spent so much precious political and moral capital on what Powell viewed as a culture-war issue of gays in the military.[90] To top off Clinton's problems with the military, the new president had trouble figuring out how to salute the troops he might send off to die.

And yet, despite the issues and personalities that divided the Clintonites from the military, two years before Clinton even took office, events began to conspire that would force a candidate elected on domestic issues to face extremely difficult choices in foreign affairs. In 1991, Yugoslavia came undone and within a year the city of Sarajevo—which had hosted the Olympics in 1984—lay in ruins. Christian Serbs embarked on a campaign of genocide against Bosnia's Muslims. Reports of concentration camps and atrocities not seen since the Second World War began to enter the conscience of the West. Armed with the weapons of the former Yugoslav military, the Serbian forces committed brutalities that shattered illusions about peace. Early on Clinton and his foreign-policy team watched as European countries proved hopelessly inadequate in their responses. The whole time this moral morass deepened, Powell advised staying out.

In a series of essays published in America's leading foreign-affairs journals in 1992 and 1993, Powell laid out his "doctrine" for American military intervention. Not surprisingly, it resembled the strategy of the Gulf War, in which fewer than two hundred Americans had died, and was designed to keep America out of another Vietnam, in which over fifty-six thousand Americans died. Powell explained:

> When the political objective is important, clearly defined and understood, when the risks are acceptable, and when the use of force can

be effectively combined with diplomatic and economic policies, then clear and unambiguous objectives must be given to the armed forces. These objectives must be firmly linked with the political objectives. We must not, for example, send military forces into a crisis with an unclear mission they cannot accomplish—such as we did when we sent the U.S. Marines into Lebanon in 1983. We inserted those proud warriors into the middle of a five-faction civil war complete with terrorists, hostage-takers, and a dozen spies in every camp, and said, 'Gentlemen, be a buffer.' The results were 241 Marines and Navy personnel and a U.S. withdrawal from the troubled area.

Powell addressed the new reality of deploying American power in small operations for specific and relative brief periods. Gone were the days of large-scale wars that would lead to deaths in such high numbers that terms such as *sacrifice* might be employed. But Powell also underscored that any time troops were sent to do violence—to kill—they were being sent to make war, not to create peace or make the world a better place. War, he asserted, "is the scourge of God. We should be very careful how we use it. When we do use it, we should not be equivocal: we should win and win decisively."[91]

Clinton did not have time to ruminate on the Powell doctrine, for Powell's former boss had passed along a nasty situation in Somalia. The operation, from the start, looked like something from George Orwell's fiction, as American troops and media personnel in almost equal numbers stormed the coastal city of Mogadishu in a vague attempt to help people devastated by civil war. Cameras tracked Americans and the U.N. aid workers as they delivered food and medicine to emaciated Somali children. Clinton acquired a mission he was powerless to stop. But by 1993 its focus had changed from bringing humanitarian aid to a ravaged people to bringing down Somalia's bloody warlord Mohamed Farrah Aidid. The difficulty of that situation came home on October 3, 1993, when what was supposed to be a "swoop and grab" went tragically wrong, ending with eighteen American soldiers killed in a failed attempt to capture Aidid and two of his commanders. Horrific images of the botched raid were all over the media—television, magazines, and newspapers. The most iconic picture was of a dead American soldier being dragged half-naked through the streets of Mogadishu.

The *New York Times* editorialized, "The American public was right to want to scuttle the Somalia expedition as soon as American corpses appeared on the television screen."[92] But Americans were mixed about the mission overall. In polls, more Americans supported keeping American troops in Somalia to "finish the job" rather than leaving.[93] It was a view their president held as well. In Clinton's address to the nation after the Mogadishu debacle, he linked the American presence in Somalia to "the Nation's best tradition" of helping others when no one else either can or will. And, in the course of praising the bravery and valor of the soldiers who protected those shot down in the firefight, Clinton conflated their heroics with the nation's ideals: "They stayed with their comrades. That's the kind of soldiers they are. That's the kind of people we are."[94]

Richard Holbrooke called the situation "Vietmalia."[95] It was the kind of mess that Powell had warned against but Clinton was unable to prevent. Clinton might have avoided fighting in Vietnam as a young man, but he was unable to avoid its legacy as president. The United States found itself, at once, hamstrung to intervene anywhere in the world with enough military force to be effective but unable to turn away from situations in dire need of intervention. From Bosnia to Somalia to Haiti to the genocide in Rwanda, Clinton experienced the two things that undermine American moral authority: botched interventions and interventions that never happened.[96]

Bush had a dream that after the Cold War an international order would emerge that would be enforceable—the "good guys" would work together to isolate and slowly reduce the number of "bad guys." Clinton inherited that dream but found making it work closer to a nightmare. In his first two years as president, Clinton watched the new world order give way to atrocities. The U.N., which had seemed so effective when Bush used it to launch a war against Saddam had become in Clinton's time, at worst, a bystander to genocide. The U.N.'s role in both Bosnia and Rwanda was to do nothing and to make it difficult for the United States to intervene. But in July 1995 in the village of Srebrenica, a U.N. "safe haven," Clinton's patience with the new world order ran out. Nearly forty thousand Bosnia Muslims had sought safety with the U.N. and NATO, both under the guidance of European powers. The result was genocide. Serb militias raped women and girls and then took thousands of men and boys away from Srebrenica and executed them. With the Rwandan genocide still haunting Clinton and his advisors, the latest Serb atrocities against Bosnia Muslims pushed the United States to scrap the U.N. and take control of NATO once again. NATO would now have authority to bomb Serb positions in order to stem the atrocities committed by the Serbian militias. The new American policy disregarded the U.N., upset a diplomatic balance with the Europeans, but coerced the Serbs to enter into talks held at an air force base in Dayton, Ohio, that ultimately halted the war in Bosnia.

What Clinton had learned from his experience with the war in Bosnia added an addendum to Bush's belief that the Gulf War had kicked the Vietnam Syndrome. Bush believed his success made it possible for Americans once again to believe in the ability of the nation to use its power for good. In reality, the Gulf War had illustrated American willingness to support a short-term, low-casualty war that asked relatively little of most people. No doubt, Americans wanted that kind of experience, but it fell short, as Bush learned, of creating a new understanding of the nation itself. The culture wars, not sacrifice and duty, came to define the era of Bush and Clinton. Yet Clinton differed from Bush in a specific way: the war that framed Clinton's thinking was not World War II or even the Cold War but Vietnam. So, whereas Bush hoped that the Gulf War would do for the American spirit what World War II had done, Clinton approached the effect of war differently. In one sense, Clinton's view of war was quite limited; he seemed to propose that war could be right as long as it wasn't righteous—in other words, when bad things are being done by bad people, the United States could do good by stopping such actions. In another sense, Clinton's approach could appear to be wildly ambitious—criticized as warmed over Wilsonianism and global meliorism—because it suggested a strategy to replace containment. In a speech to the U.N. in 1993, he argued, "During the cold war we sought to contain a threat to the survival of free institutions. Now we seek to enlarge the circle of nations that live under those free institutions. For our dream is of a day when the opinions and energies of every person in the world will be given full expression, in a world of thriving democracies that cooperate with each other and live in peace."[97] Given the disasters of the first two years of his presidency, how would Clinton salvage this vision?

Two speeches a year apart from each other provided an answer. Clinton went to Georgetown in July 1995 and to George Washington University in August 1996 to deliver speeches that came to define the latter half of his presidency. In 1995, he spoke about realizing what he had called in his first inaugural address the New Covenant. This idea—his contention that "you don't have to choose between being personally right and having common goals"—was his alternative to the divisiveness of the culture wars. Like all presidents, Clinton pined for national unity but presided over a period that was better defined by fractious debate. "I think we have got to move beyond division and resentment to common ground," Clinton pleaded. "We've got to go beyond cynicism to a sense of possibility." But how? In light of his recent experience with ethnic conflicts, Clinton contended that because "America is an idea," Americans should be able to find common ground. If they could not find it in domestic politics, Clinton contended Americans would find it abroad.[98]

A year later, Clinton sought to unify Americans at home by directing their vision outward, away from the culture wars and toward America's role in the world. As the imperative of the Cold War had unified Americans at home, so Clinton believed the imperatives of the post–Cold War world would do the same. The president declared, "The fact is America remains the indispensable nation. There are times when America and only America can make a difference between war and peace, between freedom and repression, between hope and fear. Of course, we can't take on all the world's burden. We cannot become its policemen. But where our interests and values demand it and where we can make a difference, America must act and lead." Clinton suggested that America could not remake the world. He was not succumbing to the charms of Wilsonianism and imagining that the force of morality and logic would push the arc of history toward peace on earth. But he was also aware that the United States could not simply abide tragedies because they didn't directly affect American national interests.[99]

Clinton came under intense scrutiny for practicing a muscular form of bleeding-heart liberalism that included a rash of public apologies for an assortment of crimes. He apologized on behalf of the federal government for medical experiments conducted on hundreds of black men with syphilis—a study that spanned forty years, from 1932 to 1972. On a trip to Africa in 1998, Clinton made two apologies—one for a historic and long-term crime; the second for an atrocity committed under his watch. In Uganda, the president apologized for the slave trade and slavery as an institution in Europe and the United States. However, Uganda was not a country from which the United States received slaves, and slavery, as an institution, had a history much longer that the European-controlled Atlantic slave trade. But perhaps Clinton was simply acknowledging the general mistreatment of Africans because his next apology took place in Rwanda. Here Clinton issued a personal apology that he attributed to the rest of the world: "We did not act quickly enough after the killing began. . . . We did not immediately call these crimes by their rightful name: genocide."[100]

However, Clinton's repentance had limits: in 1995, in preparation for the fiftieth anniversary of the end of World War II, Clinton did not issue an apology to the Japanese people for the atomic bombing of Hiroshima and Nagasaki. In reply to a reporter's questions, Clinton responded that his predecessor Truman had made a decision "based on the facts he had before him," and it was right.[101] Furthermore, Clinton's apology in Africa for slavery did not translate into an official apology in the United States. Rather than entertain the idea of reparations to the American ancestors of former slaves, the president convened a commission on race headed by historian John Hope Franklin to defuse a critique about America itself.

Clinton's approach to American moral authority confounded previous categories. As a realist might, he put a great deal of faith in the utility of American military strength but still operated, as a revisionist would, under the influence of the Vietnam Syndrome. He believed that America should be a force of good in the world but also admitted, as had many mainline Protestant leaders and Catholic bishops, that the United States had done bad things in the past that had to be accounted for. And while he entered office with the hope that in the wake of the Cold War Americans could turn inward to embrace an opportunity to build a "New Covenant" among themselves, he also believed that the promise of the United States should be accessible to almost anyone around the world.

Clinton and his advisors appealed to a global civil religion, one that Bellah had theorized about in the conclusion to his 1967 essay. "There seems little doubt," Bellah wrote, "that a successful negotiation of this third time of trial—the attainment of some kind of viable and coherent world order—would precipitate a major new set of symbolic forms." In the wake of the Cold War, or this third time of trial, Bush had hoped a new world order would take shape. When that new world order failed to hold its shape, Clinton proposed a next stage, an era of globalization that united people under democratic capitalism. Bellah had speculated that "a world civil religion could be accepted as a fulfillment and not a denial of American civil religion. Indeed," Bellah concluded, "such an outcome has been the eschatological hope of American civil religion from the beginning."[102]

In his second inaugural address, in January 1997, Clinton confirmed such a vision: "At the dawn of the twenty-first century, a free people must now choose to shape the forces of the information age and the global society, to unleash the limitless potential of all our people, and yes, to form a more perfect Union." For Clinton, his appeal to unity was expansive. He hoped to unite a divided public at home by projecting the ideals of their nation abroad. He remarked that while voters had returned one party to the White House and another to Congress, "surely they did not do this to advance the politics of petty bickering and extreme partisanship they plainly deplore. No, they call on us instead to be repairers of the breach and to move on with America's mission. America demands and deserves big things from us, and nothing big ever came from being small." Clinton made clear that divisiveness at home would undermine the nation's ability to realize a future that it had fought a world war and the Cold War to create. The moment had arrived, he believed, for America to redeem the world by acting in line with ideals that were supposed to be universal. Bellah had observed, "To deny such an outcome would be to deny the meaning of American itself."[103]

Clinton did not believe such broad redemption could happen without war. And the war that became the new standard was the NATO campaign in Kosovo. Slobodan Milosevic was once again carrying out ethnic cleansing of a minority population, this time in the tiny Balkan province of Kosovo. On the face of it, this situation failed to meet any standard of American national interest. Yet Clinton chose to appeal to a standard that existed beyond the nation itself. In doing so, he made an argument for investing American faith through American force and sacrifice in a global civil religion.

At a White House ceremony celebrating the millennium, Clinton delivered a set of remarks that established the moral rationale for his vision. He approached the podium after Noble Prize winner and Holocaust survivor Elie Wiesel had delivered the keynote address, entitled "The Perils of Indifference: Lessons Learned from a Violent Century." Cognizant of the tone set by Wiesel, Clinton said, "The history of our country for quite a long while had been dominated by a principle of non-intervention in the affairs of other nations. Indeed, for most of our history we have worn that principle as a badge of honor, for our Founders knew intervention as a fundamentally destructive force." But horrific events of the twentieth century and the American experience following World War II had changed the American moral temper. "Now, at the end of the 20th century," the president observed, "it seems to me we face a great battle of the forces of integration against the forces of disintegration, of globalism versus tribalism, of oppression against empowerment." The dilemma facing the United States was not whether to intervene but when and how. He declared that America was in Kosovo because in a world with so much promise, the mightiest nation could not be indifferent to "the oldest demon of human society, our vulnerability to hatred of the other." Thus, Clinton proposed, "We can't, perhaps, intervene everywhere, but we must always be alive to the possibility of preventing death and oppression and forging and strengthening institutions and alliances to make a good outcome more likely."[104]

American intervention did indeed lead to a relatively good outcome in Kosovo. The bombing stopped Milosevic's campaign against the ethnic Albanians, and the United States paid nothing in casualties—not a single casualty. But debates did erupt over what many considered an illegal war. The campaign in Kosovo had many ironies. Liberals, who had grown wary of war because of Vietnam, now embraced what war could do if done "correctly." Clinton chose to use NATO rather than the U.N. to launch a war that, according to the president's rhetoric, fit the charter of the U.N. rather well. And while the war undoubtedly stopped Milosevic, Clinton and his allies justified it by appealing to a grander legacy—it was the first humanitarian war. And yet the world that Clinton hoped to conjure for Americans to unite around did not materialize. A global civil religion was a pipe dream.

That did not prevent another version of a national theology from taking shape however. At the same time Clinton proposed the idea of humanitarian war, a group of young conservative intellectuals—the neocons—offered a theology of American exceptionalism. The generation of neocons who dominated discussions in the 1990s, unlike Hauerwas and Neuhaus, were not especially religious; but they did have faith. They "had a more dramatic idea of politics than other kinds of conservatives," historian Gary Dorrien noted about the neocons and their agenda for a "Pax Americana." At its core, their view "featured a radical, expansive faith in American power." The patron saints of this generation of neocons were Teddy Roosevelt and Reagan. They appreciated the unalloyed patriotism of both former presidents. "Their blend of ideology, idealism, and an increasingly frank neo-imperialism offered a coherent view of what the United States should do with its unrivaled economic and military power."[105]

The label *neoconservative* had been around since the mid-1970s, when former leftists and Democrats, including Irving Kristol, Norman Podhoretz, and Seymour Martin Lipset, turned against liberal causes such as Lyndon Johnson's Great Society and the foreign-policy strategy of detente and took up more pessimistic views of social policy and engagement with communist powers. But this brand of neoconservatism fizzled out with the end of the Cold War and the success of the Gulf War. A new wave of neocons emerged during Clinton's presidency, in part as a corollary to his vision of democratic enlargement, which many neocons generally agreed with, and in response to the culture wars that Clinton seemed unable to rise above. Much like the older generation of neocons, the 1990s version also saw a crucial link between domestic behavior and global vision. For the new generation of neocons, such as William Kristol, editor of *The Weekly Standard,* and Robert Kagan, co-founder with Kristol of the New American Century Project, the evaporation of national unity had left Americans with two equally egregious choices: retrenched isolationism or an ill-defined multinationalism.

One author has noted that these "third generation" neocons believed that "a nation's foreign policy is a mirror in which it can see a reflection of itself, its health, and its moral condition. A prudent, timid, and cynical (in other words, realist) approach to international affairs is not worthy of America, it neither inspires nor edifies its own citizens."[106] The crux of the neocon theology of American exceptionalism rested on the notion that the United States was unlike any empire that had ever existed and would operate so differently from empires of the past that a Pax Americana would usher in an era of global benevolence. This was a twist on the idea of a global civil religion, but, unlike Bellah and Clinton, the neocons saw America as the god of civil religion, not as something to be judged through civil religion. Columnist David Brooks wrote in a famous essay on national greatness that the creed by which to measure the nation was not a set abstract ideals but a "set of physical goals" such as building the interstate highway system, exploring space, waging the Cold War, and "disseminating American culture throughout the world." Americans shouldn't spend time ruminating on their inability to live up to some unrealistic notion of goodness; such an abstraction could be expressed as anything from isolationism to global meliorism. Rather to be great meant eliminating "barriers to ambition." "The first task of government is to convey a spirit of confidence and vigor that can spill across the life of the nation." There was no need to seek redemption in light of past crimes such as slavery, genocide, and atomic bombs; a future based on an energetic American hegemony would make such gestures irrelevant. Most important, though, the neocons of the late 1990s believed the exercise of American power was crucial to reinvigorating faith in the nation, for only then would Americans understand what the nation was and why it would be worth sacrificing for.[107]

In their celebrated 1996 essay, "Toward a Neo-Reaganite Foreign Policy," Kagan and Kristol put their charge succinctly: "The remoralization of America at home ultimately requires the remoralization of American foreign policy." The point was that throughout the 1990s, the American public had been distracted—had been allowed to grow distracted—by the lack of a coherent martial vision. Kagan and Kristol believed that the American military was not some unfortunate appendage of a peace-loving, civic polis but an essential branch of the American system of ideals. "It is foolish to imagine that the Untied States can lead the world effectively while the overwhelming majority of the population neither understands nor is involved, in any real way, with its international mission," they asserted. They clearly believed that the military stood as the sole institution in American public life that should command universal admiration. Americans needed to be reminded, educated, and trained, Kagan and Kristol claimed, in "military virtues." "The president and other political leaders can take steps to close the growing separation of civilian and military cultures in our society," they advised. "They can remind civilians of the sacrifices being made by U.S. forces overseas and explain what those sacrifices are for." These neocons saw no contradiction between the military's being both the embodiment of the highest ideals of American life and the force charged with unleashing violence and death. At base, Kagan and Kristol said, "There is no more profound responsibility than the defense of the nation and its principles." The public needed the "moral clarity" that an activist, interventionist foreign policy provided. America needed a big war.[108]

CHAPTER 6

Civil Religion Forsaken

ON OCTOBER 11, 2000, Bill Clinton's vice president, Al Gore, debated his opponent in the presidential election, Texas governor George W. Bush. Somewhat like George H. W. Bush, Gore was an heir apparent. He intended to follow a president who had, over all, enjoyed considerable success. Like Ronald Reagan, Clinton had his crises, but he had also presided over an era so economically vibrant that the federal government ran a surplus. Gore intended to ride that prosperity into the White House. The nation was at peace. In contrast, Bush could claim little experience in administering a government—that was simply the fate of a Texas governor—and had even less expertise in foreign affairs. In an era defined by culture wars more than real war, Bush presented himself as a moderate on social issues, a conservative on fiscal issues, and outright cautious on foreign affairs. A few minutes into the debate, moderator Jim Lehrer asked Bush, "Should the people of the world . . . fear us, should they welcome our involvement, should they see us as a friend? How would you project us around the world, as president?" The Texas governor paused for a moment, looked down at some notes, and responded in a way consonant with his father's conservative foreign policy.

> Well, I think they ought to look at us as a country that understands freedom where it doesn't matter who you are or how you're raised or where you're from, that you can succeed. I don't think they'll look at us with envy. It really depends upon how our nation conducts itself in foreign policy. If we're an arrogant nation, they'll resent us. If we're a humble nation, but strong, they'll welcome us. And it's—our nation stands alone right now in the world in terms of power, and that's why we have to be humble. And yet project strength in a way that promotes freedom. So I don't think they

ought to look at us in any way other than what we are. We're a freedom-loving nation and if we're an arrogant nation they'll view us that way, but if we're a humble nation they'll respect us.

Lehrer nodded and repeated "a humble nation" as he looked over at Gore for his response. Gore, as always, was eager to reply. "I agree with that. I agree with that," he said with enthusiasm. "I think that one of the problems that we have faced in the world is that we are so much more powerful than any single nation [that] . . . there is some resentment of U.S. power. So I think that the idea of humility is an important one." Then, Gore switched gears a bit and pronounced the kind of doctrine that made the Clinton years somewhat paradoxical—Gore supported humility but with zest. "I think that we also have to have a sense of mission in the world. We have to protect our capacity to push forward what America's all about," he declared. "That means not only military strength and our values, it also means keeping our economy strong." Like Clinton, Gore imagined that America had an obligation to the world: "The fact that we have the strongest economy in history today is not good enough. We need to do more. But the fact that it is so strong enables us to project the power for good that America can represent." Bush jumped in, adding: "We do have an obligation, but we can't be all things to all people. We can help build coalitions but we can't put our troops all around the world. We can lend money but we have to do it wisely. We shouldn't be lending money to corrupt officials. So we have to be guarded in our generosity."[1]

Bush was a moderate, perhaps because he was a political neophyte. However, the campaign team around him was not. He signaled where he stood ideologically in his choice for vice president. He picked Dick Cheney, a veteran of the Executive Branch since the administration of Richard Nixon. In Cheney's debate against Gore's running mate, Joe Lieberman, a U.S. senator from Connecticut, Cheney echoed Bush's moderate conservatism and, frankly, did not score points against his Democratic opponent save on one topic—the military. When Cheney spoke about the military, he made sure to remind his audience that because he had served as secretary of defense, the military would be in better shape once the Republicans returned to the White House. "There is no more important responsibility for a President of the United States than his role as Commander in Chief," Cheney counseled, "[particularly] when he decides when to send our young men and women to war." Cheney took a shot at the Clinton administration, intimating that he and Bush understood how to treat the military with the respect it deserved. "When we send them without the right kind of training, when we send them poorly equipped or with equipment that's old and broken down, we put their lives at risk," Cheney said. "We will suffer more casualties in the next conflict if we don't look to those basic problems now. This administration has a bad track record in this regard, and it's available for anybody who wants to look at the record and wants to talk to our men and women in uniform, and wants to spend time with the members of the Joint Chiefs."[2]

The military was the only issue that Bush-Cheney could use to attack Gore. On almost every other issue, even the economy, there was little difference between the two parties. Use of American troops was a wedge issue—but an ironic one. The Clinton administration had lost fewer soldiers during its eight years in office than any previous eight-year period since the end of World War II. Thus, Cheney's charge made little sense in light of the reality that the military's image had actually improved in large part because Clinton's foreign policy had avoided ground wars and, instead, killed from the skies. And while Bush-Cheney went after the Clinton-Gore record of fighting "humanitarian wars," such efforts had created an image of American troops doing good across the world. Ironically, then, Clinton's policies allowed Bush, Cheney, and the neocons to use the military as a unique expression of American virtue—as the embodiment of American civil religion.

The 1990s had been a decade of overcoming the effects of war. The first president Bush hoped to kick the dreaded Vietnam Syndrome only to see the nation bogged down in the culture wars. Clinton had attempted to elevate the vision of Americans to points above their own noses, only to hear the neocons retort that the nation failed to achieve "greatness" because it had lost its martial spirit. The neocons, though, did not determine the 2000 presidential election, the U.S. Supreme Court did. In the closest election in U.S. history, Bush defeated Gore in the Electoral College by taking the hotly contested state of Florida. The presidential election of 2000 mirrored America itself—it was divided. The combination of economic prosperity and little fear of foreign challengers allowed Americans room to argue over everything from homosexuality to the Bible and to elect a candidate who had a familiar last name but relatively little executive experience.

The day that the second president Bush took office, America seemed far from great. In his first inaugural address, Bush acknowledged that he now presided over the "divided" states of America. "Sometimes our differences run so deep," Bush said, "it seems we share a continent but not a country." He pledged to "work to build a single nation of justice and opportunity" and appealed to Americans to find unity of purpose in "ideals that move us beyond our backgrounds, lift us above our interests, and teach us what it means to be citizens." The new president added that he believed such unity was in "our reach because we are guided by a power larger than ourselves, who creates us equal, in His image." That remark was characteristic of Bush's faith in the promise of America, a sense that sounded innocuous because it was so familiar. The new president, like many before him, truly believed that the United States was one nation under God. Yet Bush presided over a nation with many divisions, including serious disagreements over the existence and implications of an American civil religion. Bush observed that in the absence of "depression and war, when defeating common dangers defined our common good," Americans had only legacies to "inspire us or condemn us." It was time, the new president concluded, to "achieve [God's] purpose . . . in our duty." He defined this duty obliquely as "service to one another."[3] But service for what? Why would Americans come together? What would make Americans look beyond their differences toward something greater? The answer was war.

On the morning of September 11, 2001, Father Richard John Neuhaus was on his way to say mass at the Church of the Immaculate Conception on Fourteenth Street and First Avenue in lower Manhattan. He looked further downtown and saw a fire in one of the two towers of the World Trade Center. He remarked to a few people standing on a corner that they should pray for the safe exit of the people from the building. Only after mass did he learn that he had glimpsed the beginning of an American tragedy. He made an interesting observation that morning: "It is weird," he wrote. "We can look down avenues and see the still billowing smoke, as though watching a foreign country under attack, but of course it is our city, and our country." That vision was ominous—his nation had been attacked, and would soon be at war. Neuhaus, like many others, anticipated major changes.[4]

Perhaps nothing changed more than the new president. Bush spoke to the nation on the evening of September 11 from his desk in the Oval Office. In the first few seconds of his remarks, Bush introduced terms that defined his era: "Thousands of lives were suddenly ended by evil," Bush intoned, "despicable acts of terror." It was not entirely clear at that moment who committed these acts or what America's response might be. However, one theme did emerge in his speech: far from "changing everything," the attacks on 9/11 had, according to the president, only revealed how solid America was. "Terrorist attacks can shake the foundations of our biggest buildings," Bush said, "but they cannot touch the foundation of America. These acts shattered steel, but they cannot dent the steel of American resolve." Bush sought to reassure the nation that evening by explaining that the government would function as normal and that the economy was fine. He vowed to track down those responsible for "these evil acts," making "no distinction between the terrorists who committed these acts and those who harbor them." He intended to do this by joining with "friends and allies . . . who want peace and security in the world." "We stand together," Bush declared, "to win the war against terrorism." At the end of his brief speech, Bush invoked the memory of Pearl Harbor, stating "America has stood down enemies before, and we will do so this time." But unlike Franklin Roosevelt, President Bush did not pledge merely to defeat a foe but "to defend freedom and all that is good and just in the world."[5]

Bush was transformed. He was a wartime leader now, and his posture, rhetoric, and purpose changed dramatically. When Bush spoke the next day from the cabinet room at the White House, he did so in new terms: he declared that the attacks the day before had been more than merely acts of terror; "they were acts of war." As a result, the president explained, "this will require our country to unite in steadfast determination and resolve. Freedom and democracy are under attack." Bush aimed to use his authority "to conquer this enemy" and prevent that enemy from "changing our way of life or restricting our freedoms." Going forward, Bush emphasized his role as the nation's commander in chief in a way that illustrated his belief that the presidency had changed.

The nation was at war, and his prosecution of war would determine his relationship to the nation.[6]

The divisions in America that characterized the 2000 election had not disappeared. Yet the resort to war illustrated that war has an appeal that can shift public discussion toward speaking about the nation in an abstract sense. Rather than focus on specific problems such as God in schools or gays in the military, war idealized the nation, making it whole and seemingly indivisible. Thus for Bush it was not much of stretch to launch a war that was in itself rather abstract against an amorphous enemy who attacked the values of an idealized nation. Without a formal declaration of war, America resorted to unspecified force for an unspecified length of time to defend the idea of freedom. The abstract nature of this moment made it ripe for a dramatic redefinition of civil religion.

The unveiling of this new civil religion happened at a site befitting the occasion—the National Cathedral in Washington, D.C. Bush had declared September 14 a National Day of Prayer and Remembrance, an act that presidents had used throughout American history to call the nation to reflect on tragedy. Abraham Lincoln had famously declared such a day in the middle of the Civil War because, he said, "it behooves us . . . to humble ourselves before the offended Power, to confess our national sins, and to pray for clemency and forgiveness."[7] Bush was moved by a martial spirit.

On September 14, 2001, an enormous audience of American dignitaries, including four former presidents, scores of members of Congress, military officials and personnel, and religious figures, filled the National Cathedral to join in a solemn remembrance of those lost in the attacks and to pledge to redeem their deaths. The religious leaders who presided over the ceremony were a vision of the ecumenical American civil religion. There was an Episcopal bishop, a Roman Catholic archbishop, a Jewish rabbi, and because this was twenty-first-century America, a Muslim imam. And while each had a chance to make a statement about the tragic events of September 11, they were clearly set-up acts for the main attraction—Billy Graham.

An elderly and slightly hobbled Graham slowly walked to the lectern and delivered a sermon reminiscent of his early Cold War days. He began by thanking the president and Mrs. Bush for calling a day of prayer. "We need it at this time," Graham said, because it allowed

Americans "to come together . . . to affirm our conviction that God cares for us, whatever our ethnic, religious or political background may be." Graham declared that "September 11 will go down in our history as a day to remember." True, of course, but how? "We're involved in a new kind of warfare . . . facing a new kind of enemy . . . and we need the help of the Spirit of God." This enemy had reminded Americans of "the reality of evil." But "the lesson of this event," Graham preached, "is not only about the mystery of iniquity and evil, but . . . about our need for each other." Indeed, he returned to a theme that had defined the civil religion for most of the postwar period: through war and the moral imperatives it placed on the nation, a diverse people found unity and purpose. "A tragedy like this could have torn our country apart," he observed, "but instead it has united us and we've become a family." In an age of fracture, following a badly divisive election, Graham found that Americans "were more united than ever." He pointed to the "very moving way . . . members of Congress stood shoulder to shoulder and sang 'God Bless America'" as an exemplar of this unity. And then, perhaps sensing the vague nostalgia for the early Cold War among the American people, Graham proclaimed it was time for another "spiritual renewal in this country." It was time to "repent our sins and . . . turn to Him and He will bless us in a new way." Graham warned once again that the consequences were grave for failing as a nation to be humble before God. "We have a choice: whether to implode and disintegrate emotionally and spiritually as a people and a nation—or, whether we choose to become stronger through all this struggle—to rebuild on a solid foundation." Knowing that his president supported such a national renewal, Graham spoke confidently: "This is going to be a day that we will remember as a day of victory."[8]

Graham gingerly made his way from the lectern, and as he reached the other religious leaders, a growing roar of applause filled the cathedral. The congregants stood and clapped for the only time that day. Graham greeted his counterparts and took his seat still professing the national faith.

Then the minister-in-chief spoke: President Bush stood and strode confidently to give his address. His speech wasn't long, but he took pains to appear resolute. He began by recognizing those who had died and vowed to redeem their deaths: "Our responsibility to history is already clear," he announced, "to answer these attacks and rid the world of evil." As commander in chief, Bush had made his decision; as minister to the nation, he astutely managed civil religion. He admitted that in "tragedy . . . [God's] purposes are not always our own." The president could not claim God's will for the violence he was about to unleash—at least not with four religious leaders sitting next to him. But then, with subtlety, he doubled back, stating he knew that "this world He created is of moral design." Indeed, Bush needed to make clear that while he did not intend to launch a war in God's name, he did believe that 9/11 had a single interpretation—and Bush's was it. The president assured Americans that the attacks on 9/11 had not succeeded; they had only revealed the depth of the American character. Like Graham, Bush saw in these attacks a moment to affirm the soul of the nation; there was no need to doubt it. He concluded by consoling Americans that "neither death nor life, nor angels nor principalities nor power, nor things present nor things to come, nor height nor depth, can separate us from God's love." Bush asked God to "bless the souls of the departed," "comfort our own," and "guide our country."[9]

America had left behind the world of moral ambiguity. Before 9/11 people debated among other issues whether America was still the last best hope for humanity. After 9/11, the world would make sense again, Bush assured Americans. God was where he should be—watching over a nation that believed in his grace.

Civil religion went back to war. And Robert Bellah was none too pleased. In an interview with the *Washington Post*, the scholarly voice of American civil religion decried Bush's brief address at the National Cathedral, calling it "stunningly inappropriate" that the president had "invoked civil religion to make a case for war." Religious scholar Mark Silk took issue with Bellah's outrage. While not associated with the term as much as Bellah, Silk had written about civil religious debates since World War II in a well-received 1988 book entitled *Spiritual Politics*. Silk found Bellah's reaction somewhat odd, considering that "if civil religion is about anything, it's about war and those who die in it."[10] In one sense, Bush had simply applied Bellah's own terms to the tragic situation at hand.

Silk was correct: civil religion is about war and the people who die in it. But that's not how Bush had used it. After all, there was no war—at least no formal declaration of war. What Bellah objected to was Bush's deployment of civil religion as a way to make war. Bush needed to build unity and deter scrutiny, and he used civil religion to make a case that had the feeling of biblical truth. Bush believed that while it might be impossible to know God's will (to claim God's favor for America), history had revealed God's plan to those willing to notice. In other words, Bush had revived the conflation of reason and faith that had characterized a version of American civil religion leading up to the Civil War. Lincoln had cast devastating doubt on that confidence as he attempted to make sense of the war's carnage. War had not brought victory to either side, Lincoln argued, and, what's more, it had undermined the notion that God's relationship to America was even discernible. For most of the postwar period, Lincoln's bequest hung over debates about America's ability to wage war. But Bush seemingly returned to a time that resembled antebellum America: he asked Americans to believe in war in order to believe in their nation. The nation would use war to project what was best about itself. This was a war unlike any since the Civil War. This war would not merely reveal the American soul; it would redeem it.[11]

Less than a week after Bush's speech in the National Cathedral, he addressed the nation again, employing a biblical sense of judgment to explain the actions the nation would take. Bush stood in the Capitol addressing a Congress that had not been this united in forty years. The audience gathered gave the president rousing ovations. Not surprisingly, Bush wasted little time delivering the point of his address: "Tonight we are a country awakened to danger and called to defend freedom. Our grief has turned to anger and anger to resolution." Then pausing slightly to prepare his audience for his most important point, Bush spoke at a deliberately slower pace: "Whether we bring our enemies to justice or bring justice to our enemies, justice will be done." Bush claimed a mandate unlike that of any recent president; he was perhaps the most popular person alive at that moment. People around the world responded with expressions of solidarity for Americans; makeshift memorials appeared at American embassies and major public sites. Congress rallied together, singing "God Bless America" on the Capitol steps and authorizing $40 billion for the president's use. The British prime minister, Tony Blair, flew to Washington to attend Bush's speech. In such a moment, Bush did not exaggerate when he declared, "The civilized world is rallying to America's side."[12]

But an enormous question had emerged: What had the terrorist strikes revealed about America? Bush believed that 9/11 had revealed the core of American ideals—the best in the nation—and the nation's response to the attacks would be a war to express those ideals. "On September 11, enemies of freedom committed an act of war against our country," he declared. He made clear that the day of the attacks ended an era of confusion about America's role in world and had begun a new era in which America understood clearly its role in history. The relationship between foreign policy and history was crucial here. Clinton had attempted to end savage conflicts through the indirect use of American power. Bush and neocon critics of Clinton's foreign policy saw such action as pseudo-war—a poor use of American military might because it was based on a misunderstanding of the nation's ability to understand and shape history. After 9/11, Bush resurrected a faith that war need not be an anomaly of civilized life; it could be the most noble expression of the core values of a society dedicated to the promise of good. Thus, 9/11 had not undermined American civil religion but, rather, had made it apparent, had made it incarnate.[13]

For Bush, America did not change on 9/11; the nation only became more profoundly American. For that reason he could both tell the American public to expect "a lengthy campaign, unlike any other we have ever seen," and promise that Americans wouldn't be called on to sacrifice as they had been to defeat fascism and communism. He asked Americans to "live your lives" and to "uphold the values of America." We might imagine that in making such an appeal Bush simply wanted to allay the fears of his people. However, near the conclusion of his address, Bush outlined a set of assumptions on which a new civil religion rested. Bush declared that Americans need not let fear dominate their lives: "This country will define our times, not be defined by them. As long as the United States of America is determined and strong, this will not be an age of terror; this will be an age of liberty, here and across the world." Bush believed that history could be understood and pushed in a direction that was right and good. And it was a second assumption that gave him such confidence. Bush acknowledged that the "course of this conflict is not known" but added, "Its outcome is certain." "Freedom and fear, justice and cruelty have always been at war, and we know that God is not neutral between them." Bush had not declared a holy war but had defended American moral authority: because the attacks were wrong, America's response would be right. While few people disagreed with the first part of that contention, the second invited (demanded) scrutiny.[14]

Bush believed 9/11 had revealed a union between heaven and earth; others saw his rhetoric as utterly sanctimonious and ultimately very dangerous. In the week following the terrorist attacks, the *New Yorker* published reflections from an array of intellectuals. Susan Sontag, a veteran of wars over ideas, words, and culture, leveled a devastating analysis.

> Our leaders are bent on convincing us that everything is O.K. America is not afraid. Our spirit is unbroken, although this was a day that will live in infamy and America is now at war. But everything is not O.K. And this was not Pearl Harbor. We have a robotic President who assures us that America still stands tall. A wide spectrum of public figures, in and out of office, who are strongly opposed to the policies being pursued abroad by this Administration apparently feel free to say nothing more than that they stand united behind President Bush. A lot of thinking needs to be done, and perhaps is being done in Washington and elsewhere, about the ineptitude of American intelligence and counter-intelligence, about options available to American foreign policy, particularly in the Middle East, and about what constitutes a smart program of military defense. But the public is not being asked to bear much of the burden of reality. The unanimously applauded, self-congratulatory bromides of a Soviet Party Congress seemed contemptible. The unanimity of the sanctimonious, reality-concealing rhetoric spouted by American officials and media commentators in recent days seems, well, unworthy of a mature democracy.

Sontag argued at this early date that the manipulation of organic unity would define the period begun by 9/11. "Those in public office have let us know that they consider their task to be a manipulative one," she wrote: "confidence-building and grief management." Much to her utter chagrin, "Politics, the politics of a democracy—which entails disagreement, which promotes candor—has been replaced by psychotherapy." She closed with a piece of advice that drifted over American history for the next decade: "Let's by all means grieve together. But let's not be stupid together."[15]

Responses to Sontag's essay were predictable. Conservative intellectual and blogger Andrew Sullivan named a special award after Sontag for writers who failed to honor America properly. Richard Brookhiser at the *National Review* dismissed Sontag as the dean of the "we deserved it" school of intellectuals, which included other figures such as Noam Chomsky and Katha Pollitt. Charles Krauthammer at *Time* said Sontag was "morally obtuse." Generally, many intellectuals and pundits thought Sontag stood as the exemplar of anti-Americanism at a moment of frenetic American patriotism.[16]

Sontag was most certainly an effective antidote to the "soft despotism" of civil religion that extreme historical moments create, but hers was a decidedly minority position. Alexis de Tocqueville had made that observation at the birth of American democracy:

> Above this race of men stands an immense and tutelary power, which takes upon itself alone to secure their gratifications and to watch over their fate. That power is absolute, minute, regular, provident, and mild. It would be like the authority of a parent if, like that authority, its object was to prepare men for manhood; but it seeks, on the contrary, to keep them in perpetual childhood: it is well content that the people should rejoice, provided they think of nothing but rejoicing. For their happiness such a government willingly labors, but it chooses to be the sole agent and the only arbiter of that happiness; it provides for their security, foresees and supplies their necessities, facilitates their pleasures, manages their principal concerns, directs their industry, regulates the descent of property, and subdivides their inheritances: what remains, but to spare them all the care of thinking and all the trouble of living?[17]

Indeed, Sontag's concern dwelled on the precipitous lack of critical thought at a time in which America needed to be something other than an echo chamber. In his 2005 book, *The Abuse of Evil*, philosopher Richard Bernstein argued that the Bush administration and its neoconservative supporters peddled an "uncritical or unreflective appeal to objective certainty, absolutes, and rigid dualisms," perpetrating a "dangerous abuse of evil." Bernstein observed that rather than promoting a vigorous discussion worthy of a "complex and precarious world," the administration's public discourse "stifled thinking" about the morality of war. He ended his essay with a plea: he wanted "ordinary citizens . . . to oppose the political abuse of evil, challenge the misuse of absolutes, expose false and misleading claims to moral certainty, and argue that we cannot deal with the complexity of the issues we confront by appealing to—or imposing—simplistic dichotomies."[18]

Yet the most common refrain became that 9/11 changed everything—the intellectual ground had shifted under the feet of people like Sontag and Bernstein. Edward Rothstein wrote in the *New York Times* the same week that Sontag's essay appeared that the terrorist attacks challenged "the intellectual and ethical perspectives of two set of ideas: postmodernism . . . and postcolonialism." He hoped that both would be summarily rejected. The events of 9/11 seemed "to cry out for a transcendent ethical perspective," something that the relativism of post-everything ideologies was incapable of offering. Rothstein argued that postmodernism complicated "objective notions of truth," and post-colonialism sought to undermine the West's ideological dominance; such "rejections of universal values and ideals have little room for unqualified condemnations of a terrorist attack, particularly one against the West." However, the promise of a system that housed transcendent values—civil religion—lay in its ability to help people discern moral action in a time of crisis. The implication of Rothstein's argument was fairly simple: Americans had the power to claim truth, and that truth would set them free from the culture wars.[19]

Perhaps, as Roger Rosenblatt thought, the "one good thing could come from this horror [was that] it could spell the end of the age of irony." In an argument similar to Rothstein's, Rosenblatt argued that the culture wars had diverted attention from serious issues for over thirty years and by doing so had helped to create the impression that "nothing was real." But the attack snapped Americans out of their self-satisfied, narrow-interest daze. The reality of the world had returned, and "people may at last be ready to say what they wholeheartedly believe." Among the revelations people awoke to was the reality of the "greatness of the country." The collective grief, collective resolve, and collective action of the American people in the first few weeks after 9/11 convinced observers such as Rosenblatt that the nation was good—full stop.[20]

Krauthammer, Rosenblatt's colleague at *Time,* described this transformation in a colorful way: "The fire at Ground Zero burned for
exactly 100 days. . . . But not before it forged a new America." He
observed that as smoke filled lower Manhattan, "Our holiday from history, from seriousness of thought and purpose was over." Krauthammer
had consistently been among the most significant popularizers of the
neocon faith in American power. His thinking offered insight into the
perpetuation of Reagan's civil religious discourse about the need to
see the United States as a moral entity. He had grown distraught, as
had other neocons, by what he saw as the great distractions of the culture wars following the end of the Cold War. The struggle against
totalitarianism from World War II through 1991 had forged a moral
clarity for Americans that was then allowed to dissipate in the 1990s.
"Overnight, this land of 'bowling alone,' of Internet introversion, of
fractious multiculturalism developed an extraordinary solidarity," he
declared. Krauthammer gushed with pride over the "vast outpouring of
charity and volunteering; [the] suppression of partisanship and ethnic
division; [and the] coalescing behind resolute national leadership
anchored by a new, untested President who rose extraordinarily to the
occasion." Images of yellow ribbons ("emblems of America held
hostage") gave way to waving American flags at ceremonies all around
the country. In a nation that often longs for and celebrates moments
of moral certainty, Krauthammer was sure that "this generation of
Americans—post-Vietnam, post–cold war, never challenged—has had
no finer hour."[21]

The theme of self-mobilization and grassroots prayers for the nation
also impressed intellectual historian Wilfred McClay. In an era that had
hotly debated the place of religion in public life—for that was a central
topic of the culture wars—McClay observed that one would not have
been surprised if 9/11 had only confirmed the need to marginalize religion even more. Some expressions of religion confirmed such fears. For
example, Jerry Falwell and Pat Robertson engaged in a brief, well-worn,
and quickly publicized exercise of seeing the attacks on New York and
Washington as God's direct retribution against the United States for its
sins of abortion and homosexuality. The response to such claims was so
overwhelmingly negative that the two preachers publicly recanted.
McClay noted, "The more common public reaction was something

much simpler and more primal. Millions of Americans went to church in search of reassurance, comfort, solace, strength, and some semblance of redemptive meaning in the act of sharing their grief and confusion in the presence of the transcendent." The collective reactions of millions of Americans to act religiously indicated to McClay that American civil religion had not died of irrelevance in the 1990s but had laid dormant, waiting, it seemed, for a great revitalization.[22]

McClay's reaction to the popular expression of civil religion reflected a broader hope among many intellectuals—especially those who tended to be conservative—that the nation had found its way out of the culture wars and back to an older and more authentically American moral authority. While he acknowledged that civil religion had the capacity to grow intolerable in its most extreme forms, he also defended the tradition in the United States "to conflate the realms of the religious and the political" in order to affirm a higher set of ideals to guide and judge the nation. "Religion and the nation are inevitably entwined," McClay noted, "and some degree of entwining is a good thing. After all, the self-regulative pluralism of American culture cannot work without the ballast of certain elements of deep commonality." Yet McClay also recognized that the diversity of American culture did not operate in a religious vacuum; there was a dominant tradition, and it exercised considerable influence in the aftermath of 9/11. Among the most evocative examples of the Christian dominance of Bush-era civil religion was the discovery of cross-shaped girders in the wreckage of the Twin Towers. Ground zero in Manhattan had quickly become a kind of holy site for the nation's reformed civil religion. "What," McClay wondered, "does this object mean to the people viewing it, many of whom are not Christian and not even Americans?" He had struck upon the perilous nature of civil religion's power. He claimed that there was ambiguity in this image and that ambiguity made civil religion problematic. Yet, it seems to me, there was little ambiguity in the "discovery" of the cross at ground zero—it emerged as a clear symbol of a Christian-dominated civil religion. The post-9/11 civil religion was as much an evangelical Christian response to the culture wars as to the imperative of the war on terror itself. McClay noted that the "September 11 attacks reminded us . . . that the impulse to create and live inside of a civil religion is an irrepressible human impulse." What followed 9/11 was a rush to use civil religion as a source of revelation, as a way to discover the righteous path of the nation and to compel others to recognize it.[23]

A particular kind of civil religion emerged that appeared to be the opposite of the messy postmodernism of the previous thirty years. In a sense, post-9/11 civil religion reinvigorated the assumption that a single, unified religious understanding of America was best for the nation. That notion had persisted for much of American history because evangelical Protestants had exerted considerable influence over an American moral order. But in the aftermath of World War II and Vietnam, it was not a single church but a civil religion that re-established a single American moral order. Bush's efforts were the apotheosis of this development.[24]

Feeling this strong sense of moral unity, Bush confidently chose war. On October 7, 2001, an American-led war in Afghanistan began. Bush declared, "We defend not only our precious freedom but also the freedom of people everywhere to live and raise their children free from fear." Defeating a particular enemy was almost beside the point. Bush now offered a war worthy of the deaths it would produce. In the past, Americans had killed and died for just causes, but the world had not changed in some fundamental way. In a moment when the world, much less the American people, seemed prepared to stand behind U.S. action in a way utterly unprecedented in world history, Bush proclaimed that it was not he alone who wanted this war; support for it came from a massive, popular swell of faith in the American idea. "Since September 11," Bush said, "an entire generation of young Americans has gained a new understanding of the value of freedom and its cost in duty and in sacrifice." With such support, it is no wonder he ended almost chanting: "We will not waver; we will not tire; we will not falter; and we will not fail." Indeed, he understood how much goodwill and confidence was riding on this war.[25]

In Bush's first State of the Union since the attacks, he consummated his civil religion. The nation's representatives gave the president long ovations, just as they had the last time he appeared before Congress, four months previously. In January 2002, Bush reported that Afghanistan had been liberated, terrorists had been captured, and the world was a far safer place than it had been, but this was the State of the Union, after all, and Bush spent considerable time delivering ringing proclamations about America itself. In a signature moment, the chamber erupted when Bush declared, his voice rising with enthusiasm, "As we act to win the war, protect the people, and create jobs in America, we must act, first and foremost, not as Republicans, not as Democrats but as Americans." He would need such unity, not merely bipartisanship, to plow forward with policies that would remake the executive branch, the military, and, Bush proposed, the economy. The speech was interrupted so often by applause and shouts of support that one might doubt that the election of 2000 had actually been so divisive. The America of the culture wars had disappeared. Bush made that understanding the foundation of his concluding remarks.[26]

"During these last few months, I've been humbled and privileged to see the true character of this country in a time of testing. Our enemies believed America was weak and materialistic, that we would splinter in fear and selfishness. They were as wrong as they are evil," Bush said with a staccato delivery. "After America was attacked," Bush observed, "it was as if our entire country looked into a mirror and saw our better selves. We were reminded that we are citizens with obligations to each other, to our country, and to history." In a sentence, he dismissed the three decades of wrangling about ethics, identity, even history, asserting that self-centered catch phrases such as "If it feels good, do it" had given way to "a new ethic and a new creed" exemplified by the final words of a passenger on United Flight 93, "Let's roll." And as other presidents had realized in their time of trial, Bush understood the time was ripe to offer his theology of America. "This time of adversity offers a unique moment of opportunity, a moment we must seize to change our culture," Bush pleaded. "I know we can overcome evil with great good. . . . We have a great opportunity during this time of war to lead the world toward the values that will bring lasting peace."[27]

In the post-9/11 world, Bush imagined a unity based on the recognition that there are sacred values that all people share, regardless of whether they are on opposite sides of the political divide or opposite sides of the world. "We seek a just and peaceful world beyond the war on terror," Bush intoned. "Together with friends and allies from Europe to Asia and Africa to Latin America, we will demonstrate that the forces of terror cannot stop the momentum of freedom." How would this unity be made apparent to all? Bush's answer was at once enlightening and tragic: "In a single instant," he declared, "we realized that this will be the decisive decade in the history of liberty, that we've been called to a unique role in human events. Rarely has the world faced a choice more clear or consequential." September 11 sparked a great awakening of historical consciousness, according to Bush, because of its theological profundity. In tragedy, Bush preached, we discover that "God is near."[28]

Neuhaus and Stanley Hauerwas debated the theological implications of that confidence. In a debate that filled pages in *First Things* and spilled out across editorial pages, scholarly journals, and books, Neuhaus and Hauerwas took up the issue of war, the nation, and Christian witness once again. Neuhaus's experience in the culture wars—he had become a leading opponent of abortion—had soured him on imagining that an abstract notion of civil religion was viable. Instead he advocated a Catholic version of public culture. In essays just prior to 2001, Neuhaus asserted a stark ideological contrast: on the one side were those who believed in moral truth—the idea of good and evil; on the other side were those who rejected truth as a normative term and instead constructed ethics based on argument, with the most convincing argument carrying the moment. According to Neuhaus, "The Word of God, or the *logos* that is the ordering reason of all things, is incarnate in history and is the guarantee that the search for truth is not in vain." Instead of a Bellahesque civil religion, Neuhaus offered the Catholic concept of natural law. "This is not, as some claim, a formula for theocracy," Neuhaus explained. "It is an exercise of democratic authority through republican or representative means by which the people place a check upon their own power by designating the higher authority to which they hold themselves accountable."[29]

Neuhaus was not a neocon, per se, but a theocon who like Bush and other conservatives saw an opportunity in 9/11 to reorient the nation.[30] He wrote a few days after the attacks that the crisis would "inaugurate a time of national unity and sobriety in a society that has been obsessed by fake pluralism while on a long and hedonistic holiday from history." A few days later, *First Things* issued a remarkably strong editorial, making clear that it too pined for the moral clarity that so many presumed had reigned in early times and that had to return to snap Americans back to reality. "This is war," Neuhaus and the editors thumped. After all, terrorists had struck a few blocks from where Neuhaus preached, an act that had to provide moral clarity to a world now at war. In Bush's speech at the National Cathedral, the editors saw resoluteness, not hubris. From those who criticized the speech *First Things* demanded:

> Let them make the case that between freedom and fear, between justice and cruelty, God *is* neutral. . . . Assured as we are and must be of the rightness of our cause, the President submits that cause in prayer to a higher authority. In a time of grave testing, America has once again given public expression to the belief that we are "one nation under God"—meaning that we are under both His protection and His judgment. That is not national hubris. Confidence that we are under His protection is faith; awareness that we are under His judgment is humility.

In short, the editors declared Bush's undeclared war a just war. "It is, if just, a positive duty, the doing of which, while it may entail much suffering, is to be counted as a good." However, the editors did offer a caveat: "Not immediately, but in due course, we need a clear statement on how we will know that the war is over and a just peace is reasonably secured."[31]

Neuhaus and his colleagues at *First Things* had made a similar argument in regard to the Gulf War. In the intervening years, though, Neuhaus had seemingly grown more strident not only in his war talk but in his tolerance of dissenters. The editors allowed that "because we are a democracy, we will tolerate a large measure of dissent from our national purpose in this war—some of it honorable, much of it contemptible." The morally debilitated professoriate, the editors believed, "test the patience of ordinary Americans who view reality from the moral pinnacle of common sense, but so far Americans have passed the test and they will likely continue to do so."[32]

"Nonviolent resistance" the editors argued, was "implausible" and the tactics that following from it were "not idealistic" but "dumb." To *First Things* the stakes and terms of the war were clear: "Those who in principle oppose the use of military force have no legitimate part in the discussion about how military force should be used. They only make themselves and their cause appear frivolous by claiming that military force is immoral and futile, and, at the same time, wanting to have a political say in how such force is to be employed. The morally serious choice is between pacifism and just war. Here, too, sides must be taken."

The religiosity that followed the attacks revealed yet again, according to a position struck by Neuhaus and other theocons, that the United States was not a secularized nation but a religious people—that was the real state of America. In terms that even Bush was careful to avoid, Neuhaus's journal decided that 9/11 had revealed a religious war. That struggle had come to define part of the culture wars, but the terrorist attacks allowed it to go global. "Today many in the West are asking, Who are they? We cannot ask Who are they? Without also asking Who are we?" the editors contended. "More and more, as this war continues, we may come to recognize that we are, however ambiguously, who they think we are, namely, the Christian West."[33]

Hauerwas was furious, but not surprised. As a member of the editorial board of *First Things* and a theologian as substantial as Neuhaus, Hauerwas believed the vigorous embrace of war and equally vigorous denunciation of pacifism had been directed at him. In a long letter printed by the journal, he wrote bluntly, "Silenced. I have been silenced and I find it tempting to accept being silenced." But silent he would not remain. "For me to remain silent cannot help but suggest I accept the position taken in '[Religion] in a Time of War,' when the exact opposite is the case."[34]

Much as in the debate during the Gulf War, Neuhaus and the theocons once again used Niebuhr's break with pacifism in the 1930s as a way to determine a valid response to the terrorist attacks. While substantial issues existed over how to apply the idea of nonviolent resistance and just-war theory to September 11, the issue that loomed over this spat was not how Niebuhr had responded to Nazis in World War II. Rather, still at stake was the application of the word *we*. Hauerwas wrote, "I fear the 'we' [in]'[Religion] in a Time of War' is the American 'we.'" Indeed, according to Hauerwas, the issue was whether 9/11 and the war that followed from it had turned everyone into a one-dimensional American. "The refusal to recognize that Christians are Americans," the editors of *First Things* stated, "is an attempt to avoid our duty." To this notion, Hauerwas expressed his utter frustration: "I simply cannot comprehend the Editor's celebration of the new patriotism occasioned by September 11." Hauerwas did not believe patriotism had much to do with the question of war; at least it should not be an issue if one was a Christian. Thus, as a Christian who lived in the United States, Hauerwas did not believe that his passport determined how he expressed his faith. In short, for Hauerwas the nature and destiny of America were irrelevant to the truth of Christ crucified.[35]

Now Hauerwas had to battle not merely catastrophes such as war but the way an alternative faith—an American civil religion—had effectively replaced the Christian church in its response to war. While he rejected civil religion as unnecessary (Americans had plenty of faiths to choose from), he observed, "What a horror it would be if the nation is morally to be renewed by war. Surely a nation capable of fighting a just war must be one that does not need to find its moral substance through war." Through his argument, Hauerwas raised a question that had haunted Americans at least since the time of Lincoln: "Is the American response to September 11 a confirmation of Hegel's suggestion that bourgeois states periodically need to be renewed through war?"[36]

First Things shot back: "We do not as a society 'need to be renewed through war,'" the editors declared, "but the readiness to do our duty in response to great injustice may entail a measure of moral renewal." In the end, the editors recognized that this war was just in part because it had an effect on the soul of their nation—such an effect, the editors hoped, that the sickness they had identified while fighting the culture wars would be overcome. This was a war fought to renew American civil religion. Hauerwas was correct: when *First Things* used the word *we*, it meant Americans, not Christians.[37]

The moment Bush and Neuhaus both exclaimed, "We are at war," Hauerwas signaled the nation's loss of moral credibility. That declaration became "magic words to reclaim the everyday. . . . We are frightened, and ironically war makes us feel safe." But those words also transformed the nation from one in which people mourned victims while at peace to one that was at war seeking revenge for heroes. Hauerwas put it bluntly: "The flag that flew in mourning was soon transformed into a pride-filled thing; the bloodstained flag of victims [was] transformed into the flag of the American indomitable spirit."[38] September 11 invigorated a flagging civil religion: through war, as Bellah suggested, Americans understood the transcendent meaning of their nation.

Hauerwas understood this well and reflected on his need to change how he behaved in public. After the attacks and the national transformation, Hauerwas stopped singing "The Star-Spangled Banner."

He stood when it was played at baseball games, but would not sing—
"a small thing that reminds me that my first loyalty is not to the United
States but to God and God's church." Hauerwas's response reflected
a combination of elements that cut across the debate over war and
nation in America since 1945. As a child growing up in Texas, Hauerwas
had a working-class father who physically embodied the American
dream. Then Vietnam came, and Hauerwas recalled while he and his
colleagues were critical of the war, they did not think their opposition
made them other than American. "Indeed the criticisms of the war were
based on an appeal to the highest American ideals." In the aftermath of
9/11 and in reference to the critics who spoke out against the war in
Afghanistan, Hauerwas said, "I do not even share their allegiance to
American ideals."[39]

"Where does that leave me?" he asked. "Do I forsake all forms of
patriotism, failing to acknowledge that we as a people are better off
because of sacrifices that were made in World War II? To this I can only
answer 'Yes.' If you call patriotism 'natural,' I certainly do disavow that
connection." Did that make him ungrateful for being an American?
Hauerwas took care to explain that he was not anti-American; rather, he
rejected patriotism not because it was a popular position to take up but
because it was the only position seen as legitimate. In a time of war,
Hauerwas saw clearly the pull civil religion could have not merely on
Americans but on all those who, by the very nature of their other beliefs,
had to have other options for faith. "Indeed," Hauerwas wrote, "I fear
that absent a countercommunity to challenge America, [Osama] bin
Laden has given Americans what they so desperately needed—a war
without end."[40]

Unlike other critics of American foreign policy and war who saw
Bush simply expanding a paradigm of American exceptionalism or manifest destiny, Hauerwas understood that the significance of war for the
United States was in the understanding Americans had of their own
nation. As had been seen in the Vietnam War, Americans could turn
against the actions of their nation, but they found it more difficult to
imagine a position with enough distance to be critical of the nation as an
idea. That was why Vietnam led, rather quickly, to a rededication to
civil religion as a way to salvage what has always been the last best hope
not for the world but for Americans.

For Hauerwas, 9/11 sparked another episode of war in a period that, since World War II, has consistently found moral sustenance in wars. "War names the time we send the youth to kill and die (maybe) in an effort to assure ourselves the lives we lead are worthy of such sacrifices. . . . War makes clear we must believe in something even if we are not sure what that something is, except that is has something to do with the 'American way of life.'" Moreover, 9/11 had revealed that unlike his colleagues at *First Things* Hauerwas did not emerge out of the culture wars in search of a real war. For him, moral clarity and truth had undoubtedly been affected by postmodernism and the "soap opera of Bill Clinton," but war was not the best way to return to reality; it was a flight from faith. Ironically, during the culture wars, Hauerwas shared with Neuhaus and others the conviction that postmodern America had failed to understand the truth of a Christian faith; in the post-9/11 world, that same faith had become the opponent of an American civil religion that Neuhaus and others believed transcended the sectarianism of Hauerwas's Christianity. Hauerwas believed that Neuhaus and his allies in this debate were playing a dangerous game.[41] Was he right?

If it was a dangerous game, Neuhaus and *First Things* were far from the only ones playing it. In February 2002, a bold open letter "from America" appeared in major periodicals and newspapers around the world under the heading, "What We're Fighting For." Written mostly by Jean Bethke Elshtain, a highly regarded scholar of social ethics at the University of Chicago, the statement was signed by a variety of intellectuals who came from think tanks and academia and who, it seemed, were joined more by where they stood in the recent culture wars than by how they voted in presidential elections or even how they viewed war. Elshtain made clear that 9/11 forced Americans to address what she and others believed were fundamental and unresolved issues from the decade just past. She made clear that because there was no argument over the justness of the attacks on September 11, the question thus became one of response—in other words, what would Americans be fighting for. They would not be fighting for all things that America had become, Elshtain acknowledged. For this group of intellectuals, at least, "some values sometimes seen in America are unattractive and harmful." She pointed to consumerism, unfettered freedom, and "the notion of the individual as self-made and utterly sovereign, owing little to others or to society."

This group also believed that 9/11 would reinvigorate the ethic of sacrifice and, through it, a new moral unity would emerge. In the aftermath
of 9/11, America would awaken to its core values and dispense with
both the postmodernist confusion of the 1990s and the terrorism that
plagued the modern world.[42] But how?

Behind the war lay a set of assumptions that was pure civil religion.
Elshtain argued that Americans fought for the dignity of all human
beings; that the only legitimate government was one that protected
"universal moral truths" accessible to all people; that in pursuit of guar-
anteeing these "universal truths" all people had a right to offer "reasonable arguments in pursuit of truth"; that religion was a legitimate form of
argument for pursuing truth; and that "killing in the name of God is
contrary to faith in God and is the greatest betrayal of the universality of
religious faith." However, killing in the name of the nation would not
constitute a betrayal of these basic assumptions but would be an expression of the right to "defend ourselves and to defend . . . universal principles." Elshtain anticipated attacks from her adversaries in the culture
wars and so added, "Some people assert that these values are not universal at all, but instead derive particularly from Western, largely Christian
civilization." Elshtain waved away such notions, writing, "We believe
that certain basic moral truths are recognizable everywhere in the
world." And those truths would be fought for and would triumph in
the wars launched after 9/11. "As Americans in a time of war and global
crisis, we are . . . suggesting that the *best* of what we too casually call
'American values' do not belong only to America, but are in fact the
shared inheritance of humankind, and therefore a possible basis of hope
for a world community based on peace and justice." The period begun
by the attacks on September 11 would internationalize American civil
religion just as Clinton had envisioned but, as Elshtain and other opponents to Clinton would have pointed out, in the "right way" this time.[43]

Elshtain followed this section on the defense and projection of
American values with a section on how the nation might remain right in
a moral sense while employing tactics that would have grave moral
implications. To do this, Elshtain referred to the ageless idea that the
United States would find its way through war because it would fight
as one nation under God's judgment. Even though the signatories of
this statement did not all share a common church or religion, they did,

according to Elshtain, believe that religion mattered. They all shared the sociological view that around the world religion both unified and divided people. But they also seemed to believe together that the United States had gotten the role of religion about right because America sought "to be a society in which faith and freedom can go together, each evaluating the other." The popular expression of this combination was, Elshtain suggested, a diverse population of religious and nonbelievers all reciting as one citizenry "a Pledge of Allegiance to 'one nation, under God.'" Yet again, intellectuals used a civil religious argument as a touchstone for an American genius that couples reason and faith to produce a society free of tyranny but beholden to a higher judgment. As Elshtain explained, "Politically, our separation of church and state seeks to keep politics within its proper sphere, in part by limiting the state's power to control religion, and in part by causing government itself to draw legitimacy from, and operate under, a larger moral canopy that is not of its own making."[44]

Using such logic, Elshtain moved from suggesting how Americans understood national morality to explaining how they would preserve that position even in war. Not surprisingly, Elshtain placed her faith in an American ability to apply correctly the principles of just war. Regarded as an expert on just-war theory, the University of Chicago professor contended that "the primary moral justification for war is to protect the innocent from certain harm." However, because 9/11 necessitated an unconventional response, Elshtain argued that a broader tradition of just war could be employed. That application included the legitimate use of force by the U.S. government not merely to protect its citizens, many of whom were believers in religions that did not permit them individually to support such force, but also to protect people around the world who were threatened by a force that was the same as or similar to the force that endangered Americans. "If one has compelling evidence that innocent people who are in no position to protect themselves will be grievously harmed unless coercive force is used to stop an aggressor," then, Elshtain concluded, "the moral principle of love of neighbor calls us to the use of force."[45]

In June 2002, Bush signaled his intention to shift America's focus from one "neighborhood" to another; from Afghanistan to Iraq. He traveled to the U.S. Military Academy at West Point to deliver the commencement address. Bush saw the young cadets as an audience to whom he could speak about the moral value of war and sacrifice. By mid-2002, the war in Afghanistan had succeeded in toppling the Taliban, but the Americans had failed to capture the primary target, bin Laden. Apparently undeterred by that unfulfilled promise, Bush told the young cadets that they had a new mission to accomplish. "We will defend the peace against threats from terrorists and tyrants. . . . And we will extend the peace by encouraging free and open societies on every continent." The war against terrorists was about to get bigger and bolder.[46]

In a line that was repeated in the president's ambitious 2002 National Security Strategy, he contended that "the gravest danger to freedom lies at the perilous crossroads of radicalism and technology." That description certainly fit the hijacking of airliners for use as ballistic missiles. But Bush made clear that an even more grave and perhaps pressing threat came from "tyrants who solemnly sign nonproliferation treaties and then systematically break them." He called on Americans to maintain the kind of "moral resolve" they showed during the Cold War under leaders such as John F. Kennedy and Reagan. These presidents had not coddled tyrants; "they gave hope to prisoners and dissidents and exiles and rallied free nations to a great cause."[47]

If the American operation in Afghanistan had been a disaster, as some had predicted, then Bush's speeches in the summer of 2002 might have been considerably different. But Afghanistan was initially a success. Peter Beinart noted in his book on the period, "From a standing start, America had gone to war in a forbidding, landlocked country half a world away, a legendary graveyard of empire that had brought the mighty U.S.S.R. to its knees."[48] The cost of toppling the Taliban had been less than two billion dollars with few American casualties. Such success, though, had significant ideological and moral implications. The approval rating of the president and his administration soared; popular faith in the military reached a new post-Vietnam high point; and critics of Bush and his team were sent reeling, opening a vacuum of power. The combination of national unity after 9/11 and a successful military mission against its perpetrators made it seem reasonable that America could move history in a direction to its liking. At least Bush saw things this way. He ended his introduction to the 2002 National Security

Strategy with a statement that expressed a confidence born of the nation's recent experience in Afghanistan: "Freedom is the non-negotiable demand of human dignity; the birthright of every person—in every civilization. Throughout history, freedom has been threatened by war and terror; it has been challenged by the clashing wills of powerful states and the evil designs of tyrants; and it has been tested by widespread poverty and disease. Today, humanity holds in its hands the opportunity to further freedom's triumph over all the foes. The United States welcomes our responsibility to lead in this great mission."[49] With this heady mix of success, faith, and military might, Bush and his closest advisors looked at the Persian Gulf and began to imagine the new world order that had eluded both his father and Clinton.

In October 2002, Bush traveled to Cincinnati, Ohio—a stronghold for him politically—to deliver an unusually long and detailed speech on the next great threat—Iraq. "We resolved [on September 11] and we are resolved today to confront every threat, from any source, that could bring sudden terror and suffering to America." He quoted from a U.N. report that concluded that "Saddam Hussein is a homicidal dictator who is addicted to weapons of mass destruction." And, therefore, Bush added, "the danger [he poses] is already significant, and it only grows worse with time." Bush spent considerable time constructing the proposition that because both Al-Qaeda and Saddam were enemies of the United States and both had killed Americans, they had a relationship dedicated to harming Americans in the future. "We have seen that those who hate America are willing to crash airplanes into buildings full of innocent people. Our enemies would be no less willing—in fact, they would be eager—to use a biological or chemical or nuclear weapon." Bush argued that Iraq hoped to and probably already did possess such "weapons of mass destruction," and thus it was only a matter of time before those weapons were used by unknown terrorists to strike at the United States. "The time for denying, deceiving, and delaying has come to an end," Bush declared in a typical rhetorical moment. "Saddam Hussein must disarm himself, or for the sake of peace, we will lead a coalition to disarm him." "I am not willing to stake one American life," Bush barked, "on trusting Saddam Hussein." A future that Saddam contributed to was a future of fear, Bush said. "That is not the America I know. That is not the America I serve. We refuse to live in fear," he declared. "This Nation, in World War and in cold war, has never permitted the brutal and lawless to set history's course. Now as before, we will secure our Nation, protect our freedom, and help others to find freedom of their own."[50] It was a Herculean task that Bush proposed, and it had all the makings of a Greek tragedy.

On March 19, 2003, Bush began an American campaign to set a new course. In an address that lasted a little over four minutes, the president announced in a clear, calm tone that the American military had begun a campaign to "disarm Iraq, to free its people, and to defend the world from grave danger." Bush said that this mission was joined by a coalition of thirty-five nations, all sharing "the honor of serving in our common defense." That latter comment reflected the unparalleled unity that existed immediately after the September 11 attacks throughout the world and that had, for the most part, persisted through the early stages of the war in Afghanistan. The world had joined the United States in its grief and had supported America in its act to avenge the 9/11 attacks. Certainly there had never been a moment during which the world seemed to validate America as an idea more than in the months following September 11. Bush hoped to extend that support to another act, not to avenge an attack but, as he said, to meet a "threat now with our Army, Air Force, Navy, Coast Guard, and Marines, so that we do not have to meet it later with armies of firefighters and police and doctors on the streets of our cities." But he also clearly understood that this mission depended on the American military. On the shoulders of the soldiers, he said, was "the peace of a troubled world and the hopes of an oppressed people." And he believed that such "trust is well-placed." "The enemies you confront will come to know skill and bravery. The people you liberate will witness the honorable and decent spirit of the American military."[51]

Bush placed an enormous burden on America's military when he asked it to invade and liberate Iraq less than two years after the war in Afghanistan had begun. Two wars for the defense of America; two wars to expand Bush's vision of freedom; two wars that had the potential for unparalleled achievement and untold disaster. The confidence that Bush possessed during the period from September 2001 through the first half of 2003 was an expression of faith in the nation. That kind of faith had existed throughout American history but rarely had been advanced by military force; it had not been during the postwar era. Bush's self-confidence belied his civil religion; he imagined because he led a nation under the judgment of a God that he understood, he had an obligation to drive that nation toward extraordinary accomplishments.

What was the source of Bush's confident civil religion? Bruce Bartlett, an old Republican hand from the administrations of Reagan and George H. W. Bush, told Ron Suskind in 2004 that Bush "truly believes he's on a mission from God. Absolute faith like that overwhelms a need for analysis. The whole thing about faith," Bartlett said, "is to believe things for which there is no empirical evidence." That characterization—echoed by many who heard Bush expound his vision around that time—missed a crucial distinction. There are plenty of things we believe in without the support of empirical evidence—love, freedom, hope. These ideas move history just as surely as armies do. So it was not Bush's faith in the unseen or the seemingly impossible that led him to invade Iraq. Moreover, Bush's confidence in himself and the nation was not necessarily unique either. Cockiness and self-assuredness have been a trademark of leaders throughout time, American presidents included. Suskind came close to capturing the essence of Bush's civil religion when he argued that what made Bush different from other American presidents was his belief "in the power of confidence." "At a time when constituents are uneasy and enemies are probing for weaknesses," Suskind argued, "he clearly feels that unflinching confidence has an almost mystical power. It can all but create reality." Indeed, Suskind related a remarkable insight from a senior advisor to Bush: "We're an empire now, and when we act, we create our own reality," he told Suskind. "And while you're studying that reality . . . we'll act again, creating other new realities, which you can study too, and that's how things will sort out. We're history's actors," the aide said in true Bush fashion, "and you, all of you, will be left to just study what we do." Reflecting on such wisdom, Suskind concluded that this comment got "to the very heart of the Bush presidency."[52]

The heart of the Bush presidency was that the president had the confidence to believe that he was history's most powerful actor and that he had the ability to understand and advance the plan of history's God. "The life of the nation and the life of Bush effortlessly merge," Suskind observed; "his fortitude, even in the face of doubters, is that of the nation; his ordinariness, like theirs, is heroic; his resolve, to whatever end, will turn the wheel of history." There were a number of ways to turn the wheel of history. Bush's combination of vision, confidence, and faith might have been channeled toward solving the endemic problem of poverty, as it seemed might be his intention in his original campaign for president. But because he presided over a nation under attack, the civil religion that Bush employed was not the self-reflective type offered by Martin Luther King Jr. nor the ironic civil theology of Niebuhr, but an absolutist moral theology of the nation. It was a civil religion of America defined by war.[53]

Like other Americans, Bush had religious faith, which could have countered or critiqued American civil religion. But his religious faith, also like that of many Americans, was not important to understanding the nation. The way Bush's religious faith operated in relation to his civil religion was significant.

Famously, Bush had a born-again experience at the age of forty, during which he was shepherded by Graham from his father's mainline Episcopal faith to the Methodist Church. He paid tribute to this transition by entitling his campaign biography *A Charge to Keep* after a popular religious hymn from Methodist Charles Wesley. The lyrics of the hymn are important for the insight they provide into Bush:

> A Charge to keep I have,
> A God to glorify,
> A never dying soul to save,
> And fit it for the sky.
> To serve the present age,
> My calling to fulfill;
> O may it all my powers engage
> To do my Master's Will!

Such thought brought together a confidence that God's will would be done, and that will, while unknown in specific terms, would be carried out only by those who, like Bush, gave themselves over to God as an agent. Thus, Bush's acceptance of God as a guide in his life was not metaphorical but historical: while we cannot know what history will create, we can know, if we believe, that God still has expectations for us.

In his 2003 State of the Union address, Bush pronounced this philosophy as a way, yet again, to turn what was a war against terror into a
larger war against moral laxity in America. In the concluding section of
his address, the section that was meant to be soaring and lasting, Bush
asserted, "In two years, America has gone from a sense of invulnerability
to an awareness of peril, from bitter division in small matters to calm
unity in great causes." The culture wars were, as many neocons had
argued, a vacation from history. History had returned, Bush declared.
"And we go forward with confidence, because this call of history has
come to the right country." He knew America was the "right" country
because he had a chance to make it so. Bush believed he had a mandate
from heaven, not in some abstract sense, but out of experience. The war
on terror had a purpose to Bush beyond national security, a purpose that
accorded with Bellah's understanding of civil religion. "Americans are a
resolute people who have risen to every test of our time. Adversity has
revealed the character of our country, to the world and to ourselves.
America is a strong nation and honorable in the use of our strength. We
exercise power without conquest, and we sacrifice for the liberty of
strangers." In short, this was the moment to create a civil religion that
reached out to all the world. "Americans are a free people who know
that freedom is the right of every person and the future of every nation.
The liberty we prize is not America's gift to the world; it is God's gift to
humanity." "We Americans have faith in ourselves, but not in ourselves
alone," Bush explained. "We do not know—we do not claim to know
all the ways of providence, yet we can trust in them, placing our confidence in the loving God behind all of life and all of history." The
president delivered this address less than two months before the start of
the Iraq War. He concluded by asking for God's assistance: "May He
guide us now. And may God continue to bless the United States of
America."[54] William Abraham, a professor of Wesley studies, concluded
that such pronouncements illustrated "the liberationist, emancipatory
side of [Bush's] theology in full song. . . . He insists that moral and
anthropological principles are at stake as well as American domestic and
security interests. It is not accidental that some have referred to his
theology as a version of liberation theology, even as they despise his policies and actions."[55] Indeed, the power of Bush's civil religion seemed to
leave little room for any other faith to counter his interpretation of

history and God's role in it. As Jim Wallis pointed out bluntly around that time, "American Christians will have to make some difficult choices. Will we stand in solidarity with the worldwide church, the international body of Christ—or with our own American government?"[56]

In 2003, most religious Americans appeared to stand with Bush. Mark O'Keefe reported in the *Christian Century* in May 2003 that "opinion polls showed that the spiritual movement opposing the U.S.-led invasion of Iraq had little impact on churchgoers, much less on the American public—both overwhelmingly support both the war and President Bush." O'Keefe cited a Gallup poll that showed two out of every three Americans who attended church at least weekly supporting the war. A Pew study registered 62 percent of Catholics and an equal number of Protestants supporting the war, and 77 percent of evangelical Christians behind the war effort. Thus, O'Keefe noted that while "leaders of mainline Protestant denominations, including the Episcopal, Evangelical, Lutheran, and United Methodist churches, opposed war, and Pope John Paul II worked passionately against it . . . the flocks disagreed with their shepherds."[57]

A few of those shepherds, though, were also divided. Again, the conservatives at *First Things* lent their support to Bush's mission. In his first essay on the justness of the war in Iraq, Neuhaus understood that his view placed him in a minority among Catholic intellectuals. He offered, as he said, no essentialist defense of the United States nor of war, but tried only "to contribute a measure of moral clarity in a time of great confusion." During the first years of the George W. Bush administration, he reached his apex of political power as an informal advisor to the president on matters of morality. Accordingly, he pronounced that, as "a theologian and moralist, [I] had no special competence to assess the threat posed by Iraq. On the basis of the available evidence and my considered confidence in those responsible for making relevant decisions, I was inclined," Neuhaus explained, "to believe and I earnestly prayed that they would do the right thing."[58]

William Cavanaugh, a student of Hauerwas's in the 1980s, offered a scathing rebuttal to Neuhaus's moral clarity regarding the Iraq War. Writing in the Catholic journal *Commonweal*, Cavanaugh argued, "Moral judgment in the Christian tradition is primarily a matter not of information, but of being formed in the virtues proper to a disciple of

Christ. There is no reason to assume that the leaders of a secular nation-state are so formed, nor that the principles guiding the Christian moral life are at the heart of American foreign policy. War planners are always going to think their wars are justified. There is also no guarantee, to put it mildly, that moral considerations will trump those of narrowly defined national interest and corporate profit when the foreign policy establishment creates its agenda. The notion that we should hand over responsibility for judging the justice of war to the president on the basis of his superior access to information is profoundly undemocratic."[59]

The next year, in the same journal, Peter Dula put the stakes in the game Neuhaus and others were playing more bluntly: "If they have been wrong, especially theologically wrong about the justice of this war, it should matter to those who share [George] Weigel and Neuhaus's belief that religion should play a major role in the public square." Indeed, the civil religious debate over Iraq had the potential to be a "game changer" in the culture wars. September 11 seemed to give the upper hand to Bush and those who supported his configuration of moral authority. But what if the wars that followed from 9/11 went badly. What would happen then to moral authority?[60]

In the immediate wake of the invasion of Iraq, Bush stood almost as high in the polls as he did in the immediate aftermath of the September 11 attacks. He was so emboldened that on May 1, 2003, he made a remarkable visit to the *Abraham Lincoln*, an aircraft carrier off the coast of San Diego, to announce that in Iraq it was "mission accomplished." Bush wore a fighter-pilot suit and flashed a "thumbs-up" as he strode away from his plane. He announced that major combat operations in Iraq were over and that America and its allies were now "engaged in securing and reconstructing that country." Following that announcement, Bush swiftly returned to the moral justification for the invasion: "In this battle, we have fought for the cause of liberty and for the peace of the world," he reminded his audience. "Our Nation and our coalition are proud of this accomplishment; yet it is you, the members of the United States military, who achieved it. Your courage, your willingness to face danger for your country and for each other, made this day possible. Because of you, our Nation is more secure. Because of you, the tyrant has fallen, and Iraq is free."[61] Bush was smart to praise the military. At the time, polls illustrated an astonishing popularity for the military among Americans. In those same polls, Bush was usually a distant second. War had made civil religion incarnate for Bush; and he believed that history and history's "author" had smiled on the United States. And then history turned.

By August 2003, the war had grown increasingly sectarian and began to appear unmanageable for U.S. troops and American leaders in Iraq. Not surprisingly, as the images and reports of the war darkened, public perceptions of the war darkened too. By early September, polls showed that less than 50 percent of Americans polled approved of the way Bush was conducting the war in Iraq. That number would hover around 50 percent for the next three months before dropping precipitously.[62]

By 2004, reality began to mock Bush's view of history. His declaration aboard the *Abraham Lincoln* was supposed to be the beginning of a new moment in history—a moment in which American military might carried forward by American soldiers would liberate a nation from a tyrant and affirm a sacred mission for America itself. But those soldiers began to die in increasing numbers as 2003 dragged on into 2004. And in March 2004 media reports revealed that American soldiers had tortured captured Iraqis at Abu Ghraib, a notorious prison under Saddam that had been resurrected by the American military. Mission accomplished had turned into mission forsaken.

The Abu Ghraib scandal broke when two media outlets—*60 Minutes II* and the *New Yorker*—ran reports on an internal military investigation into the torture and abuse of detainees in the American-run prison. Both reports included photographs and accounts of military police, intelligence officers, and military contractors forcing Iraqis under their control to submit to horrific, painful, and utterly degrading acts. Among the photographs was one that became canonical of a man, hooded, forced to stand on a box holding wires in his outstretched arms; he was told that if let go of the wires he would be electrocuted. Responses to these revelations circulated throughout the world's media in the spring and summer of 2004. Bush was asked to account for the torture of detainees in a number of interviews that he gave to foreign and American reporters. In a lengthy interview with *Al-Ahram* on May 6, 2004, just a few days after the stories broke, Bush offered what became his stock reply to questions about Abu Ghraib. He told the reporter that he had not seen pictures from the prison until they were aired by CBS.

He intimated, though, that he was aware of an investigation into the "abuse" of detainees. Bush did not and would not call what happened at Abu Ghraib torture. He did apologize and promised a "full" investigation that would be "transparent." Bush argued that under a "dictatorship" if there were torture "we would never know the truth. In a democracy, you'll know the truth, and justice will be done." Bush was adamant about telling the Arab world, in particular, that "we reject this kind of treatment of people. It's abhorrent, and it's not America. . . . This is not our country."[63]

At the same moment that Bush was beginning to lose control of the perception of the mission in Iraq, his administration's people in Baghdad were losing control of Iraq. The reporter from Al-Ahram who was interviewing the president cited a poll taken of Iraqis at that time in which 71 percent regarded the United States as an occupying power and not, as Bush had once championed, the liberator of Iraq. "People don't really understand our intentions," he acknowledged. "Obviously, our reputation has been damaged severely by the terrible and horrible acts, inhuman acts that were conducted on Iraqi prisoners." The president attempted to apologize: "Today I can't tell you how sorry I am to them and their families for the humiliation." But he added that he was also sorry "because people are then able to say, 'Look how terrible America is.' But this isn't America. That's not—Americans are appalled at what happened. We're a generous people. I don't think people understand that, so I've got to do a better job of explaining to people that we're for a lot of things that most people who live in the Middle East want."[64]

While many people were appalled by the revelations of Abu Ghraib, a few, like Susan Sontag, fused their outrage with a searing critique of Bush's dangerous confidence. Sontag had leveled a devastating critique of Bush's initial response to 9/11—a critique that, like her response to Abu Ghraib, was met with a cacophony of denunciations of her as anti-American. Sontag was indeed anti-something, but she didn't need to be simplistically anti-American to make a point about the dangers of Abu Ghraib. "The torture of prisoners is not an aberration," Sontag observed. "It is a direct consequence of the with-us-or-against-us doctrines of world struggle with which the Bush administration has sought to change, change radically, the international stance of the United States, and to recast many domestic institutions and prerogatives. The Bush administration," she feared, "has committed the country to a pseudo-religious doctrine of war, endless war." Abu Ghraib was a grotesque expression of a perverted national faith. "Shock and awe were what our military promised the Iraqis. And shock and awful are what these photographs announce to the world that the Americans have delivered." What made Sontag's essay an extension of her early view of 9/11 was the way in which American public culture didn't just absorb Bush's view but enabled it. "What is illustrated . . . by these photographs," Sontag believed, "is as much the culture of shamelessness as the reigning admiration for unapologetic brutality." In this sense, the mourning of the nation was all of one piece with Bush's sacralizing of the nation; the torture of Iraqis was consonant with the general degrading of American culture. In short, Americans were apparently incapable of seeing moral limits. "The issue is not whether a majority or a minority of Americans performs such acts but whether the nature of the policies prosecuted by this administration and the hierarchies deployed to carry them out make such acts likely." The question was not how was it possible for America to commit such crimes, but whether people were surprised. "To acknowledge that Americans torture their prisoners," Sontag asserted, "would contradict everything this administration has invited the public to believe about the virtue of American intention and America's right, flowing from that virtue, to undertake unilateral action on the world stage."[65] While it was true that Abu Ghraib undermined American standing abroad, the more pressing concern for Bush—and the American public in general—was what this scandal said about the claim to America's moral authority. In other words, would Iraq undo what Vietnam had not? Would Bush witness the final deconstruction of postwar American civil religion?

If a moral reckoning regarding Bush's civil religion was to come, the presidential election in 2004 presented an opportunity. Throughout most of 2004, polls showed Bush and his challenger, Senator John Kerry of Massachusetts, running in an almost dead heat. Bush's approval ratings hovered around 50 percent, which was quite a fall from the 92 percent rating a week after 9/11 and the 77 percent rating in the month following the invasion of Iraq. However, Kerry's poll numbers rarely pushed much higher than 50 percent throughout 2004, and he simply didn't offer much of an alternative to Bush other than to suggest that he wasn't Bush. During 2004, in the many opinion polls taken about a variety of issues, there was general consistency regarding whom the public trusted and why. While Bush's approval ratings dipped below 50 percent at times, satisfaction with the nation itself also dipped below 50 percent. However, in other polls, public dissatisfaction appeared focused on domestic issues rather than international actions. Public opinion on the war in Iraq also stood around the 50 percent mark as did trust in the government to handle the war itself. There was an institution, though, that consistently polled strongly in 2004 despite setbacks and abject failures— the military. Americans continued to regard quite highly the military as an institution, especially when compared to almost any other institution (other than small businesses). And when polled about the specific situation of Abu Ghraib, Americans were quite conflicted. Americans believed both that Bush handled the situation well and that he was covering up the details of the scandal; Americans blamed the military leaders in Washington and the specific personnel charged with crimes, but they still looked up to the military as an institution. And throughout 2004 most Americans believed that what happened at Abu Ghraib should not have been considered torture, only abuse. On that issue, they agreed with their president.[66]

And so did John Kerry. In the presidential debate that focused on foreign affairs, Kerry did not once mention Abu Ghraib or suggest that the American mission in Iraq was immoral or even wrong. He did state that "winning the peace" in Iraq was an imperative. "We have to succeed. We can't leave a failed Iraq," he told moderator Jim Lehrer. "But that doesn't mean it wasn't a mistake of judgment to go there and take the focus off of Osama bin Laden. It was. . . . I think we need a president who has the credibility to bring the allies back to the table and to do what's necessary to make it so America isn't doing this alone." Bush shot back with a response he used a number of times throughout the ninety-minute debate: Kerry had been among the senators who gave the administration the authority to invade Iraq. "What my opponent wants you to forget is that he voted to authorize the use of force and now says it's the wrong war at the wrong time at the wrong place. I don't see how you can lead this country to succeed in Iraq if you say wrong war, wrong time, wrong place," Bush remarked. "What message does that send our troops? What message does that send to our allies? What message does that send the Iraqis?"[67]

Bush had, somewhat inelegantly, pointed out the basic problem with Kerry's position: the senator could criticize the president but couldn't go after the role the troops or the nation had played in creating the developing debacle in Iraq. As a highly decorated naval officer who fought in the Vietnam War, Kerry could speak with authority on military issues and combat experience. But because of that experience he was also painted as a disenchanted veteran who saw foreign policy through the lens of an era that Bush and his administration had hoped to dispel once and for all. Many Americans apparently shared Bush's hope. Even as the war in Iraq grew increasingly unpopular, most Americans continued to regard abstract notions about their nation—that it was dedicated to freedom and individual rights—as sacrosanct and to support unconditionally the idea that the troops defended such ideals with an impressive selflessness. Other than the troops, who else in the United States was willing to offer the ultimate sacrifice for the nation? Bush had a simple message in his debate with Kerry regarding the war: if one opposed the war, then one also opposed the troops. In the popular remembrance of the Vietnam War, in which Americans gave up on the troops when they gave up on the war, Bush offered the opposite pledge: he wouldn't give up on the troops because he believed in their mission to "win" the war in Iraq. In this instance, Kerry's military service did not serve him well.

Bush won his second presidential race by yet another narrow margin. As in the 2000 election, one state proved decisive in his victory—in 2004 it was Ohio. Yet in this election, unlike his first election, the cause of division was Bush as much as the culture wars. The president had grown less popular with Americans, and the mission in Iraq had become a drag on his ability to frame a moral vision for the nation. Bush's ability to use the war on terror as an ideological construct that could keep the culture wars at bay had become tenuous. But in his second inaugural address Bush hoped to reclaim the moral authority that had defined his first two years in office.

On a clear, cold day, Bush, with noticeably more gray hair than he had four years before, began his speech with a reference to both the culture wars—"years of sabbatical" he called them—and the terrorist attacks—"a day of fire." The problems with the American occupation in

Iraq had sorely tested the ideological validity of Bush's civil religion. And far from war advancing his cause, the two wars Bush had launched challenged his contention that history had a discernible arc and that America had a role to play in that history. History had played havoc with Bush's dreams. In his second inaugural, Bush made clear that forces beyond the United States moved history. "There is only one force of history that can break the reign of hatred and resentment and expose the pretensions of tyrants and reward the hopes of the decent and tolerant, and that is the force of human freedom." The United States had a decision to make, he said, either to move with the flow of history or to stand by and watch and wait for another attack. "The survival of liberty in our land," he declared, "increasingly depends on the success of liberty in other lands. The best hope of peace in the world is the expansion of freedom in all the world." In short, the United States was not exceptional, it did not stand outside history, its past was part of a history that Bush offered as the rationale for all his foreign ventures. "Advancing these ideals is the mission that created our Nation," Bush explained. "It is the honorable achievement of our fathers. Now, it is the urgent requirement of our Nation's security and the calling of our time."[68]

In early 2005, it had became hard, if not nearly impossible, to listen to Bush deliver this address and imagine that Iraq and even Afghanistan were not rather hopeless causes. And while the public had not completely given up hope, Bush had to do something to appeal to a deeper sense of mission than the one that resided in the trials of two faltering wars. The leap Bush made was to conflate his moment of history with the most profound experience in American history—the Civil War. Bush chose not dwell on the history of that conflict; that would have complicated his argument far too much. Rather he contended that the "ultimate goal [of the United States] was ending tyranny in our world." This was the "concentrated work of generations," he admitted, but it was also a legacy inherited from Lincoln, whom Bush quoted: "Those who deny freedom to others deserve it not for themselves and, under the rule of a just God, cannot long retain it." Thus, somewhat like Lincoln, who claimed that the American Civil War served to spark a new birth of freedom, Bush hoped to reimagine the short-term tragedies of two wars as a long-term struggle against tyranny.[69] "Today I also speak anew to my fellow citizens," Bush practically sang. "From all of you I have asked patience in the hard task of securing America, which you have granted in good measure. Our country has accepted obligations that are difficult to fulfill and would be dishonorable to abandon. Yet because we have acted in the great liberating tradition of this Nation, tens of millions have achieved their freedom. And as hope kindles hope, millions more will find it. By our efforts, we have lit a fire as well, a fire in the minds of men. It warms those who feel its power. It burns those who fight its progress. And one day this untamed fire of freedom will reach the darkest corners of our world." Unlike Lincoln in the Civil War, however, Bush did not believe that the world prayed to the same God to deliver two different results. He trusted that while "history has an ebb and flow of justice . . . history also has a visible direction, set by liberty and the Author of Liberty." Thus his civil religion was built on confidence in the "eventual triumph of freedom . . . because freedom is the permanent hope of mankind, the hunger in dark places, the longing of the soul." His charge to Americans, therefore, was straightforward: "The questions that come to us are narrowed and few," he said. "Did our generation advance the cause of freedom? And did our character bring credit to that cause?"[70] This was Bush's prophetic stance toward his nation. Did he asked the right questions?

He did ask legitimate questions, but it didn't matter because the experience Americans continued to have in Iraq and Afghanistan made it impossible to imagine, as Bush had hoped, a world that had a discernible role for the United States to play. The abstract nature of the American mission faced the all-too-real circumstances of failed states. And then, in the midterm elections of 2006, the Democrats thumped the Republicans and won control of both houses of Congress. Was that a result of a public moral reckoning? No, it was a political one. But a moral reckoning of sorts did play out in a debate centered around the position *First Things* had taken on the wars.

In a long and well-written critique of that journal's role in framing (and even helping Bush to frame) the war on terror, Dula, a Mennonite aid worker who witnessed the breakdown of Baghdad, asked the right questions for his moment. He wondered, after recalling how *First Things* had pronounced the need for "moral clarity in a time of war," what had become clear in light of the American experience in Iraq. "Contemplating what is happening in Baghdad from a fifth-floor hotel room, listening to the mortar rounds landing across the river," Dula observed, "will make people beyond bookish theologians too dizzy for clarity in a time of war." Neuhaus and his associates had been relatively silent as the chaos in Iraq had escalated. Dula noted that Neuhaus in particular, the moral center of *First Things* and much of the intellectual religious right, had waited until October 2004 to even mention the Abu Ghraib scandal. Dula's point, though, was not to play a game of "gotcha," as he said, by asserting that Bush's failures reflected badly on Neuhaus's support for the president. What he wanted was a moral accounting of the war by a group that had viewed itself as national moral authorities.[71]

Dula did not reject the claim to moral authority made by Neuhaus and his associates but interrogated what they had done with it. In doing so, Dula's essay was an astute critique of Bush's civil religion and the relationship to it of moral arbiters such as Neuhaus. Dula reminded readers that the *First Things* group had not merely supported Bush's general declaration of a war on terror and the invasion of Iraq as just wars but had dismissed other religious intellectuals and members of the clergy who had challenged the idea that these wars were just. By mid-2004, Dula wondered why "theologians who argued for the justice of preemptive war in Iraq [had] yet to give a just-war accounting of the conduct and consequences of this war." In other words, what would it take to determine that the war in Iraq, at least, was no longer just or justified?

Neuhaus had openly voiced his faith in the Bush administration's ability to do what was right in their war on terror, but when that war went wrong, Dula observed, Neuhaus failed to offer an accounting of his trust in Bush. That failure was compounded by *First Things* denying the legitimacy of other religious positions to question the legitimacy of the war. "If the events and revelations of the last sixteen months have not been good enough to tilt the balance toward mistrust," Dula pointed out, "there are also good old fashioned theological reasons to side with skepticism." Indeed, *First Things* had departed from its own recent history: throughout the 1990s it had consistently stood against the Clinton administration on everything from abortion to foreign policies in Iraq and the Balkans. On the issue of Abu Ghraib, Dula found a kind of civil religious fault line. Not only had it taken far too long, according Dula, for Neuhaus and *First Things* to respond to the torture by American

troops, but when Neuhaus did take up the issue, he lamented the damage those revelations would have on the image of the United States
abroad. Dula, a bit incredulous at this response, pointedly remarked,
"There is no sense in Neuhaus's condemnation of the 'outrages
committed by Americans at Abu Ghraib' that the events in that now
notorious prison have wider implications for the war on terror, the competence of the current administration, and the moral character of the
American people." If Bush's civil religion did contain the complexity
and irony to deal with abject moral failings, then it would seem incumbent on those with a professed investment in American moral authority
to offer an accounting of the nation. In this regard, Neuhaus only
needed to remember one of his most significant mentors, King.[72]

Neuhaus did come to terms with his role in understanding this time
of war. In a piece entitled "Iraq and the Moral Judgement," Neuhaus
replied to Dula and others who had found him to be an "embedded
cleric" shilling for the state rather than a theologian who offered moral
guidance to Christians living in America.[73] Neuhaus began his reflections
on the war in Iraq by offering excerpts from an interview he gave a few
weeks before the initial invasion. He then commented on revelations
about the origins and prosecution of the war since 2003. For example,
on the issues that seemed to precipitate the war, Saddam's possession of
weapons of mass destruction, Neuhaus had nothing to say about the failure to find such weapons. He offered the view that perhaps it was simply
an intelligence failure, and therefore the lack of weapons did not undermine the "moral legitimacy of the decision to disarm Saddam." On the
"Downing Street Memo," which seemed to confirm that there wasn't an
intelligence failure but an intelligence conspiracy, Neuhaus remarked, "I
fail to see its relevance to the justice of the war." On whether the Bush
administration actually manipulated the United Nations as cover for
starting a preemptive war, he concluded, "I don't know." The question
of "whether any military action is 'worth it' is hard to answer," Neuhaus
argued. "The inevitable question is: What would have been the consequences of alternative policies?" Unlike the questions that seemed
answerable when Neuhaus had "moral clarity," as the war dragged on,
questions elicited from him only the refrain, "I don't know."[74]

His uncertainty, though, was not the antidote to a simplistic civil
religion that Niebuhr had offered in the 1950s. Rather, Neuhaus

appeared chastened. His rise to prominence during the Vietnam War, the most severe crisis of faith in the nation since the Civil War, made him a theologian of considerable influence because he boldly argued that the United States was still worthy of its people's faith. Neuhaus spent the 1980s and 1990s constructing a moral authority that he hoped would reform and redeem the nation. The culture wars defined the middle of Neuhaus's career—he spent the better part of twenty years passing judgment on America's moral temper. When the war on terror began, he, like Bush and many other Americans, believed that a moment had arrived that would reveal the soul of the nation. When the war turned out to be considerably more ambivalent and conflicted than he and Bush would have liked, Neuhaus worried about the short-term effects on his nation. He had seen this kind of situation before. When the Bush administration asked Americans to believe that the nation's "vital interests and our deepest beliefs are now one," Neuhaus responded that "we should all want to believe that, and some of us can succeed in believing that it is approximately true." He returned to a sense that he developed after the Vietnam War, when his fellow theologians, much less his congregants, were abandoning their faith in America. "On balance, and considering the alternatives, America has been a force for good in the world," he contended. Bush and his proclamations on ending tyranny considerable increased the stakes "on how much good America can be for the world. If he is wrong, and considering the alternatives," Neuhaus suggested, "the consequences would likely be disastrous, both in domestic politics and world affairs. Which is a good reason to hope he is right."[75]

Even those who didn't share Neuhaus's religion or politics hoped Bush was right too. And, as in Neuhaus's case, a misplaced hope in Bush's policies and eventual outrage over actions taken by and for the administration revealed how faith and myth sustain America. One signature example was Michael Ignatieff's profession of faith in American power just before the invasion of Iraq. On January 5, 2003, the *New York Times Magazine* published a weighty essay by Ignatieff entitled "The Burden." At the time Ignatieff was the director of the Carr Center at Harvard's Kennedy School of Government, the premier public-policy institute for the study and promotion of human rights. Among his colleagues was Samantha Power, the author of the highly acclaimed book *A Problem from Hell,* which did much to recount America's moral failure to react to genocides that had taken place throughout the twentieth century, and most particularly during the 1990s. Ignatieff was a good leader of a center that had people like Power for he too believed that America had failed to reckon adequately with history. And yet Ignatieff did not recommend simply crusading around the world in search of monsters to destroy. Rather, he captured what seemed like the central dilemma of American power and promise: "A confident and carefree republic—the city on a hill, whose people have always believed they are immune from history's harms—now has to confront not just an unending imperial destiny but also a remote possibility that seems to haunt the history of empire: hubris followed by defeat." Much like Neuhaus, Ignatieff hoped American efforts would not end in failure. He suggested that as Americans contemplated regime change in Iraq, "the difficult question for Americans [would be] whether their own freedom entails a duty to defend the freedom of others beyond their borders." Indeed, Ignatieff pointed out, "there are many peoples who owe their freedom to an exercise of American military power." The Germans and Japanese are the archetypal examples, but he included the Bosnians, Kosovars, Afghans, and, perhaps, the Iraqis. All these cases involved war and suggested what was at stake for Americans: "The claim that a free republic may sense a duty to help other people attain their freedom does not answer the prudential question of whether the republic should run such risks." But by the end of his essay, the answer seemed clear. Americans had a moral burden to act as an empire in the post-9/11 world.[76]

Within a year, that burden had become nothing less than a sin. Americans had ignited the implosion of Iraq with seemingly no idea how to stop it. There was almost no end to the recriminations of critics who told the likes of Ignatieff and other supporters of the American "burden" that their delusions of grandeur were projections of the worst—rather than the best—America had to offer. Indeed, a collective project seemed to emerge that dissected not so much how Bush and his team bungled two wars but why the American promise had gone so wrong. For example, in a review for the *Nation*, Andrew Bacevich demolished a book entitled *The Good Fight* (2006) by Peter Beinart, one of the most active and enthusiastic liberal hawks. Bacevich wrote, "When it comes to foreign policy, the fundamental divide in American politics today is not between left and right but between those who subscribe to the myth of the 'American Century,' and those who do not." Likewise, in a review of Ann-Marie Slaughter's book with a high-minded title, *The Idea That Is America: Keeping Faith with Our Values in a Dangerous World* (2007), David Rieff wrote, "What no one questions is the certainty that we are capable of, indeed accustomed to, exercising [moral] leadership, and more basically still, that our ideals as a nation *entitle* us to do so. There is contention as to which American leader is fit to assert it, whether it should be done unilaterally or multilaterally, and how much the opinion of the rest of the world should count. Beyond that, there is absolute consensus."[77]

Here was the second front in the post-9/11 war of ideas. The first front was supposed to be a face-off between democracy and terror; yet it became clear that this second front would determine the scope and nature of the first. The tension between the two fronts was over the fundamental relationship between American ideals and war. Immediately after 9/11 and through the first few months of the Iraq invasion, war became the way to deal with a terrible enemy. From the fall of 2003 on, war grew into a cancer that threatened to destroy the ideals for which soldiers were supposed to be killing and dying. And then, much as in the aftermath of Vietnam, a debate raged over the nature of American ideals: Did war violate them or incarnate them?

Cornel West seized this moment, channeling the legacy of King in a jeremiad against "the sad American imperial devouring American democracy." In *Democracy Matters*, a book that collected the spirit of West's many public appearances in the wake of 9/11, the Princeton professor and a lightening rod of contemporary American prophetic thought, thundered that the "country failed to engage in a serious, sustained, deeply probing examination of the possible answers to [the] question . . . why do they hate us." While he heaped scorn on the Bush administration's Manicheanism, he also took aim at the abdication of responsibility on the part of Americans to "turn a sufficiently critical eye on our own behavior in the world. We have often behaved in an overbearing, imperial, hypocritical manner as we have attained more and more power as a hegemon." In the long postwar period, not only had American power grown exponentially but, according to West, the nation's capacity to comprehend and critique the dire consequences of such an accumulation of power overwhelmed the "deep" democratic traditions that might rescue the nation's soul from the nation's sins. West's condemnation of American imperialism was not unique, nor was it an end in itself. Because he performed a jeremiad, West called on the nation to learn from the blues. The essence of the blues, West wrote, is "to stare painful truths in the face and persevere without cynicism and pessimism." In the aftermath of 9/11, the nation needed the blues yet again. He argued that we had "experienced the niggerization of America, and as we struggle against the imperialistic arrogance of the us-versus-them, revenge-driven policies of the Bush administration, we as a blues nation must learn from a blues people how to keep alive our deep democratic energies in dark times rather than resort to the tempting and easier response of militarism and authoritarianism."[78]

West's warnings were echoed among the liberal left in the United States. Anatol Lieven, a journalist who worked in liberal-oriented think tanks including the Carnegie Endowment for International Peace, wrote a book in 2004 on American nationalism as an ideology. He argued, like Michael Sherry had in his book *In the Shadow of War* (1993), that the Cold War had created a Manichean tendency within American nationalism that justified a large, permanent military in order to vanquish threats that existed in a polarized and perpetually dangerous world. Such anxiety, Lieven contended, turned American nationalism into a maximalistic ideology: "the absolutist character [of American nationalism] influences in turn the underlying ideology of American foreign policy, making it more difficult for even highly educated Americans to form a detached and objective view of that policy; for to do so would also risk undermining the bonds uniting diverse Americans at home." Here was the intrinsic danger of civil religion, for once a people began to worship any set of ideas with blind faith, even the best ideas—in this case, the American promise—could lead to wars that tragically undermined the promise of the nation for itself and the world.[79]

For historian Walter Hixson, war was not an accident of American history or of overenthusiasm, but a product of a dangerous ideology. Hixson's 2008 book *The Myth of American Diplomacy* stated as bluntly as any observer yet had that the disasters of the Bush administration were not anomalies: "National identity drives U.S. foreign policy," he asserted. "Foreign policy flows from cultural hegemony affirming 'America' as a manly, racially superior, and providentially destined 'beacon of liberty,' a country which possesses a special right to exert power in the world. Hegemonic nation identity," Hixson concluded, "drives a continuous militant foreign policy, including regular resort to war." Hixson's narrative, though, seemed little more than a photographic negative of American exceptionalism. If American exceptionalism posited that the United States was specially ordained to act with moral authority, Hixson propounded that America was specially designed to act brutally and with utter malice, despite stated intentions to the contrary. Nonetheless, Hixson's account of the relationship between war and American national identity represented the flip side of the way Bush had imagined war as an expression of moral authority.[80]

Religious historian Ira Chernus complicated both those views on war by dwelling on the transformation of the troops during Bush's two terms. Chernus had written extensively on the politicization of religion and civil religion and seemed acutely sensitive to the construction of popular narratives about two failing wars. In short, the American public did not appear to be deluded about the wars. For example, by 2005, when asked about the idea of democratization, 74 percent of respondents said they now rejected that as a viable rationale for war, and 72 percent said they felt worse about democratization in light of the lessons of the Iraq war. Americans did not mind democratization as a foreign-policy goal, with 49 percent saying it was somewhat important, but only 38 percent agreed that "as a rule, U.S. foreign policy should encourage governments to be more democratic." They rejected the use of military force to overthrow a dictator—55 percent to 35 percent—and also rejected the idea that the United States should threaten military intervention if a foreign government doesn't enact democratic reforms, with 66 percent saying such a strategy does more harm than good. An almost equal number said that the accusation that the United States was too quick to resort to war had been either totally or partially justified.[81]

In May 2003, 74 percent of Americans believed that waging the Iraq War was the right decision, and 67 percent supported the idea of preemptive war. By January 2007, 40 percent viewed the war as the right thing to do. Chernus noted that while the public's support for the war declined, its affection for the troops remained solid. In 2007, 84 percent of Americans polled had "very favorable" and "favorable" views of the military.[82] Chernus observed that such statistics were not lost on the

Bush administration. Iraq, he argued, served as "a crucial test case of Americans' patriotic dedication to country." The public, like Bush and the neocons before him, elevated the idea of war to the level of an abstraction to secure the nation's ideals as much as to defend America from attack. "Perhaps," Chernus wrote, "'our troops' symbolized an affirmation that the nation's traditional values and mythic structures endured despite a second failed war. By 'supporting our troops,' Americans could believe that some kind of millennialism still gives meaning to the national experience and that the quest for perfection could still be a meaningful narrative structure for their own personal experience."[83]

Over time the war on terror became a strange amalgam of two traditions: an American penchant for hand-wringing when things go bad and an impulse to look for redemption in failure. Among the many critics who attempted to untangle these traditions, the best was perhaps Bacevich. Bacevich had credentials and arguments similar to those of many other critics of the American wars in Iraq and Afghanistan. He saw them as part of a larger ideological problem as well as a patchwork of policies and assumptions about the world since 1945. But, to my mind, Bacevich had a few things going for him: he had been a soldier and so had experience with the deification of "our troops"; he became a scholar and thus sought critical distance from events (for example, he has used to great effect Niebuhr's thought in picking apart an American theology of nationalism); he is Catholic and has made clear that like Hauerwas he takes seriously the requirements of faith and the restrictions imposed by dogma; and finally he is a father who has suffered for American civil religion—he lost a son in Iraq.

This combination has made Bacevich a particularly astute and acute critic of contemporary American civil religion. Bacevich, a professor of international relations at Boston University and a well-regarded public intellectual, also graduated from West Point and served for a year in Vietnam and, as a colonel, in the Gulf War. Regarding his training at West Point, Bacevich explained that popular adulation of the military mistakes that institution for an expression of democracy when, in fact, it's not. The point is "to socialize you to the primacy of duty, while not encouraging you to assess critically whether the duty makes any sense," Bacevich observed. "One is devoted to one's country above devotion to anything else other than your family: country above the notion of humanity; country above the notion of what's right or wrong or true or beautiful."[84] When a nation's civil religion becomes increasingly defined and incarnated by war, the consequences are dire.

Bacevich and his wife personally experienced those consequences in the most tragic way when they lost their son Andrew Bacevich Jr., who was killed in the Sunni triangle north of Baghdad on Mother's Day 2007. A few weeks later, on May 21, his family buried him in a cemetery in Walpole, Massachusetts. Thousands of people lined the streets of the town to witness the funeral procession—a gesture that "profoundly moved" the Baceviches. Andrew Jr.'s death was the first Walpole casualty of the Iraq War. Andrew Sr. supported his son's decision to enlist in the military but continued to write critically about the war and President Bush's prosecution of it.

Was this a disjunction? Bacevich ruminated on it, especially after receiving two messages contending "that my son's death came as direct result of my antiwar writings." Bacevich reasoned that such a charge, while seemingly vile, forced him to consider "what exactly is a father's duty when his son is sent into harm's way?" He answered that like his son, who did his duty in service to the nation as a soldier, he, as a critic of the war in which his son fought, was doing his duty as well. But both father and son experienced the tragedy of war: Bacevich lost his son to the war he opposed and lost hope that speaking out against war would make a difference. Bacevich remarked ruefully, "Memorial Day orators will say that a G.I.'s life is priceless. Don't believe it." The cost of the war was in fact the point, he argued. It was about money—money to buy influence, money spent on a war that sank the economy, and money that was given to the family of a fallen soldier to pay them for the sacrifice they made for the nation. "I know my son did his best to serve our country," Bacevich concluded. "Through my own opposition to a profoundly misguided war, I thought I was doing the same. In fact, while he was giving his all, I was doing nothing. In this way, I failed him."[85]

Bacevich's profound sense of loss came in the two areas that matter most: the personal and the mythical. He lost his son to a war that had done a great deal to undermine the mythical nature of the nation he loves. Through his work, Bacevich has expressed his *agape* for America—his love for the nation, which has been hard-earned through suffering and extensive reflection. He is not merely a cold-water critic, dousing the hopes of Americans: he chose not to dash the wishes of his son when he wanted to serve his nation. He wrote in *The Limits of Power*, "Ironically Iraq may yet prove to be the source of our salvation. For the United States, the ongoing war makes plain the imperative of putting America's house in order. Iraq has revealed the futility of counting on military power to sustain our habits of profligacy. The day of reckoning approaches. Expending the lives of more American soldiers in hopes of deferring that day is profoundly wrong."[86] And as the wars continued, with what had America reckoned?

CHAPTER 7

Reckoning with American
Civil Religion

IF RECKONING WITH THE WARS IN Iraq and Afghanistan
has begun, then Election Day 2008 offered a start. Unlike the previous
two presidential elections, the 2008 election was not historic because
it was close; it was historic because for the first time in American history
a black man won. At his victory celebration, President-elect Barack
Obama told a massive crowd gathered in Chicago's Lincoln Park, "If
there is anyone out there who still doubts that America is a place where
all things are possible; who still wonders if the dream of our founders is
alive in our time; who still questions the power of our democracy,
tonight is your answer." And in a remark that celebrated a traditional
sense of American optimism—even exceptionalism—the new president
declared: "It's the answer that led those who have been told for so long
by so many to be cynical, and fearful, and doubtful of what we can
achieve to put their hands on the arc of history and bend it once more
toward the hope of a better day."[1]

So, as much as the election of Obama was unique in American
history, the candidate himself was not. Much like other presidential
candidates, Obama believed in and promoted a kind of patriotism—a
"theology of American exceptionalism"—that David Rieff subjected
to a withering critique. In a statement he made in 2007 before the
Chicago Council on Global Affairs, Obama declared, "I reject the
notion that the American moment has passed. I dismiss the cynics who
say that this new century cannot be another when, in the words of
President Franklin Roosevelt, we lead the world in battling immediate
evils and promoting the ultimate good. . . . I still believe that America is
the last, best hope of Earth."[2] Rieff asked rhetorically how different

Obama's sentiment was from the man he sought to replace in the 2008 presidential election.[3]

Yet, unlike George W. Bush, Obama illustrated that his patriotism contains a prophetic strand, best revealed when he became tangled up in news stories about the Reverend Jeremiah Wright, the pastor of a church the Obamas attended in Chicago. In the immediate aftermath of 9/11, Wright had asked his congregation, "What should our response be in light of such an unthinkable act?" He had an answer—it was America's fault. Recalling Malcolm X, Wright declared, "America's chickens are coming home to roost. Violence begets violence. Hatred begets hatred, and terrorism begets terrorism." In a sermon delivered shortly after the American invasion of Iraq, Wright's indignation toward the United States grew as he lashed out at Bush's civil religion. America had failed to live up to its ideals, Wright thundered. The nation had a terrible legacy of mistreating people, including those within its own borders—the Indians, Japanese, and especially African Americans. "God bless America?" Wright asked with disdain. "No, no, no . . . ," he said to his congregation. "Not God bless America, God damn America. That's in the Bible, for killing innocent people. God damn America for treating her citizens as less than human. God damn America for as long as she acts like she is God and she is supreme. The United States government has failed the vast majority of her citizens of African descent. Think about this, think about this."[4] Most people did not, at least not until Obama ran for the nation's highest office, and then Wright's jeremiad became a substantial news event.

Obama had to respond and in doing so delivered the greatest speech of his political career. He traveled to Philadelphia in March 2008 and asked Americans to imagine what "a more perfect union" meant. In the aftermath of the Wright controversy, the assumption was that as a black man Obama needed to quell concerns that his view of the United States might drift toward anger and resentment rather than upward toward the Bushesque sacralization of the nation. Obama struck a different note. "I chose to run for the presidency," he said, "because I believe deeply that we cannot solve the challenges of our time unless we solve them together—unless we perfect our union by understanding that we may have different stories, but we hold common hopes; that we may not look the same and we may not have come from the same place, but we all want to move in the same direction—towards a better future for our children and our grandchildren." Obama acknowledged that this message was not what people heard from Wright. The pastor "expressed a profoundly distorted view of this country," Obama contended, "a view that sees white racism as endemic, and that elevates what is wrong with America above all that we know is right with America." Wright was "not only wrong but divisive," Obama said, "divisive at a time when we need unity." Most of all, to the man who would be president, "the profound mistake of Reverend Wright's sermons is not that he spoke about racism in our society. It's that he spoke as if our society was static; as if no progress has been made; as if this country—a country that has made it possible for one of his own members to run for the highest office in the land and build a coalition of white and black . . . is still irrevocably bound to a tragic past." Obama rejected that understanding of history, not merely because it was politically vital to do so but because "the truth is, that isn't all that I know of the man." For Obama, Wright and the Trinity United Church of Christ offered a way for a smart, ambitious young man to find hope in a deeply unfair and flawed world; to understand tragedy as part of a larger story of redemption and even victory. Obama recounted a passage from his first book, *Dreams of My Father*, about his experience at Trinity: "At the foot of that cross, inside the thousands of churches across the city, I imagined the stories of ordinary black people merging with the stories [from the Bible]. . . . Our trials and triumphs became at once unique and universal, black and more than black; in chronicling our journey, the stories and songs gave us a means to reclaim memories that we didn't need to feel shame about . . . memories that all people might study and cherish—and with which we could start to rebuild."[5]

That rebuilding seemed possible on January 20, 2009, when well over a million people attended the inauguration of Obama as the forty-fourth president of the United States. By almost any standard, it was a remarkable outpouring of goodwill and enthusiasm that echoed an equally enthusiastic sentiment around the world. Sitting on the platform while Obama delivered his inaugural address was a president who thought a great deal about America's role in advancing what he saw as the design of history. Obama's speech no doubt made Bush uncomfortable—the new president had to give his audience hope amidst, as he said, "a nagging fear that America's decline is inevitable, that the next generation must lower its sights." But Bush also heard familiar calls for unity and resolve. Like Bush, Obama too had little nostalgia for the culture wars as he made clear in a central statement from the address: "On this day, we come to proclaim an end to petty grievances and false promises, the recriminations and worn-out dogmas that for far too long have strangled our politics." And then, turning to civil religion, Obama struck a prophetic note: he told Americans that their nation was young but followed ancient wisdom. "In the words of scripture, the time has come to set aside childish things. The time has come to reaffirm our enduring spirit; to choose our better history; to carry forward that precious gift, that noble idea, passed on from generation to generation: the God-given promise that all are equal, all are free, all deserve a chance to pursue their full measure of happiness."[6]

Unlike Bush, though, Obama carefully parsed the difference between promise and obligation and in doing so proposed a civil religion based on justice rather than confidence. The difference between their civil religions appeared most clearly in the last section of Obama's address. After spending the bulk of his speech chronicling the challenges Americans had to meet, Obama asked people to accept a "new era of responsibility—a recognition," he said, "on the part of every American, that we have duties to ourselves, our nation and the world, duties that we do not grudgingly accept but rather seize gladly, firm in the knowledge that there is nothing so satisfying to the spirit, so defining of our character than giving our all to a difficult task." Obama did not pronounce the goal of such work; he did not declare his desire to spread democracy or end tyranny or even prosecute a war on terror. He did not intimate confidence that history had a design and it was good because its designer was good. Rather, he suggested, "the source of our confidence [is] the knowledge that God calls us to shape an uncertain destiny." The point was not the ultimate victory—which is always uncertain—but the fact that Americans had joined together, seeing each other as citizens under a creed that pushed them to be better to each other.[7]

One of the subtexts of Obama's election was that Bush had squandered unprecedented American unity and international goodwill on two mishandled wars. Even if it proved too difficult for Obama to join the right and left in America, he made the case that the unity of the immediate post-9/11 period was not an anomaly. He wanted critics of Bush to believe that something other than stupidity (as Susan Sontag suggested) had joined Americans, if only briefly. The question was how Obama would reclaim this unity. Robert Bellah thought he knew. Bellah enthusiastically voiced his support for Obama because the new president spoke eloquently and powerfully about the "common good." After disowning the idea of civil religion in the early 1980s, Bellah had returned to it with the election of Obama. To Bellah, Obama fused the best traditions of civil religion by placing "the common good at the core of all" his policy proposals and calling on Americans to care for one another because they all live under a creed that demands that they "help create a more perfect union." Obama's inaugural spoke to Bellah as John F. Kennedy's had. He said of Obama's address that he was "glad to have lived long enough to see such a possibility [of civic unity] in this great but benighted nation."[8]

Expectations abounded that Obama not only would offer a substantially different administration than his predecessor had but would change America for the better. Yet he also presided over a nation still in two wars, and he inherited a civil religion still defined almost exclusively through those wars. Nothing better expressed Obama's dilemma than the announcement from Oslo, Norway, that Obama had won the 2009 Nobel Peace Prize. Less than a year after winning the election for president of the United States, Obama won an award typically given to recipients who did not have direct responsibility for military campaigns on two continents. However, the Nobel committee declared in its official statement that "only very rarely has a person to the same extent as Obama captured the world's attention and given its people hope for a better future. His diplomacy is founded in the concept that those who are to lead the world must do so on the basis of values and attitudes that are shared by the majority of the world's population."[9] Ironically, Obama's election as president of the United States provided him with the possibility to "lead the world" through the notion of universal values. Bush had attempted to do just that; his subsequent failure apparently did not discredit the world's continuing faith in the American promise.

Obama added to the irony of the prize by delivering a speech about war. He wanted all who gathered for the award ceremony to recognize that he was "responsible for the deployment of thousands of young Americans to battle in a distant land. Some will kill and some will be killed. And so I come here with an acute sense of the costs of armed conflict—filled with difficult questions about the relationship between war and peace, and our effort to replace one with the other." Echoing the rationale for American wars fought since World War II, Obama described his relationship to American power and national security by stating bluntly, "We must begin by acknowledging the hard truth: We will not eradicate violent conflict in our lifetimes. There will be times when nations—acting individually or in concert—will find the use of force not only necessary but morally justified." Obama explained that he could not and would not change two basic things from the previous administration. First, he had "sworn to protect and defend" his nation; and second, America would continue to be and made no apologies for being "the world's sole military superpower." However, he pledged to be different in the realm of applying the rules of just war to American conduct. "Even as we confront a vicious adversary that abides by no rules, I believe the United States of America must remain a standard bearer in the conduct of war. That is what makes us different from those whom we fight." Indeed, one of the devastating charges leveled at the Bush administration was that it had begun fighting a war for the defense of ideals that America promoted because they were universally accepted and ended up prosecuting two wars in ways that debased those ideals and undermined the moral authority needed to defend them with force. "We honor those ideals by upholding them not when it's easy," Obama said, "but when it is hard."[10]

The clearest break Obama made with the immediate past came over the existential meaning of war. Under Bush, American civil religion seemed defined only through war because through war Americans understood their commitment to the nation and to each other; in war soldiers became the symbol of selfless sacrifice, and because of war the disputes over issues of morality that had defined the nation since the Vietnam War had receded. Obama promised to adhere to "the law of love," which used just-war theory to limit war, not to justify it. On this point, Obama might move himself beyond what other presidents of the postwar period had achieved in their attempts to balance the way civil religion can sacralize the nation's purpose through war with the way civil religion must be about something more than a nation at war.[11]

Perhaps it should not be much of a surprise, then, that Obama has also drawn on the insight of Reinhold Niebuhr, whom Obama called "one of my favorite philosophers." In an interview with David Brooks published in the *New York Times* in the spring of 2007, then Senator Obama spoke to Brooks about his admiration for Niebuhr, explaining, "I take away the compelling idea that there's serious evil in the world, and hardship and pain. And we should be humble and modest in our belief we can eliminate those things. But we shouldn't use that as an excuse for cynicism and inaction. I take away . . . the sense we have to make these efforts knowing they are hard, and not swinging from naïve idealism to bitter realism."[12] Obama had quite clearly read Niebuhr's most enduring, popular work, *The Irony of American History.* And for the ambitious senator, Niebuhr's thought served as an antidote to the hubris so many critics understood to be a natural product of American power. Thus, in this instance, a politician used a preacher to complicate rather than to simplify an understanding of America's promise. But Obama was only one of many who employed Niebuhr to make sense of early-twenty-first-century America. And it has never been clear whether using Niebuhr ultimately helps avoid the pitfalls the theologian so precisely identified.

In the decade following 9/11, Niebuhr's thought served as a touch-stone for a theological view of America, although some appropriations of Niebuhr were weaker than others. For example, in an op-ed entitled "The War Party's Theologian," Joseph Loconte of the Heritage Foundation offered a one-dimensional portrait of Niebuhr as a defender of Western civilization. Recalling Niebuhr's break with fellow socialists and pacifists over Adolf Hitler's war in Europe, Loconte argued that Niebuhr stood against the weak-willed religious critics of war. "Niebuhr owed his own clarity of vision to a deep belief in the existence of evil." Loconte contended that Niebuhr had "restored" this concept to its "biblical meaning" in an era that had largely lost use for it and was therefore incapable of comprehending the terrible history unfolding in the 1930s. Loconte wanted his readers to understand that Niebuhr was still relevant to America because he provided a way to explain that "civilized nations must strive for justice."[13] Yet it seems reasonable to assume that Niebuhr's sense of justice did not include endless wars, torture, and preemptive invasions of sovereign nations.

In a similar vein, a year after 9/11, Brooks wrote in the *Atlantic Monthly* that it was high time to bring Niebuhr back into the American conversation because Niebuhr recognized that while "every action causes some collateral damage . . . people must act nonetheless, begging forgiveness for the evils they commit in the service of good." One wonders precisely whom they would be asking for forgiveness and to what end, but, no matter, Niebuhr provided Brooks with a way to raise up an idealistic form of American power. To Brooks's credit, he at least had the honesty to point out that Niebuhr did not go far enough in endorsing the kind of civil religion Brooks wanted. Brooks said he disagreed with "two thirds of what Niebuhr wrote," mostly because Niebuhr was not useful in rallying people to a cause: the theologian was a cold-water critic. Like other neocons, Brooks believed that the post-9/11 era offered an opportunity to sweep away the remnants of the culture wars and get people fired up about defending a nation not merely against terrorists but also against those agnostic Americans who weren't quite sure they wanted to express faith in their nation. Yet, according to Brooks, "Niebuhr overlearned the lessons of his age." "Because communism and fascism were fomented by zealous idealists, he came to suspect all displays of passion, all righteous indignation, and all poetic elements of public life. But," Brooks declared, "idealism in defense of democracy is no vice, at least not on balance." The trick, it seemed, was to feel a sense of sorrow while destroying enemies and dismissing critics.[14]

Wilfred McClay also turned to Niebuhr to help him make sense of 9/11, but he did so to endorse what had become a central trope of post-9/11 thought: that the war on terror ended the distractions of the culture wars. We could be moral now. McClay was an outspoken champion of Bush's general response to 9/11: "I agree that our cause is just," he wrote, "and frankly feel a thrill [of] moral satisfaction when I hear our President say so, bluntly and confidently. When the President says, 'Let's Roll,' I'm ready." However, McClay's confidence in Bush had as much to do with the need to fill the vacuum that was created following the terrorist attacks as with making war on terror. "On September 10 many of us had grave, profound, and well-founded misgivings about the moral direction of our country," McClay said in a lecture in December 2001. And he admitted that while September 11 galvanized a certain kind of moral authority, it did not undo the problems that McClay and many others had identified as fundamental issues in the cultural wars. Yet if the issues had not changed completely because of 9/11, the sense of struggle did. McClay believed that Niebuhr's thought made clear to him that "just as the sinful and imperfect Christian is obliged to work intently for the cause of good, despite his incapacities, so a morally imperfect America was and is obliged to employ its power decisively in the world. Opting out is not an option."[15] In short, let's roll.

McClay was attracted to Niebuhr's thought by the central premise of Niebuhr's *Irony of American History*, that the "manifest strength" of the United States "becomes a crippling weakness." In this regard, McClay pointed to the fact that "the same prowess we use to defeat mass murderers a world away is threatening us too, arising out of our greatest areas [of] strength—our scientific and technological skills." Such skills, McClay and many others at *First Things* believed, had led to a "medical and biotechnological degradation of human life." Thus, in the dawning of a better world of American unity post-9/11, McClay had hope that Americans might awaken to the "better angels of their nature" and return to a "broadly biblical understanding of the sources of the dignity of the human person."[16]

In a cover story for the November 2007 *Atlantic* entitled "A Man for All Reasons," editor and author Paul Elie excoriated the contemporary revival of interest in Niebuhr because all the abusers of Niebuhr's legacy used the theologian to advance their own particular ends. Elie especially lamented the way operators across the American political spectrum had made claims about Niebuhr as they staked out positions on the Iraq War. Such appropriation distressed Elie because it underscored the trends that led to Iraq in the first place. "He [Niebuhr] foresaw that the American struggle in the postwar years would be a struggle with our addiction to power, and that our national story would be a story of our efforts to distinguish between the courageous and the foolish uses of that power—a story of our reluctant recognition that power can bring about necessary change, but that it can also have brutal unintended consequences. Moreover, he saw that distinguishing one from the other would call for wisdom, a quality born of 'the triumph of experience over dogma.'"[17]

If Elie argued that the consequence of misusing Niebuhr's warnings in the Cold War was the war in Iraq, Bacevich contended that the only way out of Iraq was revisiting Niebuhr yet again. Bacevich recognized, in a Niebuhrian way, that Bush's action in Iraq was not the result of some shortsighted policy but of a national pathology. "One must acknowledge," Bacevich offered, "that in his second inaugural address, as in other presentations he has made, President Bush succeeds quite masterfully in capturing something essential about the way Americans see themselves and their country. Here is a case where myths and delusion combine to yield perverse yet important truths." For Bacevich, Niebuhr showed a way for Americans to extricate themselves not merely from Iraq but from the mindset that got them there in the first place. "America's stubborn unwillingness to acknowledge the truths Niebuhr describes in [*The Irony of American History*] has produced disastrous consequences, in our time and before our very eyes. To persist any longer—to indulge further the fantasy that we can force history to do our bidding—will inevitably even produce greater catastrophes."[18]

From the original reception of *Irony* through to the contemporary revival of its popularity, a hope has persisted that using Niebuhr (or some version of his "thought") could break an American addiction to exceptionalist views of history. This is not a foolhardy belief considering the thoroughness of Niebuhr's critique of American delusions. Peter Viereck had good reason to call Niebuhr a "doctor of the soul." However, I think that tag explains why Niebuhr's work continues to attract adherents and why his work has seemingly failed to get the job done. Niebuhr is not a doctor but a pathologist. He diagnosed the disease that afflicted America; he never intended to offer a cure. His work has remained relevant because he took the irony of American history so seriously and offered a remarkable accounting of the ways in which "our moral perils are not those of conscious malice or the explicit lust for power. They are," Niebuhr insisted, "the perils which can be understood only if we realize the ironic tendency of virtues to turn into vices when too complacently relied upon; and of power to become vexatious if the wisdom that directs it is trusted too confidently. The ironic elements in American history can be overcome . . . only if American idealism comes to terms with the limits of all human striving, the fragmentariness of all human wisdom, the precariousness of all historic configurations of power, and the mixture of good and evil in all human virtue."[19]

Niebuhr used prophetic religion to critique more than simply American exceptionalism, and he did more than simply denounce the self-delusion that all nations traffic in. Rather he registered a prophecy that alerted the nation to disasters that would befall it because the nation was part of history—something it could neither avoid, remake, or necessarily bend to its liking.

Ultimately what Niebuhr did in *Irony*—as is evident in the responses from Viereck through Obama—was to create space for the nation's post-exceptional understanding of itself, to offer a way to use America's faith in itself—its civil religion—to recognize those national tendencies that exacerbate the historical perils that come with being a powerful nation. Such a civil religion requires an appreciation for and accounting of America's contradictions; Americans have a national creed that they cannot simply reject. Thus Niebuhr continues to make so much sense because he understood and captured the way Americans can be both Abraham Lincoln and George W. Bush; Martin Luther King Jr. and Jerry Falwell; and the way the United States is both a nation despised by many around the world as well as a nation that most in the world could not do without. Niebuhr got us—we are the last, best hope of Earth, except when we're not.

The American myth in isolation is a good one; that is why we consistently hear support for it from all quarters of American society and around the world. However, when that myth is shielded from critique, its gets commodified into something that resembles an advertisement for America itself, rather than something worthy of popular investment or sacrifice. Believing in the myths that sustain American civil religion does not require the reduction of civil religion to a theology of war. And critiquing civil religion does not inevitably produce cynicism, for losing national myths can be as dangerous for the health of a people as believing in bad ones.

William McNeil made that point in 1982, at a time when Ronald Reagan had attempted to dismiss the critical reflection embodied by Jimmy Carter and to replace it with an optimism that seemed to have little regard for reality. As a historian whose work chronicled long-term, large-scale trends in world history, McNeil offered a view of post-Vietnam America that looked beyond partisanship and toward the potential consequences for a nation without a viable civil religion. "In human society," he explained, "belief matters most. Evidence supporting belief is largely generated by actions undertaken in accordance with the belief. This is a principle long familiar to students of religion. In Christian terms, faith comes first, works follow. The primacy of faith is equally real for the various civil religions that since the eighteenth century have come to provide the practical basis for nearly all of the world's governments." McNeil did not categorically endorse Reagan's campaign, pointing out that the president had reduced cultural pluralism and global-historical complexity to a binary of the free world versus the unfree world. Reagan's tactics surely worked in the short term—he beat Carter—and would work for others who wanted to manipulate the nation's civil religion for their partisan purposes. But pointing out the perils of civil religion did not destroy the impulse for constructing one. McNeil noted, "Discrediting old myths without finding new ones to replace them erodes the basis for common action that once bound those who believed into a public body, capable of acting together."[20] Neither sectarianism nor blanket uniformity is healthy for a body politic.

We cannot live without myths and the symbols that represent them. And we cannot function as a people without a way to talk about, believe in, and yes, critique those myths. Civil religion does not exist outside of the group that uses it. And while it is prone to manipulation, civil religion is also the only way to acknowledge that we still need to believe in something worthy of the sacrifices that have been and will continue to be made in the name of the nation.

NOTES

CHAPTER 1 LINCOLN'S BEQUEST

1. James G. Meeks, "My Solemn Meeting on Veterans Day with President Obama," *New York Daily News* (November 12, 2009), http://articles.nydailynews.com/2009-11-12/news/17939514_1_first-lady-michelle-obama-marble-headstones-president-obama.
2. Barack Obama, "Speech at West Point Military Academy" (December 1, 2009), American Presidency Project, founded by John T. Woolley and Gerhard Peters, Santa Barbara, CA, http://www.presidency.ucsb.edu/ws/?pid=86948 (hereafter: American Presidency Project).
3. Carolyn Marvin and David W. Ingle, "Blood Sacrifice and the Nation: Revisiting Civil Religion," *Journal of the American Academy of Religion* 64 (Winter 1996), 769.
4. Abraham Lincoln, "Address at the Dedication of the National Cemetery at Gettysburg, Pennsylvania" (November 19, 1863), American Presidency Project, http://www.presidency.ucsb.edu/ws/?pid=73959.
5. David Rieff, "Without Exception: The Same Old Song," *World Affairs* (Winter 2008), 104.
6. Andrew Kohut and Bruce Stokes, "The Problem of American Exceptionalism," Pew Research Center for the People and the Press (May 9, 2006), http://pewresearch.org/pubs/23/the-problem-of-american-exceptionalism. John Winthrop, "Modell of Christian Charity," in Conrad Cherry, *God's New Israel: Religious Interpretations of American Destiny* (Chapel Hill: University of North Carolina Press, 1998), 40.
7. Robert N. Bellah, "Civil Religion in America," *Daedalus* 96, no. 1 (Winter 1967), http://www.robertbellah.com/articles_5.htm. Although Bellah's essay is important for my argument, his argument is one of many I have benefited from. See Ronald Beiner, *Civil Religion: A Dialogue in the History of Political Philosophy* (New York: Cambridge University Press, 2011); T. Jeremy Gunn, *Spiritual Weapons: The Cold War and the Forging of an American National Religion* (Westport, CT: Praeger, 2009); Peter Luchau, "Toward a Contextualized Concept of Civil Religion," *Social Compass* 56, no. 3 (2009), 371–386; Emilio Gentile, *God's Democracy: American Religion after September 11* (Westport, CT: Praeger, 2008); Geiko Muller-Fahrenholz, *America's Battle for God: A European Christian Looks at Civil Religion* (Grand Rapids, MI: Eerdmans, 2007); Duncan B. Forrester, "The Scope of Public Theology," *Studies in Christian Ethics* 17 (August 2004), 5–19; Michael Angrosino, "Civil Religion Redux," *Anthropological Quarterly* 75 (Spring 2002), 239–267; Marcela Cristi, *From Civil to Political Religion: The Intersection of Culture, Religion and Politics* (Waterloo, ON: Wilfrid Laurier University Press, 2001); Cheery, *God's New*

Israel, esp. 1–21; Richard V. Pierard and Robert D. Linder, *Civil Religion and the Presidency* (Grand Rapids, MI: Academie Books, 1988); N. J. Demearth and Rhys H. Williams, "Civil and Uncivil Society," *Annals of the American Academy of Political and Social Science* 480 (July 1985), 154–166; John F. Wilson, *Public Religion in American Culture* (Philadelphia: Temple University Press, 1979); John Murray Cuddihy, *No Offense: Civil Religion and Protestant Taste* (New York: Seabury Press, 1978); Catherine L. Albanese, *Sons of the Fathers: The Civil Religion of the American Revolution* (Philadelphia: Temple University Press, 1976).

8. A good summary of the American creed and its various sources, including the symbolic significance of the Great Seal, is Richard T. Hughes, *Myths America Lives By* (Chicago: University of Illinois Press, 2004), 1–15, 100–101.

9. Arthur Schlesinger Jr., "America: Experiment or Destiny?" *American Historical Review* 82 (June 1977), 521.

10. William H. McNeill, "The Care and Repair of Public Myth," *Foreign Affairs* 61 (Fall 1982), 4.

11. Mark Noll, *The Civil War as a Theological Crisis* (Chapel Hill: University of North Carolina Press, 2006), 75, 20.

12. Ibid., 21.

13. Harry S. Stout, *On the Altar of the Nation: A Moral History of the Civil War* (New York: Viking Press, 2009), xxi.

14. Abraham Lincoln, "Meditation on the Divine Will" (undated), Brown University Library Center for Digital Initiatives, http://dl.lib.brown.edu/catalog/catalog.php?verb=render&id=1210012353437500&colid=39. Abraham Lincoln, "Second Inaugural Address" (March 4, 1865), American Presidency Project, http://www.presidency.ucsb.edu/ws/?pid=73959.

15. There are two classic academic renderings of the American jeremiad: Perry Miller, *Errand into the Wilderness* (Cambridge: Harvard University Press, 1956), and Sacvan Bercovich, *The American Jeremiad* (Madison: University of Wisconsin Press, 1978); also see Wilson Brissett, "Puritans and Revolution: Remembering the Origin: Religion and Social Critique in Early New England," in *Prophecies of Godlessness: Predictions of America's Imminent Secularization, from the Puritans to the Present Day,* ed. Charles Matthews and Christopher McKnight Nichols, (Oxford: Oxford University Press, 2008), 22–25.

16. Lincoln, "Second Inaugural Address."

17. Ibid. See also Mark Noll, *America's God: From Jonathan Edwards to Abraham Lincoln* (New York: Oxford University Press, 2002), 425–435; George C. Rable, *God's Almost Chosen Peoples: A Religious History of the American Civil War* (Chapel Hill: University of North Carolina Press, 2010), 372–378; Allen C. Guelzo, *Abraham Lincoln: Redeemer President* (Grand Rapids, MI: Eerdmans, 1999), 414–421.

18. Randolph S. Bourne, "The State," in *War and the Intellectuals: Collected Essays, 1915–1919* (New York: Harper Torchbook, 1964), 71.

CHAPTER 2   CIVIL RELIGION INCORPORATED

1. Harry S. Truman, "Radio Address to the Nation" (August 10, 1945), as quoted in Paul Boyer, *By the Bomb's Early Light: American Thought and Culture at the Dawn of the Atomic Age* (New York: Pantheon Books, 1985), 6; James Agee,

"The Bomb," *Time* (August 20, 1945), http://www.time.com/time/ magazine/article/0,9171,797639,00.html.

2. Richard J. Barnet, *The Rocket's Red Glare: War, Politics, and the American Presidency* (New York: Simon & Schuster, 1990), 250. See also Michael Sherry, *In the Shadow of War: The United States since the 1930s* (New Haven, CT: Yale University Press, 1995), 123–126; John Bodnar, *The 'Good War' in American Memory* (Baltimore: Johns Hopkins University Press, 2010), 60–64.

3. Paul Fussell, *Wartime: Understanding and Behavior in the Second World War* (New York: Oxford University Press, 1990), 267–280; Bodnar, *The 'Good War,'* 1–9; Wendy Wall, *Inventing the American Way: The Politics of Consensus from the New Deal to the Civil Rights Movement* (New York: Oxford University Press, 2008), 103–112.

4. Henry R. Luce, "The American Century," *Life* 10 (February 17, 1941), 61; Bodnar, *The 'Good War,'* 4.

5. Mark Silk, *Spiritual Politics: Religion and America since World War II* (New York: Simon & Schuster, 1988), 101.

6. Bodnar, *The 'Good War,'* 5.

7. Boyer, *By the Bomb's Early Light*, 187; polling data on 183; editorials quoted on 187, 197.

8. Ibid., 200, 203; O'Brien quoted on 215.

9. Arthur H. Compton, "The Moral Meaning of the Atomic Bomb," in *Christianity Takes a Stand: An Approach to the Issues of Today*, ed. William Scarlett (New York: Penguin Books, 1946), 58, 63. Boyer, *By the Bombs Early Light*, 240.

10. A. J. Muste, *Not by Might* (New York: Harper, 1947), 18, 86.

11. Dorothy Day, "Our Country Passes from Undeclared War to Declared War; We Continue Our Christian Pacifist Stand," *Catholic Worker* (January 1942), 1, 4.

12. Reinhold Niebuhr, "Why the Christian Church Is Not Pacifist," in *The Essential Reinhold Niebuhr: Selected Essays and Addresses*, ed. Robert McAfee Brown (New Haven, CT: Yale University Press, 1986), 118.

13. James B. Conant to Reinhold Niebuhr, March 6, 1946, Reinhold Niebuhr Papers, Library of Congress, Correspondence, Box 3, Conant File.

14. Reinhold Niebuhr to James B. Conant, March 12, 1946, Reinhold Niebuhr Papers, Library of Congress, Correspondence, Box 3, Conant File.

15. Richard Wightman Fox, "Niebuhr's World and Ours," in *Reinhold Niebuhr Today*, ed. Richard John Neuhaus (Grand Rapids, MI: Eerdmanns, 1989), 2.

16. Whittaker Chambers, "Faith for a Lenten Age," *Time* (March 8, 1948), http://www.time.com/time/magazine/article/0,9171,853293,00.html.

17. Robert Wuthnow, *The Restructuring of American Religion* (Princeton, NJ: Princeton University Press, 1988), 44.

18. William Inboden, *Religion and American Foreign Policy: The Soul of Containment, 1945–1960* (New York: Cambridge University Press, 2008), 4.

19. Kevin M. Schultz, *Tri-Faith America: How Catholics and Jews Held Postwar America to Its Protestant Promise* (New York: Oxford University Press, 2011), 68–97.

20. Federal Council of Churches, *The Christian Conscience and Weapons of Mass Destruction* (New York: Department of International Justice and Goodwill, 1950), 9, 22. On this emerging religious consensus on a relationship between God and nation in the early Cold War, see Wuthnow, *Restructuring of*

American Religion, esp. 54–70; Silk, *Spiritual Politics,* 54–86; Andrew Bacevich, *The New American Militarism: How Americans Are Seduced by War* (New York: Oxford University Press, 2005), 124–126; David Ciepley, "The Thirties to the Fifties: Totalitarianism and the Second American Enlightenment," in *Prophecies of Godlessness: Predictions of America's Imminent Secularization, from the Puritans to the Present Day,* ed. Charles Mathews and Christopher McKnight Nichols (New York: Oxford University Press, 2008), 155–173; Jason W. Stevens, *God-Fearing and Free: A Spiritual History of America's Cold War* (Cambridge: Harvard University Press, 2010), 29–63.

21. Silk, *Spiritual Politics,* 57; Michael D. Long, ed., *The Legacy of Billy Graham: Critical Reflections on America's Greatest Evangelist* (Louisville, KY: Westminster John Knox Press, 2008), xiii.
22. Inboden, *Religion and American Foreign Policy,* 5; Graham quoted in William Martin, *With God on Our Side: The Rise of the Religious Right in America* (New York: Broadway Books, 1996), 29; Stephen Whitfield, *The Culture of the Cold War,* 2nd ed. (Baltimore: Johns Hopkins University Press, 1996), 78.
23. Martin, *With God on Our Side,* 30.
24. Ibid., 31–33.
25. Graham quoted in Martin, *With God on Our Side,* 33–34; Angela M. Lahr, *Millennial Dreams and Apocalyptic Nightmares: The Cold War Origins of Political Evangelicalism* (New York: Oxford University Press, 2007), 35.
26. Lahr, *Millennial Dreams and Apocalyptic Nightmares,* 43.
27. "Urbi et Orbi," *Time* (December 14, 1953), http://www.time.com/time/magazine/article/0,9171,806801,00.html.
28. John T. McGreevy, *Catholicism and American Freedom: A History* (New York: Norton, 2003), 166–188.
29. Patrick Allitt, *Catholic Intellectuals and Conservative Politics in America, 1950–1985* (Ithaca, NY: Cornell University Press, 1993), 34.
30. Ibid., 2.
31. John Cooney, *The American Pope: The Life and Times of Francis Cardinal Spellman* (New York: Times Books, 1984), 231; Spellman quoted on 240.
32. Irvin D. S. Winsboro and Michael Epple, "Religion, Culture, and the Cold War: Bishop Fulton J. Sheen and America's Anti-Communist Crusade of the 1950s," *Historian* (2009), 212; Catholic journal quote on 225.
33. Sheen sermon quoted in ibid., 226; Fulton J. Sheen, *Communism and the Conscience of the West* (New York: Bobbs-Merrill, 1948), 55.
34. Winsboro and Epple, "Religion, Culture, and the Cold War," 226.
35. McGreevy, *Catholicism and American Freedom,* 206.
36. "City of God and Man," *Time* (December 12, 1960), http://www.time.com/time/magazine/article/0,9171,871923,00.html.
37. Ibid.
38. Ibid.; Robert W. McElroy, "He Held These Truths," *America* (February 7, 2005), http://www.americamagazine.org/content/article.cfm?article_id=3995.
39. "City of God and Man"; McElroy, "He Held These Truths."
40. "City of God and Man."
41. Walter Lippmann, *The Public Philosophy: On the Decline and Revival of the Western Society* (New York: Atlantic Monthly Press Book, 1955), esp. ch. 9.
42. Inboden, *Religion and American Foreign Policy,* 4–5, 6.
43. Wall, *Inventing the American Way,* 9–10.
44. Harry S. Truman, "Annual Message to the Congress on the State of the Union" (January 7, 1948), American Presidency Project, http://www

.presidency.ucsb.edu/ws/index.php?pid=13005#axzz1SfihUrw7. Also see Inboden, *Religion and American Foreign Policy*, 113.

45. Harry S. Truman, "Inaugural Address" (January 20, 1949), American Presidency Project, http://www.presidency.ucsb.edu/ws/?pid=13282. See also Elizabeth Edward Spalding, *The First Cold Warrior: Harry Truman, Containment, and the Remaking of Liberal Internationalism* (Lexington: University Press of Kentucky, 2006), 205.

46. "NSC-68: United States Objectives and Programs for National Security" (April 14, 1950), reprinted in *American Cold War Strategy: Interpreting NSC 68*, ed. Ernest R. May (Boston: Bedford/St. Martin's Press, 1993), 29, 26; in the same book, Bruce Kuklick, "Commentary," 156–159.

47. "Transport Sails from Japan with War Dead," *Pittsburgh Post-Gazette* (March 12, 1951), 2.

48. James Stokesbury, *A Short History of the Korean War* (New York: Harper Perennial, 1990), 253.

49. Harry S. Truman, "Address in Philadelphia at the Dedication of the Chapel of the Four Chaplains" (February 3, 1951), American Presidency Project, http://www.presidency.ucsb.edu/ws/?pid=13999. See also Schultz, *Tri-Faith America*, 3–12.

50. "The Gallup Brain: Americans and the Korean War," http://www.gallup.com/poll/7741/gallup-brain-americans-korean-war.aspx.

51. Harry S. Truman, "Farewell Address" (January 15, 1953), American Presidency Project, http://www.presidency.ucsb.edu/ws/?pid=14392.

52. Dwight D. Eisenhower, "Remarks by President-Elect Dwight D. Eisenhower at the Freedom Foundation, Waldorf Astoria Hotel, Monday Noon, December 22, 1952," quoted in Patrick Henry, "'And I Don't Care What It Is': The Tradition-History of a Civil Religion Proof-Text," *Journal of the American Academy of Religion* 64, no. 1 (March 1981), 41.

53. Dwight D. Eisenhower, "Inaugural Address" (January 20, 1953), American Presidency Project, http://www.presidency.ucsb.edu/ws/?pid=9600; see also Inboden, *Religion and American Foreign Policy*, 259.

54. Dwight D. Eisenhower, "Remarks Broadcast as Part of the American Legion 'Back to God' Program" (February 7, 1954), American Presidency Project, http://www.presidency.ucsb.edu/ws/?pid=10119.

55. George M. Docherty, "Under God" (February 7, 1954), New York Avenue Presbyterian Church Archives, http://www.nyapc.org/congregation/Sermon_Archives/text/1954/under-god-sermon.pdf.

56. Bill Broadway, "How 'Under God' Got in There," *Washington Post Weekly* (July 6, 2002), B9. Dwight D. Eisenhower, "Statement upon Signing Bill to Include the Words 'Under God' in the Pledge to the Flag," American Presidency Project, http://www.presidency.ucsb.edu/ws/?pid=9920.

57. Harry Stout, *Upon the Altar of the Nation: A Moral History of the Civil War* (New York: Viking Press, 2006).

58. Quoted in James Hudnut-Beumler, *Look for God in the Suburbs: The Religion of the American Dream and Its Critics, 1945–1965* (New Brunswick, NJ: Rutgers University Press, 1994), 50, 52, 54.

59. Dwight D. Eisenhower, "Remarks at a Luncheon of the General Board of the National Council of Churches" (November 18, 1953), American Presidency Project, http://www.presidency.ucsb.edu/ws/?pid=9768.

60. William Lee Miller, *Piety along the Potomac: Notes on Politics and Morals in the Fifties* (New York: Houghton Mifflin, 1964), 131.

61. Richard H. Crossman, ed., *The God That Failed* (1950; repr., New York: Columbia University Press, 2001), 14.
62. Quoted in Hilton Kramer, "Casanova of Causes," *New York Times* (October 7, 1984).
63. Reinhold Niebuhr, *The Irony of American History* (1952; repr., New York: Scribner, 1962), 155.
64. Reinhold Niebuhr, "To Moscow—and Back," *Nation* (January 28, 1950), 88, 90.
65. Will Herberg, "After Communism—What?" *Reconstructionist* (April 7, 1950), 31.
66. Ibid., 32.
67. Will Herberg, *Protestant, Catholic, Jew: An Essay in American Religious Sociology* (1955; repr., Chicago: University of Chicago Press, 1983), 75, 77, 82–83, 84, 89.
68. Ibid., 263, 264.
69. Kevin M. Schultz, "Protestant, Catholic, Jew—Then and Now," *First Things* (January 2006), http://www.firstthings.com/print.php?type=article&year=2007&month=01&title_link=protestant-catholic-jewthen-and-now—43.
70. Martin E. Marty, *The New Shape of American Religion* (New York: Harper, 1959); Berger quoted in Hudnut-Beumler, *Look for God*, 150.
71. Hudnut-Beumler, *Look for God*, 86.
72. Abraham Joshua Heschel, "The Religious Message," in *Religion in America: Original Essays on Religion in a Free Society*, ed. John Cogley (New York: Fund of the Republic, 1952), 244, 267.
73. James Agee and Others. "Religion and the Intellectuals," *Partisan Review* 3 (1950), 103.
74. Niebuhr quoted in June Bingham, *Courage to Change: An Introduction to the Life and Thought of Reinhold Niebuhr* (1961; repr., Latham, MD: University Press of America, 1993), 7; Silk, *Spiritual Politics*, 46. See also Daniel F. Rice, "Niebuhr's Critique of Religion in America," in *Reinhold Niebuhr Revisited: Engagements with an American Original*, ed. Daniel F. Rice (Grand Rapids, MI: Eerdmans, 2009), 317–337.
75. Martin E. Marty, "Reinhold Niebuhr: Public Theology and the American Experience," *Journal of Religion* 54 (October 1974), 336.
76. Niebuhr, *Irony of American History*, 5.
77. Ibid.,155.
78. Ibid., 149, 150.
79. Ibid., 152, 171.
80. Ibid., 172, 173.
81. Ibid., 173.
82. Peter Viereck, "Freedom Is a Matter of Spirit," *New York Times Book Review* (April 6, 1952), 1, 24.
83. Robert Fitch, "Irony of American History," *Religion in Life* (Autumn 1952), 613–615.
84. William Lee Miller, "The Irony of Reinold Niebuhr" (January 13, 1955), reprinted in Miller, *Piety along the Potomac*, 146.
85. Dwight D. Eisenhower, "Farewell Address" (January 17, 1961), Dwight D. Eisenhower Presidential Papers, http://www.eisenhower.archives.gov/Research/Digital_Documents/Farewell_Address/1961_01_17_Press_Release.pdf.
86. Ibid.
87. Ibid.

CHAPTER 3   CIVIL RELIGION REDEEMED

1. John F. Kennedy, "Inaugural Address" (January 20, 1961), American Presidency Project, http://www.presidency.ucsb.edu/ws/?pid=8032.
2. John F. Kennedy, "Speech to the Greater Houston Ministerial Association," Houston, Texas (September 16, 1960), American Presidency Project, http://www.presidency.ucsb.edu/ws/?pid=25773.
3. For a critical assessment of the notion of American religious freedom, see David Sehat, *The Myth of American Religious Freedom* (New York: Oxford University Press, 2011), Introduction.
4. Lyndon B. Johnson, "Address before a Joint Session of Congress" (November 27, 1963), American Presidency Project, http://www.presidency.ucsb.edu/ws/?pid=25988.
5. Fredrik Logevall, *Choosing War: The Lost Chance for Peace and the Escalation of War in Vietnam* (Berkeley: University of California Press, 2001), 222–251.
6. Lyndon B. Johnson, "Press Conference" (July 28, 1965), American Presidency Project, http://www.presidency.ucsb.edu/ws/?pid=27116.
7. Lyndon B. Johnson, "Remarks at the 12th Annual Presidential Prayer Breakfast" (February 5, 1964), American Presidency Project, http://www.presidency.ucsb.edu/ws/?pid=26057.
8. Lyndon B. Johnson, "Remarks at the 14th Annual Presidential Prayer Breakfast" (February 17, 1966), American Presidency Project, http://www.presidency.ucsb.edu/ws/?pid=28092.
9. Lyndon B. Johnson, "Remarks at the Presidential Prayer Breakfast" (February 1, 1968), American Presidency Project, http://www.presidency.ucsb.edu/ws/?pid=29060.
10. Martin Luther King Jr., "Beyond Vietnam" (April 4, 1967), reprinted in *Speeches by the Rev. Dr. Martin Luther King, Jr.: About the Vietnam War* (New York: Clergy and Laity Concerned about Vietnam, 1969), 1.
11. Ibid.
12. Ibid., 3, 4 (emphasis in the original).
13. Martin Luther King Jr., quoted in David L. Chappell, "A Stone of Hope: Prophetic Faith, Liberalism, and the Death of Jim Crow," *Journal of the Historical Society* 3 (Spring 2003), 142.
14. Quote from *Washington Post* in David J. Garrow, *Bearing the Cross: Martin Luther King, Jr., and the Southern Christian Leadership Conference* (New York: Morrow, 1986), 553; Rowan quoted on 553, 562; Harris poll data on 562. Quotes from King associate in Adam Fairclough, "Martin Luther King, Jr., and the War in Vietnam," *Phylon* 45, no. 1 (1984), 24, 30.
15. Quoted in Garrow, *Bearing the Cross,* 543.
16. Ibid., 546.
17. Chappell, "A Stone of Hope," 143.
18. Quoted in John Cooney, *The American Pope: The Life and Times of Francis Cardinal Spellman* (New York: Times Books, 1984), 294.
19. Quoted in James Carroll, "The Pope's True Revolution," *Time* (April 3, 2005), http://www.time.com/time/magazine/article/0,9171,1044728,00.html.
20. Quoted in Angela M. Lahr, *Millennial Dreams and Apocalyptic Nightmares: The Cold War Origins of Political Evangelism* (New York: Oxford University Press, 2007), 182.

21. William L. Lunch and Peter W. Sperlich, "Public Opinion and the War in Vietnam," *Western Political Quarterly* 32 (March 1979), 22.

22. Seth Jacobs, " 'Our System Demands the Supreme Being': The U.S. Religious Revival and the 'Diem Experiment,' 1954–55," *Diplomatic History* 25 (Fall 2001), passim.

23. John C. Bennett, "From Supporter of War in 1941 to Critic in 1966," *Christianity and Crisis* 26 (February 21, 1966), 13.

24. Quoted in Lahr, *Millennial Dreams and Apocalyptic Nightmares*, 184.

25. Anne C. Loveland, *American Evangelicals and the U.S. Military, 1942–1993* (Baton Rouge: Louisiana State University Press, 1996), 133; McIntire quoted on 122.

26. Mitchell K. Hall, *Because of Their Faith: CALCAV and Religious Opposition to the Vietnam War* (New York: Columbia University Press, 1990), 7–8.

27. Quoted in ibid., 12.

28. Ibid., 13.

29. Ibid., 18.

30. Quoted in ibid., 24.

31. Penelope Adams Moon, " 'Peace on Earth–Peace in Vietnam': The Catholic Peace Fellowship and Antiwar Witness, 1964–1976," *Journal of Social History* (Summer 2003), 1039.

32. Pope Paul VI, *Decree of the Apostolate of the Laity* (November 18, 1965), http://www.vatican.va/archive/hist_councils/ii_vatican_council/documents/vat-ii_decree_19651118_apostolicam-actuositatem_en.html.

33. William Au, *The Cross, the Flag, and the Bomb: American Catholics Debate War and Peace, 1960–1983* (Westport, CT: Greenwood Press, 1985), 19, 32.

34. Ibid., 68.

35. Quoted in ibid., 95.

36. Ibid., 109.

37. Gordon Zahn, "The Church as a Source of Dissent," *Continuum* 1 (Summer 1963), 161–162.

38. Quoted in Hall, *Because of their Faith*, 34.

39. Robert McAfee Brown, "Vietnam: A Crisis of Conscience," *Catholic World* 206 (October 1967), 5.

40. Ibid., 5; J. William Fulbright, *The Arrogance of Power* (New York: Random House, 1966), 3–4.

41. Robert McAfee Brown, Abraham Joshua Heschel, and Michael Novak, *Vietnam: A Crisis of Conscience* (New York: Clergy and Laity Concerned about Vietnam, 1967), 6.

42. Brown, "Vietnam," 7–10.

43. Quoted in Hall, *Because of Their Faith*, 55.

44. Ibid., 63.

45. Ibid., 49, 66; Neuhaus quoted on 81.

46. Lunch and Sperlich, "Public Opinion and the War in Vietnam," 25–28.

47. "Is God Dead?" *Time* (April 8, 1966), http://www.time.com/time/magazine/article/0,9171,835309–1,00.html.

48. "The Death of God," *Time* (October 22, 1965), http://www.time.com/time/magazine/article/0,9171,941410,00.html; Harris poll data and all quotes in this paragraph are from this article. See also Harvey Cox, *The Secular City* (New York: Macmillan, 1965).

49. Robert N. Bellah, "Civil Religion in America," *Daedalus* 96 (Winter 1967), 1–21; reprinted in *American Civil Religion*, ed. Russell E. Richey and

Donald G. Jones (New York: Harper & Row, 1974). References are to the reprinted edition.

50. Ibid., 22–23.
51. Ibid., 33.
52. Interview with Robert N. Bellah, "In God We Trust: Civil and Uncivil Religion in America," *Encounter* (Radio National Australia) (June 25, 2000), http://www.abc.net.au/rn/relig/enc/stories/s143139.htm.
53. Robert N. Bellah, *Beyond Belief: Essays on Religion in a Post-Traditional World* (New York: Harper & Row, 1970), xiv–xv.
54. Ibid., xvi–xvii.
55. Bellah, "Civil Religion in America," 37.
56. Ibid., 38–39.
57. Ibid., 40–41.
58. Sidney Mead, *The Nation with the Soul of a Church* (New York: Harper & Row, 1975), vi, ix.
59. Ibid., 51, 59, 60, 63, 65.
60. Sydney E. Ahlstrom, "Requiem for Patriotic Piety," *Worldview* (August 1972), 10–11.
61. Charles P. Henderson Jr., *The Nixon Theology* (New York: Harper & Row, 1972), 164.
62. Richard Nixon, "Inaugural Address" (January 20, 1969), American Presidency Project, http://www.presidency.ucsb.edu/ws/index.php?pid=1941&st=&st1=#axzz1SfihUrw7.
63. Graham invocation quoted in Henderson, *Nixon Theology*, 4–5; Nixon, "Inaugural Address."
64. Richard Nixon, "Address to the Nation on the Situation in Southeast Asia" (April 30, 1970), American Presidency Project, http://www.presidency.ucsb.edu/ws/?pid=2490.
65. Henderson, *Nixon Theology*, 168.
66. Ibid., 170; Richard Nixon, "Remarks at Dr. Billy Graham's East Tennessee Crusade" (May 28, 1970),American Presidency Project, http://www.presidency.ucsb.edu/ws/?pid=2523.
67. Cong. Rec. 30682 (1970) (speech by George McGovern in favor of the McGovern-Hatfield Amendment, September 1).
68. Richard Nixon, "Remarks at the National Prayer Breakfast" (February 1, 1972), American Presidency Project, http://www.presidency.ucsb.edu/ws/?pid=3597.
69. Richard Nixon, "Second Inaugural Address" (January 20, 1973), American Presidency Project, http://www.presidency.ucsb.edu/ws/?pid=4141.
70. Martin E. Marty, "Two Kinds of Two Kinds of Civil Religion," in *American Civil Religion*, ed. Russell E. Richey and Donald G. Jones (New York: Harper & Row, 1974), 147; Bellah, "American Civil Religion in the 1970s," 259, 260–262, 264, 272.
71. Damon Linker, *Theocons: Secular America under Siege* (New York: Doubleday, 2006), 17–18.
72. Richard John Neuhaus, *Time toward Home* (New York: Seabury Press, 1975), 14.
73. Ibid., vii.
74. Paul Tillich, "The Church and Contemporary Culture," *World Christian Education* (Second Quarter, 1956), 42; Neuhaus, *Time toward Home,* vii, 13–14.

75. Richard John Neuhaus, "The War, the Churches, and Civil Religion," in James M. Gustafason, ed., "The Sixties: Radical Change in American Religion," *Annals of the American Academy of Political and Social Science* 387 (January 1970), 128, 130–134, 138.
76. Ibid., 140.
77. Richard John Neuhaus, "American Ethos and the Revolutionary Option," *Worldview* (December 1970), 9.
78. Neuhaus, "The War, the Churches, and Civil Religion," 140; Neuhaus, "American Ethos and the Revolutionary Option," 8–9; Richard John Neuhaus, "Going Home Again: America after Vietnam," *Worldview* (October 1972), 35.
79. Jim Wallis, "Post-American Christianity," *Post-American* 1 (Fall 1971), 2–3.
80. Jim Wallis, "The Movemental Church," *Post-American* 1 (Winter 1972), 2–3.
81. Jim Wallis, *Revive Us Again: A Sojourner's Story* (Nashville, TN: Abingdon Press, 1983), 18.
82. Neuhaus, "Going Home Again," 35.
83. Wallis, *Revive Us Again*, 16, 92.

CHAPTER 4   CIVIL RELIGION REBORN

1. Christopher Capozzola, " 'It Makes You Want to Believe in the Country': Celebrating the Bicentennial in an Age of Limits," in *America in the Seventies*, ed. David Farber and Beth Bailey (Lawrence: University Press of Kansas, 2004), 40. See also John Bodnar, *Remaking America: Public Memory, Commemoration, and Patriotism in the Twentieth Century* (Princeton, NJ: Princeton University Press, 1993), 228.
2. Reinhold Niebuhr, *The Irony of American History* (1952; repr., Chicago: University of Chicago Press, 2008), 133.
3. Mark O. Hatfield, *Between a Rock and Hard Place* (Waco, TX: Word Books, 1976), 93.
4. Ibid., 94–95.
5. Ibid., 96–99. At the 2010 United States Intellectual History Conference, historian Angela Lahr also recounted Graham's response to Hatfield's remarks.
6. Ibid., 102–103.
7. Ibid., 104–105.
8. Betty Glad, *Jimmy Carter: In Search of the Great White House* (New York: Norton, 1980), 333–334.
9. Christopher Lyle Johnstone, "Electing Ourselves in 1976: Jimmy Carter and the American Faith," *Western Journal of Speech Communication* (Fall 1978), 246. Rosenblatt and Novak quoted in Glad, *Jimmy Carter,* 337–338.
10. Jimmy Carter, "Acceptance Speech at the Democratic National Convention" (July 15, 1976), American Presidency Project, http://www.4president.org/speeches/carter1976acceptance.htm.
11. Jim Wallis, "The Election and Cheap Grace," *Sojourners* (October 1976), 1; Wes Michaelson, "The Fall, the Elect, and the Elections," *Sojourners* (October 1976), 5.
12. Garry Wills, "Will the Nation Be Saved?" *Sojourners* (October 1976), 8; Mark O. Hatfield, "Schizophrenia on the Campaign Trail," *Sojourners* (October 1976), 11; John Howard Yoder, "The National Ritual," *Sojourners* (October 1976), 30; Wes Michaelson, "The Piety and Ambition of Jimmy Carter," *Sojourners* (October 1976), 16.

13. Wes Michaelson, "No King but Caesar . . . ," *Sojourners* (January 1976), 4, 6.
14. Richard John Neuhaus, "Excursus I: Patriotism and Puritans," *Worldview* (December 1, 1975), 4–5.
15. Richard John Neuhaus, "Excursus II: A Carter Presidency and the Real Watershed," *Worldview* (September 1, 1976), 29.
16. Jimmy Carter, "Inaugural Address" (January 20, 1977), American Presidency Project, http://www.presidency.ucsb.edu/ws/?pid=6575.
17. Jimmy Carter, "National Prayer Breakfast Remarks" (January 27, 1977), American Presidency Project, http://www.presidency.ucsb.edu/ws/?pid=7189.
18. Quoted in Anne C. Loveland, *American Evangelicals and the U.S. Military, 1942–1993* (Baton Rouge: Louisiana State University Press, 1996), 159–160; see also Andrew Bacevich, *The New American Militarism: How Americans Are Seduced by War* (New York: Oxford University Press, 2005), 124.
19. Jimmy Carter, "Address at the Commencement Ceremonies of the University of Notre Dame" (May 22, 1977), American Presidency Project, http://www.presidency.ucsb.edu/ws/?pid=7552.
20. Jimmy Carter, "The Energy Problem" (April 18, 1977), American Presidency Project, http://www.presidency.ucsb.edu/ws/?pid=7369; Kevin Mattson, *"What the Heck Are You Up To Mr. President?" Jimmy Carter, America's "Malaise," and the Speech That Should Have Changed the Country* (New York: Bloomsbury USA, 2009), 20–21, 80.
21. Mattson, *"What the Heck Are You Up To Mr. President?"* 134–135.
22. Jimmy Carter, "Crisis of Confidence Speech" (July 15, 1979), American Presidency Project, http://www.presidency.ucsb.edu/ws/?pid=32596; Mattson, *"What the Heck Are You Up To Mr. President?"* 144.
23. Carter, "Crisis of Confidence Speech."
24. Quoted in Lou Cannon, *President Reagan: The Role of a Lifetime* (New York: Touchstone, 1991), 80.
25. Philip Jenkins, *Decade of Nightmares: The End of the Sixties and the Making of Eighties America* (New York: Oxford University Press, 2006), 157; Kondracke quoted on 174. See also Mattson, *"What the Heck Are You Up To Mr. President?"* 172, 175–195.
26. Mattson, *"What the Heck Are You Up To Mr. President?"* 202,
27. Ibid., 182. Falwell quoted in Joseph E. Davies and David Franz, "The Seventies and Eighties: A Reversal of Fortunes," in *Prophecies of Godlessness: Predictions of America's Imminent Secularization, from the Puritans to the Present Day*, ed. Charles Matthews and Christopher McKnight Nichols (New York: Oxford University Press, 2008), 199.
28. Robert Wuthnow, *The Restructuring of American Religion: Society and Faith since World War II* (Princeton, NJ: Princeton University Press, 1988), 200–202.
29. Richard John Neuhaus, "Our American Babylon," *CTI Reflections* 8 (2005), 68–69.
30. Jerry Falwell, "Listen, America!" in *American Political Theology: Historical Perspective and Theoretical Analysis*, ed. Charles W. Dunn (New York: Praeger, 1984), 125.
31. Francis Schaeffer, *Christian Manifesto* (Westchester, IL: Crossway Books, 1981), 117–118; Falwell, "Listen, America!" 124.
32. Falwell, "Listen, America!" 119; Walton quoted in Michael Lienesch, *Redeeming America: Piety and Politics in the New Christian Right* (Chapel Hill: University of North Carolina Press, 1993), 204.

33. Lienesch, *Redeeming America*, 203; Falwell, "Listen, America!" 119.
34. Quoted in Lienesch, *Redeeming America*, 211.
35. Quoted in Bacevich, *New American Militarism*, 140.
36. Ibid., 141.
37. Falwell, "Listen, America!" 18.
38. John Patrick Diggins, *Ronald Reagan: Fate, Freedom, and the Making of History* (New York: Norton, 2007), 27.
39. Ibid., 41.
40. Kiron K. Skinner, Annelise Anderson, and Martin Andeson, eds., *Reagan in His Own Hand: The Writings of Ronald Reagan That Reveal His Revolutionary Vision for America* (New York: Touchstone, 2001), xv.
41. Ibid., 227.
42. Diggins, *Ronald Reagan*, 31.
43. Ronald Reagan, "Inaugural Address" (January 20, 1981), American Presidency Project, http://www.presidency.ucsb.edu/ws/?pid=43130.
44. Ibid.; see also David S. Fogelsong, *The American Mission and the "Evil Empire": The Crusade for a "Free Russia" since 1881* (New York: Cambridge University Press, 2007), 175–181.
45. Diggins, *Ronald Reagan*, 34, 36.
46. Ronald Reagan, "Remarks to the Annual Convention of the National Association of Evangelicals, Orlando, Florida" (March 8, 1983), American Presidency Project, http://www.presidency.ucsb.edu/ws/?pid=41023.
47. Ibid.; Diggins, *Ronald Reagan*, 32.
48. Reagan, "Remarks to the Annual Convention of the National Association of Evangelicals."
49. Fogelsong, *American Mission*, 183–184; Loveland, *American Evangelicals and the U.S. Military*, 233–235.
50. Reagan, "Remarks to the Annual Convention of the National Association of Evangelicals"; Fogelsong, *American Mission*, 188–189; Diggins, *Ronald Reagan*, 197.
51. Ronald Reagan, "Address to the Nation and Other Countries on United States–Soviet Relations" (January 16, 1984), American Presidency Project, http://www.presidency.ucsb.edu/ws/?pid=39806.
52. Ibid.
53. Ibid.
54. Fogelsong, *American Mission*, 188.
55. Greg Grandin, *Empire's Workshop: Latin America, the United States, and the Rise of the New Imperialism* (New York: Metropolitan Books, 2006), 115–116.
56. Peter Beinart, *The Icarus Syndrome: A History of American Hubris* (New York: HarperCollins, 2010), 222–224.
57. Ibid., 225; Richard J. Barnet, *The Rocket's Red Glare: War, Politics, and the American Presidency* (New York: Simon & Schuster, 1990), 378; Grandin, *Empire's Workshop*, 88.
58. Charles Krauthammer, "The Reagan Doctrine," *Time* (April 1, 1985), http://www.time.com/time/magazine/article/0,9171,964873,00.html.
59. Grandin, *Empire's Workshop*, 153; Robertson quoted in Lienesch, *Redeeming America*, 217.
60. Jim Wallis, "The Powerful and the Powerless," in *Piety and Politics: Evangelicals and Fundamentalists Confront the World*, ed. Richard John Neuhaus and Michael Cromartie (Washington, DC: Ethics and Public Policy Center, 1987), 189, 195.

61. "Chicago Declaration of Evangelical Social Concern" (November 25, 1973), http://thejustlife.org/home/2008/05/01/chicago-declaration-of-evangelical-social-concern/. Graham quoted in and polling data found in Dean Curry, "Confusing Justice and Peace," in *Piety and Politics: Evangelicals and Fundamentalists Confront the World*, ed. Richard John Neuhuas and Michael Cromartie (Washington, DC: Ethics and Public Policy Center, 1987), 238–239.

62. Mary Hanna, "From Civil Religion to Prophetic Church: American Bishops and the Bomb," reprinted in *American Political Theology: Historical Perspective and Theoretical Analysis,* ed. Charles W. Dunn (New York: Praeger, 1984), 144, 148.

63. Ibid., 149, 150, 153.

64. National Conference of Catholic Bishops, "The Challenge of Peace: God's Promise and Our Response" (May 3, 1983), http://www.usccb.org/sdwp/international/TheChallengeofPeace.pdf.

65. William J. Gould, "Father J. Bryan Hehir: Priest, Policy Analyst, and Theologian of Dialogue," in *Religious Leaders and Faith-Based Politics*, ed. Jo Renee Formicola and Hubert Morken (Lanham, MD: Rowman & Littlefield, 2001), 205, 210.

66. Ibid., 207; William Au, *The Cross, the Flag, and the Bomb: American Catholics Debate War and Peace, 1960–1983* (Westport, CT: Greenwood Press, 1985), 237–239.

67. Michael Novak, "Moral Clarity in the Nuclear Age," *National Review* (April 1, 1983), 358.

68. Ibid., 380, 383.

69. Beinart, *Icarus Syndrome*, 233.

70. Diggins, *Ronald Reagan*, 348; Reagan quoted on 347–348.

71. Ibid., 404; see also Beinart, *Icarus Syndrome*, 237.

72. Ronald Reagan, "Farewell Address to the Nation" (January 11, 1989), American Presidency Project, http://www.presidency.ucsb.edu/ws/?pid=29650.

73. Ibid.

CHAPTER 5   CIVIL RELIGION AT BAY

1. See documents from the George H.W. Bush archive on this incident: http://robsherman.com/advocacy/bush/thirdfax.pdf.

2. Michael Sherry, *In the Shadow of War: The United States since the 1930s* (New Haven, CT: Yale University Press, 1988), 432–433.

3. George Bush, "Proclamation 5962, Loyalty Day" (April 28, 1989), American Presidency Project, http://www.presidency.ucsb.edu/ws/?pid=23510.

4. Robert Justin Goldstein, *Flag Burning and Free Speech: The Case of Texas v. Johnson* (Lawrence: University Press of Kansas, 2000), 88–89.

5. George Bush, "Remarks Announcing the Proposed Constitutional Amendment on Desecration of the Flag" (June 30, 1989), American Presidency Project, http://www.presidency.ucsb.edu/ws/?pid=17232.

6. Reagan quoted in Richard J. Ellis, *To the Flag: The Unlikely History of the Pledge of Allegiance* (Lawrence: University Press of Kansas, 2005), 177.

7. Ibid., 218.

8. On the decline of a "moral establishment," see David Sehat, *The Myth of American Religious Freedom* (New York: Oxford University Press, 2011),

ch. 11; on the emergence of civil religion in the early Cold War, see William Inboden, *Religion and American Foreign Policy: The Soul of Containment* (New York: Cambridge University Press, 2008), esp. ch. 7.

9. Sidney Blumenthal, "All the President's Wars," *New Yorker* 68 (December 28, 1992/January 4, 1993), 62.

10. Robert Wuthnow, *The Restructuring of American Religion: Society and Faith since World War II* (Princeton, NJ: Princeton University Press, 1988).

11. Ibid., 210–212; Falwell quoted on 211.

12. Ibid., 213.

13. Ibid., 242.

14. Ibid., 257.

15. William Martin, *With God on Our Side: The Rise of the Religious Right in America* (New York: Broadway Books, 1997), 294.

16. George Bush, "Address to the Nation on the National Drug Control Strategy" (September 5, 1989), American Presidency Project, http://www.presidency.ucsb.edu/ws/?pid=17472.

17. George Bush, "Address to the Nation Announcing United States Military Action in Panama" (December 20, 1989), American Presidency Project, http://www.presidency.ucsb.edu/ws/?pid=17965.

18. Poll numbers in Peter Beinart, *The Icarus Syndrome: A History of American Hubris* (New York: HarperCollins, 2010), 252.

19. Sherry, *In the Shadow of War*, 440.

20. Joshua Muravchik, *Exporting Democracy: Fulfilling America's Destiny* (Washington, DC: AEI Studies, 1991), 1–2, 10, 82, 117.

21. Quoted in Derek Chollet and James Goldgeier, *America between the Wars: From 11/9 to 9/11* (New York: PublicAffairs, 2008), 9.

22. George Bush, "Address to the Nation Announcing the Deployment of United States Armed Forces to Saudi Arabia" (August 8, 1990), American Presidency Project, http://www.presidency.ucsb.edu/ws/?pid=18750.

23. George Bush, "Remarks, Aspen, Colorado" (August 2, 1990), Bush Library, Digital Collection, http://bushlibrary.tamu.edu/research/public_papers.php?id=2124&year=1990&month=8.

24. George Bush, "President's Press Conference Announcing Major Troop Increase" (November 8, 1990), American Presidency Project, http://www.presidency.ucsb.edu/ws/?pid=19019.

25. Statement of George Mitchell, Claiborne Pell, and Sam Nunn (November 13, 1990), in "War and Peace in the Gulf," *Foreign Policy Bulletin* 1 (April 1991), 7–8.

26. George Bush, "Remarks to Allied Armed Forces near Dharan, Saudi Arabia, November 22, 1990," in "War and Peace in the Gulf," *Foreign Policy Bulletin* 1 (April 1991), 9–10.

27. Ibid.

28. United Nations Security Council Resolution 678 (November 29, 1990).

29. George Bush, "Press Conference" (November 30, 1990), in "War and Peace in the Gulf," *Foreign Policy Bulletin* 1 (April 1991), 12–13.

30. Elizabeth Drew, "Washington Prepares for War," *New Yorker* (February 4, 1991), reprinted in *The Gulf War Reader*, ed. Micah L. Sifry and Christopher Cert (New York: Times Books, 1991), 192.

31. All references in this note are in *The Gulf War Reader*, ed. Micah L. Sifry and Christopher Cert (New York: Times Books, 1991); all page numbers are

from *The Gulf War Reader.* Charles Krauthammer, "Nightmare from the
Thirties," *Washington Post* (July 27, 1990), 134; William Safire, "The Hitler
Analogy," *New York Times* (August 24, 1990), 210; Patrick Buchanan, "Have
the Neocons Thought This Through?" 213; Daniel Patrick Moynihan, "A
Return to Cold War Thinking," speech delivered on January 10, 1990, 284;
Michael Walzer, "A Just War?" *New Republic* (January 28, 1991), 302.

32. Colin Powell, "Oral History," *Frontline—The Gulf War,* http://www.pbs
.org/wgbh/pages/frontline/gulf/oral/powell/1.html.

33. Alex Molnar, "If My Marine Son Is Killed . . . ," *New York Times* (August 23,
1990), in *The Gulf War Reader,* ed. Micah L. Sifry and Christopher Cerf
(New York: Times Books, 1991), 207.

34. George Bush, "Address to the Nation Announcing Allied Military Action in
the Persian Gulf" (January 16, 1991), American Presidency Project, http://
www.presidency.ucsb.edu/ws/?pid=19222.

35. George Bush, "State of the Union Address" (January 29, 1991), American
Presidency Project, http://www.presidency.ucsb.edu/ws/?pid=19253.

36. George Bush, "Address to the Nation on the Suspension of Allied Offensive
Combat Operations in the Persian Gulf" (February 27, 1991), American
Presidency Project, http://www.presidency.ucsb.edu/ws/?pid=19343.

37. George Bush, "The War Is Over, Address to a Joint Session of Congress"
(March 6, 1991), American Presidency Project, http://www.presidency
.ucsb.edu/ws/?pid=19364.

38. George Bush, "State of the Union Address" (January 28, 1992), American
Presidency Project, http://www.presidency.ucsb.edu/ws/?pid=20544.

39. Charles Krauthammer, "How the War Can Change America," *Time* (January
28, 1991), http://www.time.com/time/magazine/article/0,9171,972218,00
.html; Charles Krauthammer, "The Unipolar Moment," *Foreign Affairs* 70
(1990), 24.

40. B. Turque, "Erasing the Vietnam Nightmare," *Newsweek* (February 3,
1991), 67.

41. Jacob Weisberg, "Means of Dissent," *New Republic* (February 25, 1991),
18–19.

42. William J. Bennett, "Rebirth of a Nation," *National Review* (March 18,
1991), 42; see also Editorial, "Rush from Judgment," *National Review*
(February 11, 1991), 15–16.

43. Michael Barone, "Seeking Comfort," *U.S. News and World Report* (January
28, 1991), 19.

44. Kenneth Walsh, "Bush's 'Just War' Doctrine," *U.S. News and World Report*
(February 4, 1991), 52.

45. Jeffrey L. Sheler, "Holy War Doctrines," *U.S. News and World Report*
(February 11, 1991), 55.

46. John Howard Yoder, "Just War Tradition: Is It Credible?" *Christian Century*
(March 13, 1991), 295–298.

47. George Weigel, "The Churches and War in the Gulf," *First Things* (March
1991), http://www.firstthings.com/article/2007/10/003-the-churches—
war-in-the-gulf-28; Peter Steinfels, "War in the Gulf: The Home Front;
Church Leaders Reaffirm Opposition to War," *New York Times* (February 15,
1991).

48. Weigel, "The Churches and War in the Gulf"; Richard John Neuhaus, "Just
War and This War," *Wall Street Journal* (January 29, 1991), A18.

49. Stanley Hauerwas and Richard John Neuhaus, "Pacifism, Just War and the Gulf," *First Things* (May 1991), http://www.firstthings.com/article/2007/11/005-pacifism-just-war—the-gulf-1.

50. Reinhold Niebuhr, "Why the Christian Church Is Not Pacifist," originally published in *Christianity and Crisis* (1940), reprinted in Robert McAfee Brown, ed., *The Essential Reinhold Niebuhr: Selected Essays and Addresses* (New Haven, CT: Yale University Press, 1986), 102–119.

51. Hauerwas and Neuhaus, "Pacifism, Just War and the Gulf."

52. Ibid.

53. Ibid.

54. Ibid.

55. Richard John Neuhaus, *The Naked Public Square: Religion and Democracy in America* (Grand Rapids, MI: Eerdman's, 1984), 76–77.

56. Blumenthal, "All the President's Wars," 70.

57. Poll data in Sherry, *In the Shadow of War*, 476.

58. Quoted in ibid., 477.

59. Ibid., 479.

60. Blumenthal, "All the President's Wars," 70.

61. George Bush, "Remarks at the United States Military Academy in West Point, New York" (January 5, 1993), American Presidency Project, http://www.presidency.ucsb.edu/ws/?pid=20414.

62. Ibid.

63. Patrick Buchanan, "Speech at the 1992 Republican National Convention," known as "The Culture War" speech (August 17, 1992), Houston, Texas, http://buchanan.org/blog/1992-republican-national-convention-speech-148.

64. Sherry, *In the Shadow of War*, 438.

65. Sidney Blumenthal, "Christian Soldiers," *New Yorker* 70 (July 18, 1994), 34–35; Reed quoted on 35.

66. James Davison Hunter, *Before the Shooting Begins: Searching for Democracy in America's Culture Wars* (1991), excerpted in *Culture Wars: Opposing Viewpoints*, ed. Mary E. Williams (San Diego: Greenhaven Press, 2001), 18–19.

67. John D. Woodbridge, "The Dangers of War Talk," *Christianity Today* (March 6, 1995), and Rhys Williams, ed., *Culture Wars in American Politics: Critical Reviews of a Popular Myth* (New York: Aldine de Gruyter, 1997), both excerpted in *Culture Wars: Opposing Viewpoints*, ed. Mary E. Williams (San Diego: Greenhaven Press, 2001), 28–32.

68. Quoted in "Repenting of America, 1492–1992," *First Things* (October 1990), http://www.firstthings.com/article/2007/09/001-editorial-repenting-of-america-1492–1992-14.

69. Ibid.

70. Memorandum, November 13, 1970, Box I: 245, Folder 3, Daniel Patrick Moynihan Papers, Manuscript Division, Library of Congress, Washington, DC, as cited in Andrew Hartman, "'The Arbitrators of Political Correctness': Historians, *Enola Gay*, and the Limits of Academic Freedom" (paper presented at the annual meeting of the History of Education Society, November 4–7, 2010), 9.

71. Gary Nash, "Reflections on the National History Standards," *National Forum* (Summer 1997), http://www-personal.umich.edu/~mlassite/discussions261/nash.html.

72. Ibid.
73. John Lewis Gaddis, "On Moral Equivalency and Cold War History," *Ethics and International Affairs* 10 (1996), http://www.mtholyoke.edu/acad/intrel/gaddis.htm.
74. Air Force Association, "The Crossroads: The End of World War II, the Atomic Bomb, and the Onset of the Cold War," *Enola Gay Archive* (March 15, 1994), http://www.afa.org/media/enolagay/07–93.asp; see also Hartman, "Arbitrators of Political Correctness," 6.
75. John Lewis Gaddis, "On Moral Equivalency and Cold War History," *Ethics and International Affairs* 10 (1996), http://www.mtholyoke.edu/acad/intrel/gaddis.htm.
76. John Lewis Gaddis, "Morality and the American Experience in the Cold War," in *Ethics and Statecraft: The Moral Dimension of International Affairs* (Westport, CT: Greenwood Press, 1992), 171.
77. Ibid.
78. Gaddis, "On Moral Equivalency and Cold War History."
79. Gaddis, "Morality and the American Experience in the Cold War," 174.
80. Leo P. Ribuffo, "Moral Judgements and the Cold War: Reflections on Reinhold Niebuhr, William Appleman Williams, and John Lewis Gaddis," in *Cold War Triumphalism: The Misuse of History after the Fall of Communism*, ed. Ellen Schrecker (New York: New Press, 2001), 65.
81. William J. Clinton, "Speech in Milwaukee, WI" (October 2, 1992), reported in the *New York Times* (October 3, 1992).
82. Francis Fukuyama, "The End of History?" *National Interest* (Summer 1989), http://www.la.wayne.edu/polisci/kdk/Comparative/SOURCES/fukayama.htm.
83. Daniel T. Rodgers, *Age of Fracture* (Cambridge: Harvard University Press, 2011), 1–14.
84. William J. Clinton, "Remarks Announcing the New Policy on Homosexuals in the Military" (July 19, 1993), http://www.presidency.ucsb.edu/ws/?pid=46867.
85. Richard D. Mohr, "Military Disservice: President Bill Clinton's Policy on Homosexuals in the Military," *Reason* (August-September 1993), http://findarticles.com/p/articles/mi_m1568/is_n4_v25/ai_14171972/.
86. Thomas E. Ricks, "The Widening Gap between the Military and Society," *Atlantic* (July 1997), http://www.theatlantic.com/magazine/archive/1997/07/the-widening-gap-between-military-and-society/6158/; Lind quotes in this article.
87. Ibid.
88. David C. King and Zachary Karabell, *Generation Trust: How the U.S. Military Has Regained the Public's Confidence since Vietnam* (Washington, DC: AEI Press, 2003), ch. 1.
89. Michael Mandelbaum, "Foreign Policy as Social Work," *Foreign Affairs* (January/February 1996); see also Chollet and Goldgeier, *America between the Wars*, ch. 6.
90. Chollet and Goldgeier, *America between the Wars*, 61.
91. Colin Powell, "U.S. Forces: The Challenges Ahead," *Foreign Affairs* (Winter 1992), http://academic.brooklyn.cuny.edu/history/johnson/powell.htm.
92. *New York Times* (February 27, 1994).

93. Cori Elizabeth Dauber, "The Shot Seen 'Round the World': The Impact of the Images of Mogadishu on American Military Operations," *Rhetoric and Public Affairs* 4 (Winter 2001), 668.
94. William J. Clinton, "Address to the Nation on Somalia" (October 7, 1993), American Presidency Project, http://www.presidency.ucsb.edu/ws/?pid=47180.
95. Quoted in Chollet and Goldgeier, *America between the Wars, 83.*
96. Beinart, *Icarus Syndrome,* 274.
97. William J. Clinton, "Remarks to the 48th Session of the United Nations General Assembly in New York City" (September 27, 1993), American Presidency Project, http://www.presidency.ucsb.edu/ws/?pid=47119.
98. William J. Clinton, "Remarks at Georgetown University" (July 6, 1995), American Presidency Project, http://www.presidency.ucsb.edu/ws/?pid=51584.
99. William J. Clinton, "Remarks on International Security Issues at George Washington University" (August 5, 1996), American Presidency Project, http://www.presidency.ucsb.edu/ws/?pid=53161.
100. David Stout, "Clinton to Apologize for Tests on Blacks," *New York Times* (April 9, 1997); John Ryle, "A Sorry Apology from Clinton," *Guardian* (April 13, 1998), at guardian.co.uk; Stephen J. Pope, "The Politics of Apology and the Slaughter in Rwanda," *America* (March 9, 1999), 8–10.
101. William J. Clinton, "The President's News Conference" (April 18, 1995), American Presidency Project, http://www.presidency.ucsb.edu/ws/?pid=51237.
102. Robert N. Bellah, "Civil Religion in America," *Daedalus* 96 (Winter 1967), 1–21; reprinted in *American Civil Religion,* ed. Russell E. Richey and Donald G. Jones (New York: Harper & Row, 1974), 40.
103. William J. Clinton, "Second Inaugural Address" (January 20, 1997), American Presidency Project, http://www.presidency.ucsb.edu/ws/?pid=54183; Bellah, "Civil Religion in America," 40.
104. William J. Clinton, "Remarks at the Seventh Millennium Evening at the White House" (April 12, 1999), American Presidency Project, http://www.presidency.ucsb.edu/ws/?pid=57396.
105. Gary Dorrien, *Imperialist Designs: Neoconservatism and the New Pax Americana* (New York: Routledge, 2004), 16.
106. Justin Vaisse, *Neoconservatism: The Biography of a Movement* (Cambridge: Belknap Press of Harvard University Press, 2010), 234.
107. David Brooks, "A Return to National Greatness: A Manifesto for a Lost Creed," *Weekly Standard* (March 3, 1997).
108. William Kristol and Robert Kagan, "Toward a Neo-Reaganite Foreign Policy," *Foreign Affairs* (July/August 1996), http://www.carnegieendowment.org/publications/index.cfm?fa=view&id=276.

CHAPTER 6 CIVIL RELIGION FORSAKEN

1. Second Gore-Bush debate (October 11, 2000), Wake Forest University, Winston-Salem, NC, http://www.debates.org/index.php?page=2000-debates#oct-3-2000.
2. Lieberman-Cheney vice-presidential debate (October 5, 2000), Centre College, Danville, KY, http://www.debates.org/index.php?page=2000-debates#oct-3-2000.

3. George W. Bush, "Inaugural Address" (January 20, 2001), American Presidency Project, http://www.presidency.ucsb.edu/ws/?pid=25853.
4. Richard John Neuhaus, "September 11—Before and After," *First Things* (September 2001), 65.
5. George W. Bush, "Address to the Nation on the Terrorist Attacks" (September 11, 2001), American Presidency Project, http://www.presidency .ucsb.edu/ws/?pid=58057.
6. George W. Bush, "Remarks Following a Meeting with the National Security Team" (September 12, 2001), American Presidency Project, http://www. presidency.ucsb.edu/ws/?pid=58058. See also Gary Wills, *Bomb Power: The Modern Presidency and the National Security State* (New York: Penguin Books, 2010), 49.
7. George W. Bush, "Proclamation 7462—National Day of Prayer and Remembrance for the Victims of the Terrorist Attacks on September 11, 2001" (September 13, 2001), American Presidency Project, http://www .presidency.ucsb.edu/ws/?pid=61759. Abraham Lincoln, "Proclamation 97—Appointing a Day of National Humiliation, Fasting, and Prayer" (March 30, 1863). American Presidency Project, http://www.presidency.ucsb.edu/ ws/?pid=69891.
8. Billy Graham, "9/11 Remembrance: Sermon" (September 14, 2001), National Cathedral Digital Archives, http://www.nationalcathedral.org/ worship/sermonTexts/bg010914.shtml.
9. George W. Bush, "9/11 Remembrance: Remarks by the President" (September 14, 2001), National Cathedral Digital Archives, http://www .nationalcathedral.org/worship/sermonTexts/gwb20010914.shtml.
10. Mark Silk, "Civil Religion Goes to War," *Religion in the News* (Fall 2001), 1; Bellah quoted on 1.
11. Quite a few books have dealt with similar ideas since September 11, 2001. For example, see Geiko Muller-Fahrenholz, *America's Battle for God: A European Christian Looks at Civil Religion* (Grand Rapids, MI: Eerdmans, 2007); Emilio Gentile, *God's Democracy: American Religion after September 11* (Westport, CT: Praeger, 2008); Christopher Collins, *Homeland Mythology: Biblical Narratives in American Culture* (University Park: Pennsylvania State University Press, 2007).
12. George W. Bush, "Address before a Joint Session of the Congress of the United States in Response to the Terrorist Attacks of September 11" (September 20, 2001), American Presidency Project, http://www.presidency .ucsb.edu/ws/?pid=64731.
13. Ibid.
14. Ibid.
15. Susan Sontag, "Tuesday and After," *New Yorker* (September 24, 2001) http://groups.colgate.edu/aarislam/susan.htm.
16. Sullivan quoted in Richard Bradley, "Sizing Up Sontag" (January 3, 2005), TomPaine.common sense, http://www.tompaine.com/articles/sizing_up_ sontag.php; Richard Brookhiser, "Susan Sontag and 9/11" (September 11, 2007), *National Review Online*, http://www.nationalreview.com/corner/ 148545/susan-sontag-and-911-richard-brookhiser; Krauthammer quoted in Daniel Lazare, "The *New Yorker* Goes to War," *Nation* (June 2, 2003), 25–26. See also "Hall of Shame," *National Review* (October 15, 2001), 15–16.
17. Alexis de Tocqueville, *Democracy in America*, vol. 2, University of Virginia Digital Collection, http://xroads.virginia.edu/~HYPER/DETOC/ch4_06.htm.

18. Richard J. Bernstein, *The Abuse of Evil: The Corruption of Politics and Religion since 9/11* (Cambridge: Polity, 2005), 13–14, 121.

19. Edward Rothstein, "Attacks on U.S. Challenge the Perspectives of Postmodern True Believers," *New York Times* (September 22, 2001).

20. Roger Rosenblatt, "The Age of Irony Comes to an End," *Time* (September 24, 2001), 79.

21. Charles Krauthammer, "The Hundred Days," *Time* (December 31, 2001–January 7, 2002), 156.

22. Wilfred M. McClay, "The Soul of a Nation," *Public Interest* (Spring 2004), 6.

23. Ibid., 7, 8, 17, 18.

24. See David Sehat's argument about this in his book *The Myth of American Religious Freedom* (New York: Oxford University Press, 2011).

25. George W. Bush, "Address to the Nation Announcing Strikes against Al Qaeda Training Camps and Taliban Military Installations in Afghanistan" (October 7, 2001), American Presidency Project, http://www.presidency.ucsb.edu/ws/?pid=65088.

26. George W. Bush, "Address before a Joint Session of Congress on the State of the Union" (January 29, 2002), American Presidency Project, http://www.presidency.ucsb.edu/ws/?pid=29644.

27. Ibid.

28. Ibid.

29. Richard John Neuhuas, "The Idea of Moral Progress," *First Things* (August/September 1999), http://www.firstthings.com/article/2009/02/the-idea-of-moral-progress-5; Richard John Neuhaus, "Civil Religion or Public Philosophy," *First Things* (December 2000), 72–73.

30. Damon Linker, *The Theocons: Secular America under Siege* (New York: Doubleday, 2006).

31. Neuhaus, "September 11—Before and After," 65; Editors, "Religion in a Time of War," *First Things* (December 2001), http://www.firstthings.com/article/2007/01/in-a-time-of-war-18.

32. Editors, "Religion in a Time of War."

33. Ibid.

34. Stanley Hauerwas and the Editors, "In a Time of War: An Exchange," *First Things* (February 2002), http://www.firstthings.com/article/2007/06/002-in-a-time-of-war-an-exchange-25.

35. Ibid.

36. Ibid.

37. Ibid.

38. Stanley Hauerwas, "September 11, 2001: A Pacifist Response," *South Atlantic Quarterly* (Spring 2002), 426.

39. Ibid., 427–428.

40. Ibid., 430.

41. Ibid.

42. "What We're Fighting For" (February 2002), reprinted in Jean Bethke Elshtain, *Just War against Terror: The Burden of American Power in a Violent World*, 2nd ed. (New York: Basic Books, 2004), 193–195.

43. Ibid., 195–196.

44. Ibid., 198–199.

45. Ibid., 200.

46. George W. Bush, "Commencement Address at the United States Military Academy in West Point, New York" (June 1, 2002), American Presidency Project, http://www.presidency.ucsb.edu/ws/?pid=62730.

47. Ibid.
48. Peter Beinart, *The Icarus Syndrome: A History of American Hubris* (New York: HarperCollins, 2010), 334.
49. George W. Bush, "National Security Strategy of the United States" (September 17, 2002), reprinted in Wes Avram, *Anxious about Empire: Theological Essays on the New Global Realities* (Grand Rapids, MI: Brazos Press, 2004), 214–215.
50. George W. Bush, "Address to the Nation on Iraq from Cincinnati" (October 7, 2002), American Presidency Project, http://www.presidency.ucsb.edu/ws/?pid=73139.
51. George W. Bush, "Address to the Nation on Iraq" (March 19, 2003), American Presidency Project, http://www.presidency.ucsb.edu/ws/?pid=63368.
52. Ron Suskind, "Faith, Certainty and the Presidency of George W. Bush," *New York Times Magazine* (October 17, 2004), 47, 51.
53. Ibid., 102.
54. George W. Bush, "State of the Union Address" (January 28, 2003), American Presidency Project, http://www.presidency.ucsb.edu/ws/?pid=29645.
55. William J. Abraham, "The Political Theology of President George W. Bush" (unpublished paper, June 2007).
56. Jim Wallis, "Dangerous Religion: George W. Bush's Theology of Empire," *Sojourners Magazine* (September/October 2003), http://www.sojo.net/index.cfm?action=magazine.article&issue=soj0309&article=030910.
57. Mark O'Keefe, "Antiwar Movement Stalled in Pews," *Christian Century* (May 3, 2003), 14, 15.
58. Richard John Neuhaus, "The Sounds of Religion in a Time of War," *First Things* (March 2003), 77.
59. William T. Cavanaugh, "At Odds with the Pope," *Commonweal* (May 23, 2003), 12.
60. Peter Dula, "The War in Iraq: How Catholic Conservatives Got It Wrong," *Commonweal* (December 3, 2004), 12.
61. George W. Bush, "Address to the Nation on Iraq from the U.S.S. Abraham Lincoln" (May 1, 2003), American Presidency Project, http://www.presidency.ucsb.edu/ws/?pid=68675.
62. I used polls compiled at PollingReport.com to create this composite assessment of public opinion about the war. See http://www.pollingreport.com/iraq.htm.
63. George W. Bush, "Interview with Al-Ahram International" (May 6, 2004), American Presidency Project, http://www.presidency.ucsb.edu/ws/?pid=63380.
64. Ibid.
65. Susan Sontag, "Regarding the Torture of Others," *New York Times Magazine* (May 23, 2004), http://www.nytimes.com/2004/05/23/magazine/regarding-the-torture-of-others.html.
66. Investor's Business Daily/Christian Science Monitor poll (August 2–5, 2004), http://www.pollingreport.com/iraq14.htm.
67. "Transcript: First Presidential Debate: September 30, 2004, from Coral Gables, Fla.," *Washington Post,* http://www.washingtonpost.com/wp-srv/politics/debatereferee/debate_0930.html.
68. George W. Bush, "Second Inaugural Address" (January 20, 2005), American Presidency Project, http://www.presidency.ucsb.edu/ws/?pid=58745.

69. Ibid.; see also John Lewis Gaddis, "Ending Tyranny: The Past and Future of an Idea," *National Interest* (September–October 2008), http://www.the-american-interest.com/article.cfm?piece=459.

70. Bush, "Second Inaugural Address."

71. Dula, "The War in Iraq," 14, 15.

72. Ibid., 16–18; also see Cavanaugh, "At Odds with the Pope"; Eugene McCarraher, "The Most Intolerable of Insults: Remarks to Christian Infidels in the American Empire," in *Anxious about Empire: Theological Essays on the New Global Realities, ed. Wes Avram* (Grand Rapids, MI: Brazos Press, 2004),103–115.

73. McCarraher, "The Most Intolerable of Insults," 110.

74. Richard John Neuhaus, "Iraq and the Moral Judgement," *First Things* (October 2005), http://www.firstthings.com/article/2009/03/iraq-and-the-moral-judgement-13.

75. Ibid.

76. Michael Ignatieff, "The Burden," *New York Times Magazine* (January 5, 2003), http://www.nytimes.com/2003/01/05/magazine/05EMPIRE.html.

77. Andrew Bacevich, "The American Political Tradition," *Nation* (July 17/24, 2006); David Rieff, "Without Exception: The Same Old Song," *World Affairs* (Winter 2008). See also Tony Smith, *A Pact with the Devil: Washington's Bid for World Supremacy and the Betrayal of the American Promise* (New York: Routledge, 2007), esp. 163–194.

78. Cornel West, *Democracy Matters: Winning the Fight against Imperialism* (New York: Penguin Books, 2004), 8, 10, 12, 19, 21.

79. Anatol Lieven, *America Right or Wrong: An Anatomy of American Nationalism* (New York: Oxford University Press, 2004), 6, 15, 63, 154.

80. Walter Hixson, *The Myth of American Diplomacy: National Identity and U.S. Foreign Policy* (New Haven, CT: Yale University Press, 2008), 1–2, 14.

81. Ira Chernus, "The War in Iraq and the Academic Study of Religion," *Journal of the American Academy of Religion* 76 (December 2008); Chicago Council on Foreign Relations (CCFR), The Program on International Policy Attitudes (PIPA), and Knowledge Networks, "Americans on Promoting Democracy" (September 29, 2005), http://www.ccfr.org/UserFiles/File/POS_Topline% 20Reports/POS%202005_September/Democratization%20Report%20Sept %202005.pdf.

82. I used polls compiled at PollingReport.com to create this composite assessment of public opinion about the war; see http://www.pollingreport.com/ iraq.htm.

83. Chernus, "The War in Iraq and the Academic Study of Religion," 862–863.

84. Quoted in Wendy Murray, "U.S. Delusions: An Army Man Changes His Mind," *Christian Century Magazine* (August 11, 2009), http:www .christiancentury.org/article.lasso?id=7481.

85. Andrew Bacevich, "I Lost My Son to a War I Oppose. We Were Both Doing Our Duty," *Washington Post* (May 27, 2007).

86. Andrew Bacevich, *The Limits of Power: The End of American Exceptionalism* (New York: Metropolitan Books, 2007), 12–13.

Chapter 7   Reckoning with American Civil Religion

1. Barack Obama, "Victory Speech" (November 5, 2008), http://www.npr .org/templates/story/story.php?storyId=96624326.

2. David Rieff, "Without Exception: The Same Old Song," *World Affairs* (Winter 2008).
3. Barack Obama, remarks at the Chicago Council on Global Affairs (April 24, 2007), http://www.realclearpolitics.com/articles/2007/04/remarks_of_senator_ barack_obam.html.
4. Jeremiah Wright, "The Day of Jerusalem's Fall" (September 16, 2001), and Jeremiah Wright, "Confusing God and Government" (April 13, 2003), both accessed at http://abcnews.go.com/Blotter/story?id=4719157&page=1.
5. Barack Obama, "A More Perfect Union" (March 18, 2008), American Presidency Project, http://www.presidency.ucsb.edu/ws/?pid=76710; see also Richard T. Hughes, *Myths America Lives By* (Urbana and Chicago: University of Illinois Press, 2003), 8–15; Carl Pedersen, *Obama's America* (Edinburgh: Edinburgh University Press, 2009), 47–52.
6. Barack Obama, "Inaugural Address" (January 20, 2009), American Presidency Project, http://www.presidency.ucsb.edu/ws/?pid=44.
7. Ibid.
8. Robert N. Bellah, "This Is Our Moment, This Is Our Time," *Immanent Frame* (January 12, 2009), http://blogs.ssrc.org/tif/2009/01/12/this-is-our-moment-this-is-our-time/.
9. Norwegian Nobel Committee, "Press Release for 2009 Nobel Peace Prize" (October 9, 2009), accessed May 13, 2011, http://nobelprize.org/nobel_prizes/peace/laureates/2009/press.html.
10. Barack Obama, "Nobel Lecture—2009" (December 10, 2009), nobelprize.org. See also Stephen L. Carter, *The Violence of Peace: America's Wars in the Age of Obama* (New York: Beast Books, 2010), Preface.
11. Obama, "Nobel Lecture—2009."
12. David Brooks, "Obama, Gospel and Verse," *New York Times* (April 26, 2007).
13. Joseph Loconte, "The War Party's Theologian," *Wall Street Journal* (May 31, 2002), w13.
14. David Brooks, "A Man on a Gray Horse," *Atlantic Monthly* (September 2002), 24–25.
15. Wilfred M. McClay, "The Continuing Irony of American History," first delivered as the Witherspoon Lecture in December 2001 and reprinted in *First Things* (February 2002), http://www.firstthings.com/article/2007/06/001-the-continuing-irony-of-american-history-36.
16. Ibid.
17. Paul Elie, "A Man for All Reasons," *Atlantic* (November 2007), http://www.theatlantic.com/magazine/archive/2007/11/a-man-for-all-reasons/6337/. See also Wilfred M. McClay, "A Man for All Reasons?" *First Things* (October 15, 2007), http://www.firstthings.com/onthesquare/2007/10/a-man-for-all-reasons.
18. Andrew J. Bacevich, "Prophets and Poseurs: Niebuhr and Our Times," *World Affairs* 27 (Winter 2008); Andrew J. Bacevich, "Introduction," in Reinhold Niebuhr, *The Irony of American History* (1952; repr., Chicago: University of Chicago Press, 2008), xx.
19. Peter Viereck, "Freedom Is a Matter of Spirit," *New York Times Book Review* (April 6, 1952), 24. Niebuhr, *Irony of American History*, 133.
20. William H. McNeill, "The Care and Repair of Public Myth," *Foreign Affairs* 61 (Fall 1982), 2, 4, 9.

Index

Abraham, William, 223
Abu Ghraib, 226–230. *See also* Bush,
  George W.; Iraq War; Sontag, Susan
Adler, Mortimer, 29
Afghanistan War, 208
Agee, James, 11
Ahlstrom, Sydney, 83–84
American Bicentennial, 98–99
American civil religion, 4–6, 39,
  146–149, 253–254; and Abraham
  Lincoln, 8–9; and Afghanistan War,
  208; and the American military,
  178–182, 239–240; and American
  Civil War, 7–9; "The American
  Way of Life," 45–46; and the Cold
  War, 24, 29–32, 37–39, 46–47,
  175; and culture wars, 170–172,
  178, 181, 205–208; and humility,
  107–111; and Iraq War, 225–226,
  237–240; and 9/11, 200–201,
  207–208, 215–217; and Persian
  Gulf War, 154, 162; and Robert
  Bellah, 4, 79–81; and Vietnam War,
  63, 80–81, 88–90, 94–95, 99–100;
  and war, 5, 9, 113, 147, 150; and
  World War II, 12–13. *See also*
  individual presidents, theologians, and
  intellectuals
American Civil War, 6–9
American creed, 2
American exceptionalism: and
  differences with American civil
  religion, 3, 9; and Harry Truman,
  30–32; and neoconservatives, 151,

191–192; and public opinion, 3;
  and Ronald Reagan, 123
American flag, 144–146
American jeremiad, 7–8
American Legion, and "Back to God"
  program, 37
American military: and civil religion,
  160, 178–182, 239–240; and
  Dwight D. Eisenhower, 53; and
  George H. W. Bush, 153–156,
  158–159, 168–169, 218, 225–226;
  and homosexuals, 178–179; and
  Jimmy Carter, 111–112; and John
  Kerry, 230; and neoconservatives,
  191–192; and the New Christian
  Right, 118–121; and Ronald Reagan,
  132–133; and William J. Clinton,
  178–179, 185. *See also* Powell,
  Colin; sacrifice; *and specific wars*
American Revolution, 4, 12, 80, 98
Arlington National Cemetery, 1; and
  CALCAV march (1968), 75
atheism: and Dwight D. Eisenhower,
  39; and George H. W. Bush,
  143–144
atomic bombing of Japan, 11, 13–15,
  17–18, 173–174; and reactions from
  American churches, 14

Bacevich, Andrew: and Iraq War,
  236–237, 240–242; and Reinhold
  Niebuhr, 252
Balkan wars, 184–185. *See also*
  Clinton, William J.

279

About the Author

RAYMOND HABERSKI JR. is an associate professor of history at Marian University. For the 2008–2009 academic year he held the Fulbright Danish Distinguished Chair in American Studies at the Copenhagen Business School. He is the author of three previous books, a founding member of the Society for United States Intellectual History, and a regular contributor to the S-USIH awarding-winning blog.